Relations between State and Higher Education

# Legislating for Higher Education in Europe

## VOLUME 1

# Relations between State and Higher Education

Roel in 't Veld
Hans-Peter Füssel
Guy Neave

*Legislative Reform Programme*
*for Higher Education and Research,*
*Coucil of Europe*

KLUWER LAW INTERNATIONAL
THE HAGUE / LONDON / BOSTON

A C.I.P. Catalogue record for this book is available from the Library of Congress

ISBN 90-411-0245-0

---

Published by Kluwer Law International,
P.O. Box 85889, 2508 CN The Hague, The Netherlands.

Sold and distributed in the U.S.A. and Canada
by Kluwer Law International,
675 Massachusetts Avenue, Cambridge, MA 02139, U.S.A.

In all other countries, sold and distributed
by Kluwer Law International,
P.O. Box 85889, 2508 CN The Hague, The Netherlands.

"The authors are responsible for the choice and presentation of the facts contained in this book and for the opinions expressed therein, which are not necessarily those of the Council of Europe and do not commit the Organisation"

Cover design: Tandar, Ljubljana, Slovenia
The cover design was sponsored by the Slovenian Ministry of Education and Sport

Layout and camera-ready copy: Anne-Marie Krens, Oegstgeest, The Netherlands

*Printed on acid-free paper*

Printed in the Netherlands

"Après le pain, l'éducation est le premier besoin d'un peuple"

Georges Jacques Danton, 1759–1794

# TABLE OF CONTENTS

FOREWORD                                                      xvii

CHAPTER 1
Legislating for higher education and research
in Europe                                                       1

1.1.1      The Legislative Reform Programme for higher
           education and research                               1
1.1.1.1    Towards open societies                               1
1.1.1.2    The purpose of the Legislative Reform Programme      2
1.1.1.3    Changing objectives                                  2
1.1.1.4    The working methods                                  3
1.1.2      The design of the LRP publication project            3
1.1.2.1    The purpose of the publications                      3
1.1.2.2    The audience                                         5
1.1.2.3    The approach                                         5
1.1.2.4    Six volumes                                          5
1.1.2.5    The outline of volume 1                              6
1.2.1      Perspectives on legislating for higher education
           and research                                         7
1.2.1.1    Common issues                                         7
1.2.1.2    Legislation                                           8
1.2.1.3    Accelerating change                                  10
1.2.1.4    Modification versus codification?                    10
1.2.1.5    The quest for models and standards                   12

| | | |
|---|---|---|
| 1.2.1.6 | How to do things with rules? | 13 |
| 1.2.2 | Bridges for enlightenment and freedom | 14 |
| | CHAPTER 2 | |
| | Relations between the state and higher education | 17 |
| 2.1 | Introduction | 17 |
| 2.2 | Relations between the state and higher education | 20 |
| 2.2.1 | The evolution of the nation state in relation to education in general | 20 |
| 2.2.1.1 | Universities in former stateless societies | 20 |
| 2.2.1.2 | The classical viewpoint: the state in its capacity as benign emancipator of the "masses" | 21 |
| 2.2.1.3 | The state, economic development and standardisation of qualifications | 22 |
| 2.2.1.4 | Interconnections and dynamics, amongst others professionalisation | 23 |
| 2.2.2 | The nation state and higher education | 24 |
| 2.2.2.1 | Typologies of policy making: the human capital theory | 24 |
| 2.2.2.2 | Stages of growth of higher education | 25 |
| 2.2.2.3 | Recent macro trends in western Europe: driving forces for change | 27 |
| a | Erosion | 28 |
| b | Communication technology | 30 |
| c | Commercialisation of knowledge | 31 |
| d | Continuing education | 32 |
| 2.2.2.4 | Dramatic macro-change in society and it implications for higher education legislation in eastern Europe | 33 |
| 2.3 | Legislation as policy system | 34 |
| 2.3.1 | Policy systems | 34 |
| 2.3.2 | Law of diminishing effectiveness of steering | 36 |
| 2.3.3 | Law of policy accumulation | 37 |
| 2.3.4 | First- and higher-order learning | 38 |
| 2.3.5 | Crises | 40 |
| 2.3.6 | Internalisation | 41 |
| 2.3.7 | Life-cycle of policy systems | 42 |
| 2.3.8 | Inter-active learning | 43 |
| 2.3.9 | Dimensions of policy systems: a closer look | 44 |

2.3.9.1 Degrees of decentralisation 44
2.3.9.2 Subjects of steering: inputs, throughputs and outputs 45
2.3.9.3 Instruments: regulation, money and persuasion 45
2.3.9.4 Complex policy systems 46
2.4 Educational policy traditions in Europe 46
2.5 Towards a heuristic scheme in order to deal with societal dynamics concerning legislation for higher education 49

CHAPTER 3
Guidelines to comparison 51

3.1 Introduction 51
3.2 Organisational principles of change 53
3.2.1 The challenges of choice: academic or vocational drift 53
3.2.2 The principle of subsidiarity 56
3.3 Institutional autonomy: the decline of a monopoly 56
3.4 The private sector: an engine of subsidiarity? 59
3.5 Parity and quality assurance: situating the intermediaries 61
3.5.1 Intermediaries 61
3.5.2 Parity and quality assurance 62
3.5.3 Diversification 65
3.5.4 Budgeting and general accountability 67
3.6 Conclusion 69

CHAPTER 4
Conclusions 71

4.1 Introduction 71
4.2 Analytical framework 72
4.2.1 The eternal questions: effectiveness and legitimacy 72
4.2.2 The analytical tools refined 74
4.3 Analysis 76
4.3.1 Threats and opportunities in the future 76
4.3.2 Output-orientation 77
4.3.3 Management group thinking 80
4.4 Paradoxes and dilemmas 82
4.5 Guidelines to the future 84

| 4.5.1 | Problems within universities | 84 |
| 4.5.2 | Self-control within sensible public environments | 89 |

CHAPTER 5
Country reports                                              91

| 5.1 | *Albania* | 93 |
| 5.1.1 | Current situation in higher education; Institutional diversification | 93 |
| 5.1.2 | Higher educational system and research institutes | 94 |
| 5.1.3 | The higher education budget | 95 |
| 5.1.4 | Enrolment structure | 95 |
| 5.1.5 | Reform in higher education: strategy and policy | 96 |

| 5.2 | *Belarus* | 99 |
| 5.2.1 | The Constitution of the Republic of Belarus | 99 |
| 5.2.2 | The current legislative situation | 99 |
| 5.2.3 | Higher education | 101 |
| 5.2.4 | State and intermediate leadership in the education system | 101 |
| 5.2.5 | The current situation | 104 |

| 5.3 | *The Flemish Community of Belgium* | 107 |
| 5.3.1 | The current legislative situation | 107 |
| 5.3.2 | Main features of the higher education system | 108 |
| 5.3.3 | Finance and governance | 110 |
| 5.3.4 | Conclusion | 112 |

| 5.4 | *The French Community of Belgium* | 113 |
| 5.4.1 | Constitutional provisions | 113 |
| 5.4.2 | The current situation in higher education | 115 |
| 5.4.3 | Educational structures and quality assurance | 116 |
| 5.4.4 | Management bodies | 119 |
| 5.4.5 | Teaching, research staff and financing | 120 |
| 5.4.6 | Research | 121 |
| 5.4.7 | Political authority and intermediate bodies | 121 |
| 5.4.8 | Conclusion | 123 |

| | | |
|---|---|---|
| 5.5 | *Bulgaria* | 125 |
| 5.5.1 | The Constitution of the Republic of Bulgaria, as adopted by the Grand National Assembly in July 1991 | 125 |
| 5.5.2 | The current legislative situation | 125 |
| 5.5.3 | Legislative principles and policy objectives | 130 |
| 5.5.4 | The balance of power between the State | 132 |
| 5.5.5 | Legal protection of institutions for higher education against State decisions | 133 |
| 5.5.6 | Conclusion | 134 |
| | | |
| 5.6 | *Czech Republic* | 137 |
| 5.6.1 | The Constitution of 1993 and the List of Basic Rights and Freedoms of 1993 | 137 |
| 5.6.2 | The current legislative situation in higher education | 137 |
| 5.6.3 | The balance of power | 141 |
| 5.6.4 | Conclusion | 142 |
| | | |
| 5.7 | *Denmark* | 145 |
| 5.7.1 | The current legislative situation | 145 |
| 5.7.2 | The balance of power | 146 |
| 5.7.3 | Conclusion | 149 |
| | | |
| 5.8 | *Republic of Estonia* | 151 |
| 5.8.1 | Section 38 of the Constitution | 151 |
| 5.8.2 | The current legislative situation in higher education | 151 |
| 5.8.3 | The balance of power | 155 |
| 5.8.4 | Conclusion | 158 |
| | | |
| 5.9 | *Finland* | 159 |
| 5.9.1 | The Act amending the Constitutional Act | 159 |
| 5.9.2 | The current legislative situation in higher education | 160 |
| 5.9.3 | The balance of power | 161 |
| | | |
| 5.10 | *France* | 163 |
| 5.10.1 | Current situation in higher education | 163 |
| 5.10.2 | Universities | 164 |
| 5.10.3 | Two-year technology courses | 168 |

| | | |
|---|---|---|
| 5.10.4 | Institutes and colleges | 168 |
| 5.10.5 | Administrative organisation | 170 |
| | | |
| 5.11 | *Germany* | 173 |
| 5.11.1 | Legal provisions | 173 |
| 5.11.2 | The current legislative situation in higher education | 174 |
| 5.11.3 | Science Council | 175 |
| 5.11.4 | Extension and construction of institutions of higher education: a joint task | 175 |
| 5.11.5 | The balance of power | 177 |
| 5.11.6 | A brief onclusion | 178 |
| | | |
| 5.12 | *Greece* | 181 |
| 5.12.1 | The current legislative situation | 181 |
| 5.12.2 | The balance of power | 184 |
| | | |
| 5.13 | *Hungary* | 185 |
| 5.13.1 | The current legislative situation | 185 |
| 5.13.2 | The balance of power between the State, intermediaries and the institutions | 187 |
| 5.13.3 | Conclusion | 189 |
| | | |
| 5.14 | *Latvia* | 191 |
| 5.14.1 | The Satversme, the Constitution of the Republic of Latvia | 191 |
| 5.14.2 | The current legislative situation in higher education | 191 |
| 5.14.3 | Types and missions of higher education | 194 |
| 5.14.4 | The balance of power, accountability and quality assessment | 194 |
| 5.14.5 | Competencies, steering principles and mechanisms of the Ministry | 196 |
| 5.14.6 | Access and selection, tuition fees, loans and grants | 197 |
| 5.14.7 | Conclusion | 198 |
| | | |
| 5.15 | *Liechtenstein* | 199 |
| 5.15.1 | The current situation | 199 |
| 5.15.2 | Higher education | 200 |

| | | |
|---|---|---|
| 5.16 | *Lithuania* | 203 |
| 5.16.1 | The Constitution of the Republic of Lithuania | 203 |
| 5.16.2 | The current legislative situation | 203 |
| 5.16.3 | The current situation in higher education and research | 204 |
| 5.16.4 | The balance of power | 206 |
| 5.16.5 | Conclusion | 208 |
| | | |
| 5.17 | *Malta* | 209 |
| 5.17.1 | The current legislative situation | 209 |
| 5.17.2 | The balance of power | 209 |
| 5.17.3 | Conclusion | 213 |
| | | |
| 5.18 | *Moldova* | 215 |
| 5.18.1 | The current legislative situation | 215 |
| | | |
| 5.19 | *The Netherlands* | 221 |
| 5.19.1 | Section 23 of the Constitution | 221 |
| 5.19.2 | The current legislative situation | 222 |
| 5.19.3 | The balance of power | 226 |
| 5.19.4 | Quality assurance and quality control | 229 |
| 5.19.5 | Developments and recent discussions | 230 |
| 5.19.6 | Conclusion | 232 |
| | | |
| 5.20 | *Norway* | 233 |
| 5.20.1 | The current legislative situation | 233 |
| | | |
| 5.21 | *Poland* | 239 |
| 5.21.1 | The current legislative situation | 239 |
| 5.21.2 | The balance of power | 240 |
| | | |
| 5.22 | *Romania* | 245 |
| 5.22.1 | The Romanian Constitution, Article 32 | 245 |
| 5.22.2 | The current legislative situation | 245 |
| 5.22.3 | The balance of power | 247 |
| 5.22.4 | Conclusion | 248 |

5.23      *Slovakia*                                                    249
5.23.1    Article 42 of the Constitution of the Republic of
          Slovakia                                                      249
5.23.2    The current legislative situation                            249

5.24      *Slovenia*                                                    257
5.24.1    Article 58 of the Slovenian Constitution                     257
5.24.2    The current legislative situation                            257
5.24.3    The balance of power                                         258
5.24.4    Conclusion                                                   261

5.25      *Spain*                                                       263
5.25.1    Introduction                                                 263
5.25.2    The structure of the higher education system                 263
5.25.3    Non-university education                                     265
5.25.4    Higher vocational education                                  266
5.25.5    The balance of power                                         266
5.25.6    Conclusion                                                   267

5.26      *Switzerland*                                                 269
5.26.1    The current legislative situation                            269

5.27      *Turkey*                                                      273
5.27.1    The current legislative situation                            273
5.27.2    The structure of the higher education system                 275
5.27.3    The Higher Educational Council                               276
5.27.4    The current situation                                        279
5.27.5    Conclusion                                                   283

5.28      *The United Kingdom*                                          285
5.28.1    The current legislative situation                            285
5.28.2    The higher education system                                  287
5.28.3    The balance of power: quality assurance and financing        288
5.28.4    Conclusion                                                   292

| | | |
|---|---|---|
| 5.29 | *Ukraine* | 295 |
| 5.29.1 | The current legislative situation | 295 |
| 5.29.2 | The balance of power | 297 |
| 5.29.3 | Conclusion | 298 |
| | BIBLIOGRAPHY | 299 |
| | INDEX | 303 |
| | ACKNOWLEDGEMENTS | 311 |
| | THE STRUCTURE OF THE SERIES | 319 |

# FOREWORD

## by Daniel Tarschys
### Secretary General of the Council of Europe

In the world of higher learning, there have long been conflicting traditions of control and autonomy. On the one hand, universities have often aspired to protect their independence from political and ecclesiastic authorities. On the other hand, there have always been strong pressures on higher education from the outside, from political, religious and ideological power-centres. In our recent history, universities in many countries have been subjected to totalitarian control.

At present, powerful winds of change are blowing through this domain. Virtually everywhere in Europe, relations between the State and the institutions of higher learning are changing. In most places, tight state control gives way to more institutional autonomy. This presents a great challenge to universities and colleges and makes it necessary to consider a wide range of regulatory issues.

In the Council of Europe, much thought has been given to these problems in recent years. The Higher Education and Research Committee (CC-HER), previously known as the Standing Conference of University Problems (CC-PU), has established a Legislative Reform Programme for Higher Education (LRP). The Programme is intended to give effective support to the process of legislative reform in higher education, particularly, but not exclusively, in the new member states in central and eastern Europe.

To promote dissemination of experience acquired throughout Europe and as a complement to its ongoing advisory and multilateral activities, the Programme's Steering Group has decided to publish a series entitled *Legis-*

*lating for Higher Education and Research in Europe.* The first volume of this series, *Relations Between State and Higher Education,* is hereby presented to the general public.

*Relations Between State and Higher Education,* has been compiled in close co-operation with State Parties to the European Cultural Convention. It seeks, as will subsequent volumes, to identify core issues which countries may need to confront in their legislations and offers examples of good practice.

*Daniel Tarschys*

Daniel Tarschys

# 1

## LEGISLATING FOR HIGHER EDUCATION AND RESEARCH IN EUROPE

1.1.1   The Legislative Reform Programme for higher education and research (LRP)

### 1.1.1.1   Towards open societies

Crossing borders has become increasingly easy for persons, goods, and ideas and experience. International organisations have played an important role in accomplishing this. Six years after the changes in central and eastern Europe in 1989/1990 when the Iron Curtain dissolved before the Velvet Revolutions and the old borders ceased to exist, it may be argued that Europe did not make the most of opportunities to prevent the creation of new borders. New tensions have arisen, nationalism and intolerance have come to the surface again, and on another level, many recent interregional initiatives may cultivate soft forms of isolation. This is why the indirect consequences of international co-operation should be carefully assessed in a broader perspective in order to prevent new forms of regionalism. Since its founding, the Council of Europe has been the European conscience and forum for co-operation in pursuance of democracy, human rights, pluralism, and the quality of life, laying a foundation for lasting peace. Central to this work is the setting of minimum standards and the guiding of change in many areas of legislation. Legislation is a guide, in particular in periods of transition. Yet, changes in society need to be set down in processes of legislative change. It would be a historical mistake to then allow the resurgence of new obstacles for democratic development, peaceful co-existence and co-operation for the benefit of all the citizens of Europe.

Higher education institutions have two basic functions:
·   to provide higher education;
·   to carry out research.

Only recently a third function has been defined: a general service-function, including applied research and technology transfer. It is questionable whether this function is new or only a derivative, but it is evident that higher education and research institutions have a principal role in and responsibility for creating and maintaining a society that is enabling, prosperous, democratic and open.

### 1.1.1.2  The purpose of the Legislative Reform Programme

The LRP has been an activity of the Council for Cultural Co-operation (CDCC) since July 1991, when the first advisory mission was undertaken. The LRP functions under the authority of the Higher Education and Research Committee and the strategic supervision of a Steering Group and is funded mainly by voluntary contributions from member States to a special Cultural Fund account. Following the Declaration of the Heads of State and Heads of Government of the member States of the Council of Europe (Vienna, 1993), the LRP contributes to the realisation of the main objectives of the Council of Europe which are to strengthen pluralist and parliamentary democracy and the rule of law in a concept that is known as "democratic security". The purpose of the LRP is "to stimulate and assist in the continuous process of development of the higher education and research sector, in terms of legislation and related policy development, as well as their implementation, with a special view to central and eastern Europe".

### 1.1.1.3  Changing objectives

The LRP is a support programme for new member States and new countries party to the Cultural Convention of the Council of Europe in central and eastern Europe. New policies and new laws are required to redefine the relationship between the State and the higher education and research sector, as well as academic freedom, institutional autonomy, the organisation and management of higher education and research, quality assurance, and realising full participation and co-operation in the European academic community. Reform, however, is not restricted to those new partners. Today, as a result of its natural course, the scope of the LRP goes beyond the immediate needs for legislative reform in central and eastern Europe. It embraces strategic reforms in higher education and research in Europe as a whole. In essence, it stands as a plea for the continuous renewal of legislation in higher education and research. Looking to the future, the LRP opens an opportunity for further development as a centre for consultation and legislative assistance to policy development, legal enactment and implementation.

## 1.1.1.4  The working methods

The LRP has devised four working methods which combine the study of legislative reform with active contributions to its advancement, and are therefore complementary to one another.

- In the process of policy development and legislative reform and their implementation, advisory missions support the search for practical solutions to the immediate problems of the countries.
- Multilateral workshops analyse issues of common concern to the development of the higher education systems, especially in central and eastern Europe.
- Multilateral study programmes focus on aspects of implementation of policy and legislation in the host country.
- The publication project is a series of studies, bringing together comprehensive country reports, their comparative analysis, and a theoretical focus on the selected topics.

## 1.1.2    The design of the LRP publication project

### 1.1.2.1  The purpose of the publications

Comparative knowledge has, at least, three advantages:
- it maps, and sometimes explains, diversity;
- it stimulates and guides reform;
- and it may reveal alternatives and even minimal standards.

The Council of Europe has embarked on a series of six volumes of comparative studies based on country reports. This publication project is the first LRP venture to cover completely the territorial scope of the Council of Europe. It is, at the same time, a logical complementary instrument of the Programme. Like the LRP advisory missions, workshops and study programmes which are themselves based on the comparative principle, the series provides analyses, the aim of which is to stimulate and initiate reflection, discussion and change, to survey information, give counsel and help mutual learning, and to promote and assist development processes. Subsequently, it attempts to forge constructive partnerships across Europe.

The series should contribute to the compatibility of European higher education systems and support LRP's advisory work, as well as search for common ground. It does not seek harmonisation or standardisation. The six volumes provide the reader with an opportunity to set his or her own standards and objectives within the current as well as the future context.

An examination of the consequences which follow from the pervasive policy of internationalisation of governments and institutions over the last fifteen years is equally important and most especially for the legal categories and systems it generates within higher education. It seems that current classifications have to be abandoned as a legislative melting-pot is emerging. However, comparative studies dealing with the fundamentals of higher education legislation, legislative processes, their direction, incompatible mixtures and implementation, are still rare.

Higher education and research are held to be essential for democracy, prosperity, equity, tolerance, and the common good in a modern society. This responsibility is partly fulfilled by simply providing good higher education and good practice to the future generation of teachers, managers and opinion leaders in the public and private sector. Nonetheless, higher education and research need the ongoing stimulation of public interest in order to assure a fair share of the available public funds. This series may help in locating arguments in public discussion from a substantial, value oriented and comparative, but not primarily an economic, point of view.

### 1.1.2.2  The audience

The publication project is the outcome of ongoing scholarly debate. Equally important is to inspire and serve as a practical guide for the growing constituency of ministerial and institutional policy and decision makers at any level. The series focuses on legislation in its political, social and economic context. It is not meant as a tool for lawyers alone; the volumes are designed to bring those involved in higher education and research in all forty-three States party to the Cultural Convention, closer together and to speed the communication and co-operation between members of parliament, governments, ministries, higher education and research institutions (irrespective of their legal status), intermediaries like funding councils, accreditation committees and rectors' conferences, staff and students and their representatives, as well as unions, political parties and researchers in higher education. Everyone else who is involved or interested in higher education policy and management, in non-European countries, other educational sectors, and other sectors of public service, may also find food for thought.

### 1.1.2.3  The approach

The series will deal with the government and institutional steering of higher education institutions. The topics are examined from different perspectives: meta, governmental, institutional and individual viewpoints. It will be examined whether (legislative) traditions in higher education permit a certain classification of the national higher education systems. The volumes analyse and identify the endogenous driving forces of legislation: forces within higher education institutions and government, as well as the exogenous driving forces: economic, social and political. To the question whether legislating, in the sense of developing, drafting and implementing legislation, is itself an endogenous driving force, answers may be found in the volume "Sharing Experience".

### 1.1.2.4  Six volumes

The Editing Board has opted for the presentation of broad topics, that have been specially focused. An inventory of the most important elements has resulted in the planning of the six volumes described in the overview on page 319. "Relations between State and Higher Education" lays the foundation for the following volumes and is in consequence the widest in scope. Whereas "Relations" examines the ties between government and higher learning, "Institutional Governance" focuses on the institutional dimension, and forms a counterbalance. "Administration" complements the first two volumes and concentrates on accountability in terms of the linkage between financial management and quality assurance. The volume "Sharing Experience" is somewhat different, as it concentrates on analysing, evaluating and understanding the *process* and direction of legislative reform and implementation in higher education and research. The volumes dedicated to "Staff" and "Students" focus on research and teaching as the core business of higher education institutions, as students and staff are the basic groups within institutions. This implies that policy, legislation, implementation and management should be aimed at facilitating the well-being and functioning of the individuals within these two groups.

### 1.1.2.5  The outline of volume 1

The country reports in chapter 5 and the responses to an extensive questionnaire provide the basis for this book. The editors did not impose undue restrictions or guidelines on the authors of the country reports. Their framework was interpreted in light of the circumstances prevalent in each country, and provided the basic material for an inspiring and original country report. The countries were asked to highlight the following aspects:
·   trends most relevant to recent policy objectives determining "Relations between State and higher education";
·   the current legislative situation in higher education; in particular legal, political, educational, social, cultural and economic developments, as they affected higher education;
·   legislative principles and policy objectives, related to the main features of their implementation and effect;
·   (changes in) the balance of power between the State, intermediary organisations, and institutions of higher education;
·   legal protection of institutions of higher education against state decisions.

Apart from those countries not having a higher education and research system of their own, unfortunately, Austria, Croatia, Cyprus, Iceland, Italy, Ireland, Portugal, the Russian Federation and Sweden have not been able to submit country reports for chapter 5 of this book. Despite this, it has been considered worthwhile, even necessary, to embark on this series which explores the interface between legal comparative studies and classical higher education studies, as this is a field about which we know so little. It is hoped that all European countries will appear in Volume 2.

### 1.2.1 Perspectives on legislating for higher education and research

#### 1.2.1.1 Common issues

Since 1981, discussions in higher education in western Europe have been and are dominated by three topics: budget cuts, quality assessment and institutional autonomy. The political changes in 1990 in central and eastern Europe gave those discussions a completely new dimension about which we know little. To react to problems of, for example, mass higher education education and research structures, diversification, curricula development and research programming, an entirely new approach is needed across Europe Obviously, western Europe may learn much from the deep-cutting reforms taking place in the so-called "new democracies". Nevertheless, the policy-making audience in the west seems not yet to be fully interested in what is really happening in the east ... a lack of information perhaps?

In most of western Europe, the three topics mentioned have to a considerable extent lost their momentum as the frontiers of policy development move onward. Both the LRP and this series are an exercise in looking forward, but there are also other reasons to try to anticipate what are likely to be the issues for the next decade and, if possible, to clarify them.

· Budget discussions are an annual ceremony, but discussions on funding and allocating models are decisive. Nonetheless, this is often a game played by a small group of experts and political decision-makers. Naturally, this series will look upon financial structures as steering instruments throughout. The focus will be on the political and managerial elements, not on the technicalities of financial models.

· The new methods of quality assessment are no longer an important development issue as the time has come for fine-tuning and introducing their concepts on a broad scale. Subsequently, all the volumes of the series will touch upon issues of quality assurance, because they are changing the management culture in a national system to a great extent.

· The issue of autonomy is an underlying theme in every discussion about higher education policy. Periods of stronger state intervention on certain issues are usually followed by a loosening of the ropes and vice versa. The arguments in these discussions, however, are not particularly subject to change. Institutional autonomy is more fruitfully defined in terms of division of responsibilities and guided interaction as this approach would unscramble cacophonic discussions on any topic, avoid stalemate and bring agreements nearer, rather than perpetuate endless academic disputes on academic freedom and institutional autonomy. Legislation is effective if it provides a clear division of labour for the solving of future problems of daily and strategic management, while safeguarding both institutional autonomy and academic freedom, as well as the responsibilities of a democratic government. The rest is co-operation and interaction.

## 1.2.1.2  Legislation

Peter Noll (1973) found that no exact definition of politics or policy is needed to ascertain beyond doubt that legislation is one of the most important and probably even the most important task of politics. Legislation is both an instrument in itself and a frame for the use of other instruments of policy. As it is intrinsically meant for the future, the nature, starting point, and the style, speed, direction, impact and psychological effects of legislation, are important issues to be studied. Legislation only ensures democracy and satisfactory development if it is regularly updated. Organising changes in a democracy implies in turn that the legitimacy has also to be ensured. As legislation intrinsically defines borders between the market and the state, between the society as a whole and individual responsibilities, a highly sensitive field is entered, in particular because education has to be considered as core-business of the state, usually spending the greatest part of a state budget. Hence, it should not be a surprise that such a complex process often causes slow progress.

Legislation involves taking into account other opinions, the countries' budgets, safeguarding the rights of minorities, and not only following the willpower of the government or majority vote. To change a national law in an international environment, such as higher education and research should be, is definitely complicated. Questions like: why do something; what is to be done; how to do it; when it should be done; what are the consequences, will have to be answered. How to be accountable to the Parliament and the citizens of the country is a similarly important question. On the one hand, legislation protects citizens from state intervention and safeguards classical fundamental rights. This requires a rather passive State as well as an independent judicial power. On the other hand, an active State is needed to protect fundamental social rights. This requires an active legislature and an active administration. In higher education and research legislation is "social engineering", which should secure the legitimate operation of the institutions as well as the legal protection of institutions, staff and students against the State. At the same time legislation links democracy with social engineering.

In the LRP, as well as in this series, "legislation" or "law" has been given a wider definition which includes any legislative instrument that has a general effect: any enactment, decree, rule or regulation promulgated by public authorities at national or sub-national level. The LRP, as well as this series, focuses on legislation in its context, because legislation is only a moment in time, indeed an "Act of Parliament". Much more important and interesting is the innovative process of legislative development and the flexible, but legitimate, implementation of the law, whilst implementation is in itself a first step in developing amendments to the law. Some countries in central and eastern Europe are already entering the stage of what can be called "second generation legislation". Others are still in the process of finding the way to their first framework law on higher education and research. Countries often wait a long time with legislative revisions, encounter resistance in starting a legislative process or lack the political will or courage. As has been said, legislation requires a lot of work and it takes a lot of time. Its political impact is not always predictable, nor are its positive and negative side effects easily calculable. Despite all the pitfalls, however, the discussions on the system of higher education and its legislation need inevitably a continuous review. Continuous legislative reform safeguards democratic development and the rule of law. If a law is not updated regularly, ex ante legitimating political measures, it does not take long before people are no longer interested in what is, by democratic decision, written into it. Hence, the authority of Parliament and government will be questioned and democracy itself jeopardised.

The relationship between the State and its citizens has probably the most complex features in the higher education and research sector.

1.2.1.3  Accelerating change

Society changes the law and a new law changes society, but democracy and legislation move too slowly. Alvin Toffler (1970; 1981) wrote about the accelerating speed of the changes in a global society. International developments are dictating the national reactions of government and society. People adapt to the situation, but the accelerating change of society is not matched by an accelerating tempo of legislation. Hence, governments encounter increasingly substantial problems with the rule of law, their legitimacy and their parliamentary democracy, because their laws are simply no longer fitting. It is clear from many aspects and examples of national political crises, from the increased importance of judicial review and the increasing influence of pressure groups, that the real pitfall is not changing legislation. What should be achieved in the future is a state of continuous, partial, legislative reform to keep in tune with the accelerating speed of the changes in society. It is becoming a habit that a country revises its laws on higher education and research at least once per (regular) term of government. When the legislator remains aloof, and as long as internationally accepted values and norms are anchored in the law, stability and fairness are secured and earlier adopted laws are respected and transitional legislation well designed, this should not be regarded as a problem, but as democratic governance.

1.2.1.4  Modification versus codification?

In his analysis of the educational policies in central and eastern Europe, César Bîrzea (1994) argues that countries in a state of reform should not concentrate so much on the drafting of new education laws, as not everything can be changed by decree and a law is only an instrument, a tool of the reform and not vice versa. It may be true that, in fact, only little can be changed by decree as has been argued before. But that is not important. Basically, there are two types of legislation: codification and modification.

·   Codifying values and norms that are already legal practice is the first type. This type, as it serves consolidation, seems less interesting for countries in a stable situation and for countries in rapid transition. Nevertheless, codification of international values and norms is necessary to provide stability in times of rapid transition.

·   Modifying legislation is an attempt to achieve social goals in a democratic way with a legitimate outcome that is sometimes divided into rectification, modernisation and restructuring measures.

These are rather unnatural divisions. It is preferable to regard legislation as a holistic process, reform "par excellence", and not simply as a tool. Modification can not take place without regard to that which needs to be codified. There is a natural tension between classical fundamental rights, codification and the need for stability and consolidation that require a rather passive State on the one hand, and fundamental social rights, modification and the need for reform and innovation which require an active State on the other. The LRP emphasises the latter, not only because of its mission and principal territorial scope, but also because of the most interesting complexity and uncertainties of modification. Finding a balance between the need for both stability and change is a major challenge in the development of higher education and research systems currently taking place. Yet, codification and modification are the extremes of a continuum; in practice the single provisions of new legislation show a wide variety of mixtures.

Of course, change can take place without, or more rapidly than, legislation. This is, however, paradoxically not always necessary or desirable. Modification without a legislative process is, especially in countries during times of fast transition, political change, confusion or economic crises, sometimes even dangerous for democracy. Legislation is a public process that stimulates public debate if three conditions are fulfilled: the constituency is informed, it finds it important, and it has a say. A legislative process can also attract international attention and thus international pressure, especially when developments tend to have negative consequences. In countries that wish to build a new democratic State and seek the legitimation that they missed for so long, legislation is even the only way, in spite of the trial and error that inevitably accompanies it. In the early nineties, most reformers in central and eastern Europe rightly gave priority to legislation in order to realise democratic values and norms but, unfortunately, there are tendencies to interrupt, neglect or even reverse this process.

### 1.2.1.5  The quest for models and standards

There are many ways to provide a legal framework. Some procedures will work efficiently and effectively in one country and fail in another. Some ideas seem to work well, others will certainly never work. The present state of the higher education system, the financial situation of a country and the political priorities and managerial culture of the system are predominant constraints when choosing legitimate legal instruments. A law, or a set of laws, must be tailor-made and cover the full range of the sector, including deliberate abstinence or full withdrawal of the legislature from certain issues. There are many principles and standards that govern the higher education and research sector. There is much in common that derives from national historical developments and the traditionally wide international contacts in the world of higher education and research. However, looked at more closely, it becomes difficult to formalise those principles and standards in recommendations, legislation or conventions or even a policy. The impressive legislative efforts in many European countries during the last decade, and the literally hundreds of books and thousands of articles per year seeking to identify some of these principles, is clear evidence for this. An internationally accepted model for legislation of higher education and research does not really exist. Standards change with underlying norms and values as the recent introduction of new quality assurance methods proves. Copying parts of good pieces of work from another country is also a risky operation. The spirit of a law, and its meaning, implementation and guidance under ever-changing conditions, is more important than its coincidental verbatim. Hence, implementation and interpretation of a law demands reasoning, not just reading. Key-stones of good legislation are the embedding in the internationally accepted legal practice, democratic governance and the adequate possibilities of appeal to an independent court.

1.2.1.6 How to do things with rules?

The main functions of higher education legislation are:
·    to define the mission of higher education institutions and their relation vis-à-vis the State;
·    to define the principal rights and obligations of students, staff, institutions and the State;
·    to set down formal procedures for negotiating change, for containing conflict and for setting standards by which conflict may be handled in order to facilitate the interactive process-management of the system, including mission-money relations.

The first two functions primarily only require reconfirmation of (inter-)national values, norms and conventions and seldom need important modification. The third function provides a structure for finding consensus within the system when problems arise or change is needed. This is a more complicated matter. Meaningful legislation in higher education and research consists neither of centrally regulating substantive details of the education and research process, nor a steering of details because details are as unpredictable as the circumstances in which the legislation is intended to provide a framework and, above all, the primary responsibility of the institutions. Legislation should above all contain careful and democratic procedures of steering and governance of a sector. Subsequently, initiatives to change the law should not come only from the ministry or government. Ministers have to respond to legitimate policy propositions from students, staff, institutions and intermediate bodies. This sharing of responsibilities should be part of a legal structure of information, co-operation, and structured dialogue between all relevant parties in order to come closer to the idea of a self-steering and "inherently democratic" higher education system. The latter concept is derived from that of an inherently safe nuclear power plant, by extending the comparison to the warning that goes with nuclear power, one should be very careful with democracy. One can never be sure.

Much is possible and many changes are needed, in particular in central and eastern but also in western Europe. The dilemma is, however, that there are limits to the reforms, legislative or not, that a society, a system, an institution or a person can absorb within a given period. The question of *what* to aim at is often relatively easy to answer; to outline the process of *how* to achieve those objectives is more difficult. The last chapter of a law, the transitional provisions, is the most difficult, and usually the most neglected part. Increasing gaps between the law in the books and the law in action are becoming a visible obstacle. Subsequently, negative effects on the credibility of the government, the State, are dawning. In Europe, a new approach to legislation is urgently needed.

## 1.2.2   Bridges for enlightenment and freedom

Ralf Dahrendorf (1992) wrote in his "Betrachtungen über die Revolution in Europa", an essay in the form of a letter to a Polish friend: "Freedom above everything else is what I believe in. The goal may be clear, but the road to it is paved with traps. We could help to avoid some of them, but in the first instance it depends on your own energy and determination. The rest is luck. I keep my fingers crossed and hope for the best. I do this with all my heart."

This first volume in particular, as its title suggests, examines the links between the State and the higher education institutions. Each book of the LRP publication project should give guidance to the energy and determination that Dahrendorf mentioned. It ought as well to bridge:
· the countries of Europe;
· Parliament, government, ministry, the higher education system and society;
· democracy and professional efficiency;
· the present state of legislation and policy development, legislative reform and legitimate implementation of reforms;
· the law in the books and the law in action;
· norms and values, convictions and traditions;
· teaching and research and their daily and strategic management.

Each book in this series is a co-operative creative effort of a great number of scholars involved in higher education. Without them this book would not have been written in this unique way and with this unique result. It is challenging to read the kaleidoscope of impressions, ideas for and descriptions of higher education that the country reports provide. Recollecting the cultural differences that are incorporated in the texts and their practical approach, it is obvious that differentiation is a great virtue and will never cease to exist. Nevertheless, in a world where old borders are continuously replaced by new ones, it is a matter of survival to work consciously together on compatibility and compliance within a variety of solutions, looking for a tailor-made approach for each country. The analysis and conclusions of this book are precious contributions to this survival.

The readers may find that each volume draws on their personal practical perspective and helps generate creativity and inspiration that is demanded from politicians, managers and other workers in higher education and research, and helps provide some enlightenment, heuristic tools, incentives and ideas for 'change agents' all over the world. Only then can the series contribute to the desired equilibrium between consolidation and change.

Freedom, co-operation and enlightenment, may this book contribute to their advancement.

*Peter Kwikkers*
Programme Manager of the Legislative Reform Programme

# 2

# RELATIONS BETWEEN THE STATE
# AND HIGHER EDUCATION

## 2.1    Introduction

Today we use the terminologies and the theoretical frames of the social sciences in order to describe and interpret the statics and dynamics of historical events, processes and evolution. We utilise the underlying normative assumptions within appropiate theories as well as the explicit regularities which give shape to the hard core of those theories to create order in our minds, and to be understandable between ourselves. However, by utilising frames we create veils between "reality" and our description of it at the same time. We narrow our views in order to see, maybe this is a necessary sacrifice.

We tend to use the theoretical frames of public policy and public administration to describe governmental processes and to interpret them. So if we, for instance, detect phenomena, where purposeful influence appears to be exercised, we speak about steering. If we discover bundles of reciprocally intense relationships between social actors, we tend to speak about networks. We interpret legislation above all as a conscious act of government. Legislation functions both as a framework for steering and as a steering instrument, according to public policy analysis. Our attention is fixed upon notions of effectiveness and legitimacy; we focus upon unintended consequences and learning processes.

Of course in this manner we rewrite history. Many legislators in the past and the present have never given a thought to the above-mentioned notions.

They just revealed their preferences on the structure of higher education. We however need a toolkit for the description and analysis of legislation.

Legislation as a product of public policy making can be normatively considered in two ways, as was pointed out in § 1.2.1.4: either as a means to codify values and norms and other regularities that are already accepted in society at large, or as a reform process to modify societal events; both are true at the same time in many cases. The distinction provides a useful warning against naive legalistic reform attempts on the one hand and against the immobility of the extreme "codification argument" on the other. We analyse historical processes. Therefore we need approaches that can cope with historical dynamics. Since Marxism is no longer fashionable, we no longer have any means of disposing of a holistic, all-encompassing dynamic theory. In this volume we will use partial dynamic concepts such as learning processes in order to approach the nature of time-bound developments. To write about the relationships between states and higher education now seems to be a matter of course.

One should realise however that universities and schools existed long before one could speak about nation states. They had either a private character or were based on local or regional public regulations. They existed alongside other types of educational institutions. Later on the nation state took over authority from local and/or regional public bodies; also private institutions became dependent on financial support from the state, and the latter started to steer them through the purse strings. As the nation states accepted the conceptual framework of the Rechtsstaat, legislation became predominant as a steering instrument. Legislation either confirms or creates relationships and solidifies them at the same time. The democratic nation state reveals its preferences on societal development in the first place through legislation. It reacts to events and processes elsewhere in society, but also exercises influence on society. One should speak about mutual interdependence in a dynamic time-bound framework.

The relations between nation states and institutions of higher education have developed over the last couple of centuries in a complex manner. In general the relationships between nation states and education as a whole are of a complex nature. There are no simple explanations or theories at hand. It would be a mistake to assume that the evolution of nation states can be considered as the independent variable while the educational policies or systems are dependent variables. Many authors, like Gellert, have argued that the evolution of the nation state has been intertwined with the development of formally regulated education: so for instance, the standardisation of knowledge and skill demands by regulations on degrees and diplomas on a national basis, has not only furthered economic progress and division of labour in a certain stage of economic growth, but has also consolidated the authority of the state within each national society. The expansion of public financial support for education has not only enabled the poor to receive adequate training, but also strengthened the legitimacy of the state to collect taxes. Nation states and educational systems are in many ways intertwined; their destinies are mutually interdependent.

This observation provides us, at first sight, with a very provocative forecast in an era where Europeanisation and internationalisation in a broader sense threaten the existence of the nation state. Should the national boundaries of educational systems fade away as economic development demands global markets for goods and services, and international labour markets, therefore, demand international standards on educational performance? And also should the authority of the nation state over regulation of education be broken down? And should we then not consider national legislation on education as an outdated phenomenon?

On reflection it appears to be still too early to make sensible remarks on such possible future developments as stated above, because up until now the nation state seems to have been very successful in defending its position in the cultural domains of public interest against the "attacks of internationalism". In central and eastern Europe recent history has shown the collapse of a supranational public conglomerate or federation, and the restoration of national identities. In western Europe education is the prime domain of the nation, where the European Union has had to show modesty of ambitions and has not been in an important regulatory position.

It is still too early to come to grips with the consequences of actual economic globalisation for the relationships between nation states and education. A comparative view on legislation on higher education in Europe is worthwhile because legislators could still learn a lot from each other and their efforts are not obsolete.

Fascinating theories have been formulated on the emerging relations between global economic development, the evolution of nation states and the changes in educational systems. All these theories relate to certain stages of development. Fundamental changes in the pattern of the division of labour, and moreover, the structural character and speed of that change have deeply influenced the shape of education. Legislation has accompanied these changes.

This chapter is devoted to a partial theoretical analysis of the dynamics of the relationships between states and higher education. In the next one, as well as in chapter 5, a comparative view will be presented on the state of the art of legislation on higher education in Europe. In chapter four we will draw some conclusions.


2.2      Relations between the state and higher education

2.2.1    The evolution of the nation state in relation to education in general

2.2.1.1  Universities in former stateless societies

The origins of universities are manifold. Some have their roots in religion, others in the denial of the value of close ties between education and religious beliefs. When states did not yet exist, universities in many cases tried to emancipate themselves from the influence of churches and regional rulers. They developed primarily as professional schools, producing lawyers and physicians. They gradually gained their independence, and hence invested in an internal culture, a set of academic values, of independence. Unnecessary to say that these universities were elite institutions, although in some countries the real elite, the nobility never attended a university; moreover many of those institutions developed a very international character during the sixteenth and seventeenth centuries. In particular the hospitable European regions underwent the influence of large numbers of intellectual foreign immigrants and they developed a spiritual climate in which a humanistic culture could evolve, and scientific "free" research could begin to flourish. It remained a marginal activity in the quantitative sense. Until the nineteenth century one cannot observe any visible direct connection between the economic development of countries and their university systems. The cultural influence of universities however was already considerable.

Then, gradually, the nation state "grew up".

### 2.2.1.2 The classical viewpoint: the state in its capacity as benign emancipator of the "masses"

States are there to produce collective goods, because in an egocentric society nobody else would. Education is however not a collective good, but a private good in principle: it brings the educated private profit; and it lacks the properties of collective goods of non-exclusion and indivisibility. So it could be traded in the market place. Traditionally education had been mainly in the hands of altruistic non-state institutions, but their resources were restricted. Only the happy few could profit for a longer period of time Typically the training of workers was dealt with "on the job".

Longer formal education in specific institutions demands huge investments however, so that, in the absence of charity, either the available purchasing power or the potential to borrow money are decisive factors in determining the actual demand for education in the market place. During the nineteenth century nation states consolidated their existence, and started to formulate societal objectives as to the dissemination of knowledge and skills and to introduce them to their populations. The motives were both of a paternalistic and "distributive justice" character : the public authorities held the opinion that the population at large would underestimate the benefits of education, and moreover they wished to enable everyone, irrespective of individual purchasing power, to enjoy education. The massive financial state support for merit goods in general and education in particular began. To become educated even became an obligation for each citizen. In some countries only the public part of education became subsidised, while in others the same regulation and subsidies concerned both public and private education. Later it became clear that a well educated population was not only a cultural treasure and a necessary condition for the success of representative parliamentary democracy, but also vital for economic development.

National constitutions regularly confirmed the freedom to create schools, and the individual right to teach or to receive an education. In some cases the basis for state subsidies was also recognised at the constitutional level.

Normal legislation on education had to regulate the conditions under which schools would be entitled to receive state subsidies, how new schools could be added to the existing ones, and how subsidies could be stopped. This often resulted in the formulation of rules concerning the qualification of teachers, the equipment used, etc..

2.2.1.3  The state, economic development and standardisation of qualifications

When entrepreneurial activity started to take place in larger firms, and formal education became longer and longer, as part of a direct preparation for labour, employers began to formulate demands for the educational system. They had a major interest in educational quality. They wanted to know for sure, that a school or university would deliver graduates with a specific level of knowledge and skills, and a certain general level of competence. They wanted to avoid the enormous selection costs, that they would have to make in order to find out, which member of a random population would be fit to do a certain job. Education functions as a societal filter, as it selects young people over and over again. Some argue, (for instance Kenneth J. Arrow who formulated the so-called filter theory of education), that an educational system would have considerable economic value in national society, if it just fulfilled this selective function only, without even adding knowledge to the young people.

This filter function of education relates to the selective properties of an educational system. To meet the employers' demands it appears necessary to regulate the educational structure and above all the structure of degrees. So legislation was designed to formulate the objectives and/or contents of curricula, or at least the structure of exams. As a consequence the standardisation of education, and in particular the standardisation of degrees was furthered by legislation. This has contributed to the national character of labour markets.

2.2.1.4 Interconnections and dynamics, amongst others professionalisation

There is still another set of arguments available concerning the desirability of legislation on educational structures, and degree structures in particular: people with certain knowledge, competence or skills are in the position of gradually monopolising the supply of certain services in the labour market: they "professionalise", and build organisations in order to promote their interests and to exclude non-members from professional practice. Exclusion therefore is an important part of processes of professionalisation. This exclusion concerns in many cases, the access to professional practice which is only granted if the professional can show a specific degree. Subsequently, education and professionalisation become closely connected. The state is a necessary agency to enforce this type of exclusion by law. The *effectus civilis* tied to a certain degree has to be ascertained by public regulations. In this manner the three societal sub-systems state, education and professions reconfirm and strengthen each other´s existence. They are mutually interdependent. The legitimacy of the state is continuously strengthened by its effectiveness in protecting the entitlements of the well established professional organisations and individual professions; the effectiveness of the collective monopoly held by the professionals is guaranteed by public regulations; and the position of formal education is confirmed by its monopoly to grant access to the professions concerned by the degree structure.

It may be clear now that the interests of the employers, mentioned above in § 2.2.1.2, and those of the professional organisations in many cases go hand in hand. Economic development is characterised in our times by more and more refined patterns of division of labour. So the educational structure, and moreover the degree structure, must reflect those patterns. The complexity of educational legislation is partially explained by this evolution. On the other hand the professional structure is also due to changes as technological progress is made. So legislation should not be too rigid. It is here that the interests of employers in general and those of existing professional organisations might diverge; for employers would like to profit from technological progress and therefore demand flexibility in education and degree structures, while professional organisations might want to protect their self-interests.

It is also clear that the economic advantage for employers and organised professionals of a well established and standardised educational and degree structure is so great that they consider their tax money as well spent. So the legitimacy of the state to raise taxes is well served by educational legislation. Some analysts, amongst others Gellert, have argued that it is essentially in this way that the existence of the modern nation state is intertwined with education.


### 2.2.2    The nation-state and higher education

### 2.2.2.1  Typologies of policy making: the human capital theory

Different types of policy making may be relevant at the same time: we distinguish for instance symbolic and rationalistic approaches; the former are directed towards processes of sense-making and persuasion, while the latter aim their impact on patterns of behaviour, events, and so on. Often both approaches play their roles at the same time. Legislation plays its role inside these frameworks. So the evaluation of legislation cannot be restricted to criteria concerning effectiveness in terms of visible real effects. It should possibly also include changes of value patterns, and the like. Policy making itself is based upon ideas that could be called a policy theory. A powerful policy theory on education is the human capital theory. This framework considers education as an investment process: the value added by education should be considered as a capital good. The rate of return on investments in education should be calculated in terms of future incomes of the educated, or more precisely in terms of income differentials. The costs of education should be calculated in terms of the costs of the educational process itself plus forgone incomes. External effects of education, benefits and costs not revealed in any income or other market price, would legitimate subsidies in the case of positive effects, and taxes in the case of negative externalities.

This view has gradually become the most powerful underlying policy theory in the realm of education. Although the empirical possibilities to support specific educational policy measures prove to be rather poor, the theory appears to be very persuasive in policy debates on the funding of education. The calculations made to illustrate the consequences of certain policy measures accept income data from the past in order to forecast the future benefits of investments in education, although nobody could reasonably forecast in a scientific manner incomes for decades to come. Throughout Europe this view, known under very different labels, has essentially deter-mined expansionist educational policies during the greater part of the twentieth century. Its symbolic meaning has been very important.

2.2.2.2  Stages of growth of higher education

Until the Second World War higher education in most European countries was on a moderate scale; it was still an elite provision. The economic upswing after this war demanded a much more advanced labour force than ever before. The general level of education increased, and higher education started to grow very fast. Many of the higher education institutions, however, were not designed for mass education. Their internal culture often resisted a mass character. So in many countries new institutions were necessary to cope with the fast growth of higher education as a whole. Not only were new universities erected, but other types of institutions for tertiary education were created, some as a reincarnation of former secondary professional schools, some out of a conscious political intention, such as the polytechnics in Great Britain. The traditional universities had to undergo considerable change too, in order to receive their share of the higher education cake. In eastern Europe specific professional institutions took care of the need for advanced labour. From the eighties on higher education increasingly covers more than thirty percent of any age groups, both in eastern and in western Europe. In many countries binary systems of higher education have emerged.

Then the situation changed. Gradually it became clear, that education could also be a "positional" good. As higher education became a mass provision, the unemployment among university graduates, earlier unknown as a structural phenomenon, soon became considerable. Former expectations concerning the prospects of a certain degree are not realised. The number of jobs at higher levels are increased at a rate less than the number of graduates. The more people that graduate from higher education, the more moderate their job prospects appear to be. In order to get the job you expected you have to follow still further education. This disappointment, for the first time expressed by Fred Hirsch in his Social Limits to Growth (1976), has become, as we will observe, a major political influence in recent years.

Until the 1980s this growth of mass higher education was not seriously criticised. Effectiveness and legitimacy were the prime objectives of public policy makers all over the world, and the persuasive power of the human capital theory provided sufficient symbolic political support.

Steering is exercising influence in a thoughtful manner. In systems theory we observe the steering-relation among other relationships between the environment, the steering centre and the system that is governed. Effective steering is the main subject of theory formulation in public administration, also in education, but the perspective continuously changes. We argue, throughout this volume, that it is proper to consider effectiveness as a dynamic and flexible concept and not as a static one. Therefore we need underlying theoretical concepts that can deal with these properties, but only very partial and modest ones appear to be available.

Educational policies have been developed during the last century within an ideological frame of reference characterised by "merit good motives", later supported by the human capital theory. The emancipation of all according to talent, no longer dependent on heritage or purchasing power, has been a very socially powerful policy objective. Education was and is the prime social process in order to realise this. As economic evolution has led us into the era of knowledge-intensive productive processes, professional expertise has become the most important productive resource for a national economy too. So for a long time social and economic arguments went hand in hand in order to promote intense steering of educational systems by public authorities. The welfare state concept consolidated this approach until the 1980s.

Recently however the increasing scarcity of resources in the public domain has brought to the surface once more, some of the "eternal" problems of educational public policies: "the emperor's clothes" character of the educational process itself, the vague concept of value added by education, the visible ineffectiveness of selection through education, the shortcomings of teachers and schools, etc. Moreover the increasing wealth of citizens and the realisation of the objective of emancipation, so that nowadays everyone seems to be able to judge for him or herself in educational matters, have mobilised critical attention concerning the paternalistic aspects of recent education policies, at least in western Europe. Why should the state, i.e.

the taxpayer contribute so much to, for instance, higher education, if everyone can afford to pay for it himself?

Now that mass higher education has been reached in many countries, there
is also mass unemployment of university graduates among us. Once again
we are confronted with the "positional good" character of higher education.
Public support for the increase of public subsidies to education is eroding
in a number of countries. So we face a paradox: the overwhelming success
of education in dramatically increasing the well-educated proportion of the
population has eroded public support for the continuation of a high level
of financial support. Public steering of education has not limited itself to
financing. Education laws have regulated the shape of the school system,
the contents of curricula, the labour conditions of teachers, the exact procedures of selection and examinations, the authority of local government
in educational matters, etcetera. In many respects and in many countries
the educational sector can be considered as an overregulated system, where
public policy makers lacked self-restraint in rule-production. As a consequence the autonomy of schools and the freedom of educators has weakened
considerably.

The recent and more general crisis of the welfare state has mobilised critical
attention on the effectiveness of steering systems. As we shall observe, new
steering concepts have been developed in order to create a more limited role
for the central level of public control and to improve effectiveness of the
education sector itself by giving it more autonomy in a specific manner.

### 2.2.2.3 Recent macro trends in western Europe: driving forces for change

We argue that the interdependence of a number of macro-trends is very
crucial to the situation higher education finds itself in nowadays. We distinguish the following driving forces:
a   erosion of political motives to finance higher education with taxpayers
    money;
b   the consequences of the partial commercialisation of knowledge;
c   the threats and opportunities presented by the revolution of communica-
    tion technology, and last but not least;
d   the impact of the gradual introduction of continuing education.

*a   Erosion*

We now envisage the erosion of the, until recently powerful political motivation to subsidise the development of higher education systems brought higher education into the era of mass provision. The characteristics of education, in particular the "positional good" (Fred Hirsch) character, have caused a declining willingness of tax payers to support higher education financially. In general, one can observe the decline of the public provision of merit goods and a gradual re-privatisation in many advanced societies. Former considerations concerning distributive justice are naturally weakened in a rich society where every one can borrow in order to invest in education with the objective of future profit. The nation state, of course, provides a safety net so that the disappointment of expectations as to the return on investment in higher education will not cause the financial breakdown of the individuals concerned. The possibilities of a student loan system under these conditions seem rather favourable. Higher education is booming in so far that the demand for initial and post-initial higher education is still increasing irrespective of the emergence of considerable unemployment among graduates.

In particular within national systems where traditionally higher education is free of charge, sometimes even guaranteed in the constitution, this waning of political support leads to considerable tensions, because it is impossible to introduce student fees, even if, for example Lithuania and Belarus, provisionally may have found some sort of way out.

On the other hand many government agencies are also heavily involved in the financial support of scientific research. There is no general crisis visible here, but the prevailing tendencies are to support applied research primarily; as a consequence there is relative negligence of fundamental, and in particular from an economic point of view, useless research. This type of research is produced, in general, by classical universities. The collective good character of fundamental research leads to the possibility of negligence as no public actor feels responsible for it any longer.

In the internal organisation of national government two tendencies can be observed; in some cases, the ministry of education adds other assignments such as "employment", to its original mission while in other cases ministries for trade and industry, transport or health care fulfil tasks within the domains of science and/or research policy, or even interfere with general higher education. So the complexity of relationships between institutions and governments generally has increased. Multi-actor perspectives for strategies on behalf of institutions and their representative organisations therefore should predominate.

Free rider problems emerge in so far as both nationally and internationally the neglect of sufficient provision of means for fundamental research could remain unpunished.

Until now, governments based their strategies upon an economistic utilitarian paradigm. But in fact the structure of the labour market has changed considerably as a consequence of the massification of higher education and the technological revolutions. The filter function of higher education of Arrow a.o. has partially disappeared. Employers have organised their own selective thresholds by creating an outside ring of temporary jobs inside their sphere of influence. Long-term appointments for the happy few after careful selection among many, are based upon observations and experiences collected during that period of temporary assignment. Thus new filters have been constructed.

The traditional concept of "the job" as stable or even as lifelong employment is also gradually becoming obsolete. Intermediate employer federations in their lobbying positions concerning education, genererally present very conservative points of view, but individual employers act quite differently. We now envisage a process of flexibility within the labour market. In that market only temporary labour is traded; the suppliers of labour acting like entrepreneurs. Of course this observation is only valid for a certain part of the total labour force, but that part is increasing. Relative incomes in the labour market are changing very much faster than in the past too; the relative scarcity of certain professions may change, maybe not overnight, but at a rate so fast that present relative incomes are now altogether deficient as a basis for prognoses.

Moreover, continuing education by professionals in order to update their knowledge and skills fundamentally changes the position and scope of the first-tier initial programmes in higher education. Government agencies and professional organisations design sets of conditions for the continuity of professional practice, so that public regulation of professional practice and the realisation of continuing education go hand in hand: the Europeanisation of recognition of degrees and diplomas has many complicating features. Nation states and professional organisations once more have found each other as allies in order to maintain strong legitimate regulation, they have become the gatekeepers of the exclusive character of certain professions.

The traditional economistic paradigm, based upon some variant of the human capital theory, is in fact obsolete now, and it has become a hindrance for necessary change. International organisations such as the World Bank and OECD are gatekeepers of this obsolete paradigm. Educational policies are still based upon labour market prognoses although all experts realise that the reflexive character of the labour market does not allow that type of forecasting. In fact relying on prognoses has become more or less fraudful. The advice to future students to choose specific studies where the labour market perspective now seems favourable has a random character too, as in many cases five years hence the picture will have changed dramatically. The time has come to rethink the general cultural meaning of higher learning as a source for the redefinition of policy paradigms.

The main characteristics of a new paradigm (or policy theory) should amongst others be based upon a careful analysis of the major trends in the development of the structure of the labour market, and the evolution of continuing education.

## b   *Communication technology*

Not only is the structure of the labour market experiencing profound change, but also professional practice itself is changing very fast. In the future computers will be far more trustworthy than men as continuously updated advanced databases. Human labour will be characterised by social interaction as well as man-machine interaction of a very high intensity, where human properties such as intuition, wisdom, dealing with ambiguity, paradoxes, dilemmas etc. will be of great value. The future educational system will have to prepare for this.

Moreover the technological revolution in the domain of communication, publishing, broadcasting and computing should bring about far reaching measures to enrich the learning environments of students and researchers inside universities. The presence of world wide databases necessitates dramatic changes in the contents and teaching methods in the whole domain of education. In Europe this process is proceeding far too slowly in many disciplines.

But also the higher education system and policy makers around it should design a concept in order to cope with the powerful conglomerates that are going to dominate the high tech communication industry (e.g. Negroponte). The Disney merger is neither an incident nor a joke, but has led to the formation of a powerful global conglomerate; in Europe one finds similar cases. It is not impossible that these conglomerates will start to interfere with universities. For that industry will be and will remain hungry for substance, besides games and pay-TV, and would education not be an ideal future branch? And would it not be logical then, that conglomerates would buy educational suppliers? Financially probably one global conglomerate could afford to buy ten or twenty universities in Europe. How could the necessary independence and integrity of science be maintained in such situations?

So legislators face very old questions again: how to preserve the necessary independence of institutions for higher learning.

## c   Commercialisation of knowledge

A further complicating factor is the gradual commercialisation of knowledge that causes a more hybrid culture in universities. This hybrid culture increases the probability of future conflicts between regulating and incentive producing governments and higher education institutions. It is hard to answer chicken-egg causality questions. Have the recent budget cuts led to this process of commercialisation, or were the budget cuts made possible by the already strongly stimulated commercialisation process? However, universities in Europe have now started to earn a considerable part of their income through contracts. They operate in markets for applied research, consultancy and advanced post-initial education. Instead of the pure collective sector task-organisations they had become, they have now developed into partially market-oriented institutions. On the one hand they are accountable in a public sector perspective and framework, while on the other hand they are subject to market forces. This duality causes major tensions inside European public universities: for instance the public authorities penetrate vertically in universities, through the presidency down to departments, and finally to individual scientists, while the market penetrates horizontally.

For individuals the fringe benefits resulting from market transactions are in many cases more attractive than those allied to classical tasks. The reformulation of the law of Gresham: "bad money drives out good money", in certain cases could be: "market drives out task". A return to a past where market influences were absent, is of course impossible because the declining public resources would not enable the university to survive. Also governments tend to design barriers to a further increase in the financial independence of institutions,as derived from market transactions, because they fear the disappearance of their influence. For legislators this situation is quite complicated. The relationships between the nation state and a university are given shape in the realm of public law. Very often universities are legal personalities, and in some cases even faculties possess legal personality. But the contractual relationships between universities and third parties are framed by private law. The hybridity of universities confuses legislators who sometimes react by denying the problem and by stating that public law prevails.

*d   Continuing education*

Continuing education which refreshes the knowledge and skills of all professionals is now a regular feature of professional life. Conditions for the continuity of professional praxis in terms of teaching have been formulated and reinforced by public regulation. However the consequences of continuing education for initial education have not been considered thoroughly until now. If each new employee is to be reeducated during professional practice, should the curriculum of the initial higher teaching not be reformulated dramatically? Should curricula aim at:

·   competence and learning skills rather than knowledge?
·   the learning of learning and inquisitiveness rather than learning?
·   meta-science instead of science?

·   the development of a harmonious personality instead of instrumental
    skills?

Should not subjects such as philosophy of science, logic, epistemology, meta-
informatics, meta-technology be very important? Taking this perspective
it seems amazing that no major movement for the reformulation of initial
higher learning is visible yet.

Moreover we have already observed that the global introduction of advanced
communication technology will necessitate dramatic changes in educational
contents. Is possibly the complex and rigid character of the existing educational legislation a major hindrance to this necessary adaptation to important
societal driving forces?

These driving forces will inevitably play a major role in future legislative
praxis on education in western Europe. It still has to be seen, if they will
be less important in eastern Europe.

### 2.2.2.4   Dramatic macro-change in society and its implications for higher
education legislation in eastern Europe

It is probably still too early to analyse the consequences for educational
legislation of the dramatic macro-changes that took place in eastern European
societies at the end of the 1980s. We could observe the hectic legislative
activity during the first half of the 1990s, and we will take a closer look
at it in the next chapter, but the overall picture remains rather clouded or
even gloomy.

The political revolutions that took place, had dramatic consequences for the
whole institutional structure of the nation states involved. Supranational
influence disappeared, and national or even regional steering processes
replaced it. Sometimes fragmentation prevailed, even as far as the number
of institutions for higher education is concerned, but there has also been
new alliances between institutions. The solidifying effects of new legislation
have not yet become altogether visible. The learning processes around
regulations have hardly begun.

On the surface it seems clear that the reform has strengthened university autonomy considerably. But a look under the cover of symbolic legislation often shows immediately that the very detailed regulations from national governments are found, not in formal legislation, but have been derived from it or have even been independently specified as administrative conditions allied to state subsidies. Moreover the number of intermediate organisations between the nation states and universities has increased dramatically. Some analysts call these intermediaries "buffer organisations", suggesting that they protect institutions against the national authorities. However, history has often shown that such organisations gradually evolve into allies of the state, and instead bitter hostility between the intermediaries and individual universities emerge. In chapter four we will take a closer look at this.

Is it worthwhile describing the evolution of education for Europe as a whole? Are the differences in scope and stage of development between western and eastern Europe not so striking, that we should refrain from any attempt to catch both in the same net? We do not think so. Firstly, because both parts of Europe share a past that covers the largest part of university history. Secondly, because eastern Europe now appears to accept an economic model that is similar to the western European one. Of course one might find major differences in wealth for the time being, but they will be of gradually diminishing importance. Only a return to Soviet bureaucracy would cause a breach, that could not easily be bridged.

## 2.3      Legislation as a policy system

### 2.3.1     Policy systems

Public policies are implemented in very complicated interrelated combinations of rules, procedures and measures. We call such a combination a policy system. In the concept of the Rechtsstaat a policy system is given shape by law.

A policy system is characterised by three dimensions:
- the level of decision-making;
- the points of reference for steering;
- the policy instruments.

The first dimension has to do with the degree of (de)centralisation; the second with the orientation on either inputs, throughputs or outputs of the system under steering; and the third with the choice between the three main categories of policy instruments, enforcement, money and persuasion. In a mature policy system there will easily be hundreds of components. In most analyses such a policy system is considered as a "presence" that is unrelated to time. Here we argue that the effectiveness of a policy system will gradually erode; or at least its impact will be far from constant.

Policy makers in designing a policy system concentrate on the foreseen and desirable effects of a policy system. This may seem logical, but in doing so they neglect the unforeseen effects by definition, and will tend to consider these as the undesirable side effects of favourable development. The organisations and individuals who perceive the impact of a policy system however, react in an intelligent manner. This reaction pattern is based upon reflexivity.

We speak of reflexivity concerning individual human beings when recognising their capacity to reflect upon their environment, events, threats, norms, history, expectations, etcetera, and when changing their behaviour, their tastes or preferences, and their values or norms as a consequence. We assume that reflexivity is the essential characteristic of human existence, that it is omni-present although its intensity, speed and outcomes may differ considerably. Reflections may concern any regularity, observed or detected earlier in individual behaviour, and therefore in social relations. Therefore the outcomes of reflection may transcend the earlier observed regularity. As a consequence the regularity may potentially lose its validity, because the underlying assumptions concerning human behaviour have undergone change. Elsewhere we have described the relevance of this fact for social science itself. If we define the social aspect of our world as the domain that is determined by human behaviour, the foregoing means that social systems do not bear a deterministic character. Any regularity or law concerning social systems therefore, once formulated, in principle has only a temporary validity.

However, it takes time to reflect. Moreover, it may depend upon the specific characteristics of the environment, whether and how soon, the results will show in human behaviour. If the environment, for instance, is of a very repressive nature, societal change based upon reflection will have a relatively long build-up. Moreover, the behavioural reactions will correspond to the character of the environment. So in a very repressive environment the results of reflection may emerge as explosions, revolutions or other forms of severe social unrest, while only very moderate reactions would be sufficient to bring about the same change in a relatively tolerant environment.

The reflexive character of social systems is also relevant in situations where regulation or steering prevails. Both the regulators and the "regulated", those at whom steering is directed, will be reflexive. But reflection is bound to roles and interests so it is not at all certain whether the results of both processes of reflection will converge. Of course there might also emerge different, or even contradictory, outcomes of reflection by different groups within each of the above-mentioned categories. At any rate, the evolution of steering practices will be determined by mutual and interactive reflection of both parties concerned.

## 2.3.2    Law of diminishing effectiveness of steering

In most policy analyses the effectiveness of a policy system is considered to be a concept that concerns the relationship between objectives and effects of a certain policy. According to this concept a sensible choice of tools or instruments will further effectiveness, and in general be unrelated to time. Here we argue, on the basis of the existence of reflexivity in the social system under consideration, that gradually the organisations and the individuals at whom the steering is directed will react to the steering measures in a reflexive manner. That is to say, at first they will experience any potential sanction, any force, however indirect, that is caused by the steering measures themselves, as an incentive to change their behaviour in a direction that corresponds to the will of the regulating body. That change at the same time contains a deviation from their own most preferred alternative, and therefore is experienced as a disagreeable event. If this deviation had not been brought about by the regulation, the regulation would have been redundant. So in due course the reflecting actors will utilise their learning capacity to avoid the disagreeable effects of the policy concerned, and in general they will gradually succeed better and better at this as time goes by. Avoidance, sabotage, disobedience, resistance, and any other kind of creative activity

to restore the original level of satisfaction will be observed. The consequence
of this first-order pattern of reactions is that the objectives of the regulating
body will gradually be realised less and less. We name this tendency, this
regularity the "law of diminishing effectiveness of steering". As we shall
see later on, this law is not omnivalent. Its validity is restricted by reactions
on behalf of the regulated by a higher order in the longer run. But short
term reactions to steering will be generally characterised by the above-mentioned law. Ceteris paribus one might expect a gradual decrease of effectiveness. One may assume however that reflexivity is not restricted to the
regulated organisations and individuals, regulators and policy-makers may
also reflect.

### 2.3.3    Law of policy accumulation

One would expect that the above-mentioned law would be of only minor
importance because the policy makers, the regulators, would use many
resources to correct their policies in reaction to observed decreases in their
effectiveness. However, reality is not as simple as that. Policy-makers have
invested heavily in present policies. A policy measure is not an isolated case,
but is embedded in wider and larger comprehensive sets of policies. Usually
such a set consists of regulations, of planning and budgeting procedures,
of implementation processes and, last but not least, of procedures for evaluation and control. Institutional and organisational arrangements have been
grouped around the nucleus of present policies and often costly information
systems have been designed and implemented in order to serve their execution. So it would be a major, and above all very costly operation to remove
an existing set of policies, a policy system, and replace it by another one.
The typical characteristics of the combination of the Rechtsstaat and the
welfare state or post-modernist variations upon it, in most cases dominate
the policy system's architecture. In particular the large care systems in our
society, economically known as merit goods, are characterised by an historical evolutionary process, and as a consequence allocative and distributive
objectives are approached through very large, complex policy systems, which
are very coherent as well as very hard to change. Resistance to fundamental
change also characterises less complex policy arrangements. The costs of
a more than marginal change are quite considerable, and therefore reactions
to decreasing policy effectiveness are generally given shape as piecemeal

adaptations within the existing policy framework. These adaptations attempt to correct or to compensate for the unfavourable effects of the learning processes on behalf of citizens and organisations subject to the policies concerned. In most cases the broad character of these adaptive piecemeal policy changes will be to refine the norms underlying the present policies, to fine tune the tools through which the policies are implemented, and tighten control, and so restore the earlier effectiveness of the policies. This means in general that norms will be refined, rules will be formulated in greater detail, the number of digressions into particular cases will increase, etcetera. We call this the "law of policy accumulation". The regular reaction to diminishing effectiveness of policies is to intensify or to accumulate them. Rudely stated, the reaction to ineffectiveness is "more of the same". Both the above-stated laws are operational at the same time, so we might expect that after a corrective accumulative policy measure a new period of diminishing effectiveness will start. So a seemingly infinite series of interactive actions could take place. In a following paragraph we will observe however, that gradually the corrective adaptations will decrease in impact, and that as a consequence effectiveness will decrease more and more until crisis emerges.

But let us first look a little deeper into the different categories of learning experience that are feasible, apart from the one described in the last paragraph.

2.3.4    First- and higher-order learning

Many authors have pointed out that learning is a multi-layered concept. The adaptation of behaviour under constant preferences and norms is only the most direct and superficial reaction to any disagreeable change in the environment of a human being. Gradually, however, other changes might take place in the minds of citizens and in the decision-making centres of organisations which could also be considered as learning processes. Citizens might change their attitudes towards present policies by a gradual shift of their insight into, as well as support for, the ideological, normative patterns underlying those policies. Goal displacement (Wildavsky, 1979) could very well be described as a more fundamental reaction to policy effects and their dynamics, among which is decreasing effectiveness. We call these reactions second-order learning processes, and they lead us to yet another type of policy dynamic. If support for initial policies erodes because citizens gradually shift their normative attitudes towards present policies, then the support for the necessary adaptations – brought about as a consequence of the functioning of the law of diminishing effectiveness – might also drift away. In this way the arrival of an effectiveness – as well as a legitimacy – crisis will be hastened.

A yet more fundamental category of higher order learning processes is to be detected in the "constitutional" area. We assume, along with many other public choice analysts, that our public institutions and our procedures for social choice are based upon a relative consensus as to the basic principles of operation of these institutions and procedures. This consensus relates to fundamental demands such as equality, liberty, and sovereignty of citizens in so far as social choice is concerned. Based upon these fundamental demands are more detailed values concerning the actual shape of and relations between specific institutions. Citizens have invested emotionally and normatively both in their ideological positions and in their attitudes towards institutions – take for instance the royal family, parliamentary democracy or socialism. Once people start to feel very strongly about the deficiencies of certain policies, they might start to wonder in more abstract terms, whether the present political system or a present set of policy-making institutions in a certain policy arena is still fit to produce any effective policies in the long run at all. As a result constitutional values might change, with of course very explosive potential consequences. This type of learning is related to the aforementioned categories of first- and second-order learning as a "meta-category", because it concerns the organisational aspects of the steering entity, or the steering of steering, and so two logical steps away from the subject matter itself.

We might distinguish a still different type of learning, called by earlier authors deutero-learning. The essential characteristic of this type is in the improvement of the ability to learn, the learning capacity; to learn how to learn is the nucleus of the concept. In organisational terms this type of learning relates to developments such as the establishment of citizen's movements or consumer organisations in order to protect citizen's rights against involuntary public "deliveries"; and to the improvement of an organisation's memory bank. It also relates to the introduction of think-tanks, or the instalment of antennae to observe any relevant change in the societal environment, or to the regular repetition of simulation exercises in order to get a better ex ante grip on the potential future effects of feasible policy measures. Both the steering actors and the regulated citizens might profit from their own mode of deutero-learning. Although this category of learning process is of a fascinating nature, it will not be dealt with it further because it is not directly related to the key issue of policy dynamics.

A general observation when comparing different types of learning, is that the higher the order of the learning process, the longer it will take and the more fundamental it will be.

## 2.3.5    Crises

First- and second-order learning processes will in many cases reinforce each other. The interactive relationship of both the law of diminishing effectiveness and the law of policy accumulation will lead to a problematic situation. Policy accumulation will increase the complexity of the policy system, the historical aggregate of measures, and therefore will increase the costs of operation of the system, so that efficiency will gradually decrease. Moreover, the original level of effectiveness will generally not be completely restored by policy accumulation. In due course both the effectiveness and the efficiency of the policy system will decrease further and further. An effectiveness crisis will suddenly emerge from this development. A neat example of such a crisis is found in the "Laffer-curve" which illustrates a situation where both an increase and a decrease of the marginal income tax rate causes a decrease in total tax revenues. When this curve represents reality, it becomes clear that no change within the framework of the existing arrangement will provide a reasonable solution any longer. An effectiveness crisis may coincide with or even be proceeded by a legitimacy crisis that might emerge from second-order and/or constitutional learning processes concerning the normative attitudes towards the policies under consideration.

As soon as policy-makers have become aware of the existence of a crisis, they will realise that the only available method for restoring normal circumstances, or better, for regaining a future perspective on sustainable relations, is to change the existing framework, either by creating a new steering system, or by abstaining from any regulation in the future. They could also utilise the existence of the crisis, assuming that the citizens and organisations concerned are also aware of its existence, and build the momentum necessary to overcome the difficulties of a change of frame. As has already been explained, a change of frame demands sacrifices, both emotional and monetary. However, the crisis will modify the outcomes of cost-benefit analyses by citizens in a direction favourable to a change of frame; and it will gradually become clear that the status quo is not a feasible alternative any longer.

According to the words of a famous Dutch lawyer: "gouverner, ce n'est pas prevoir, it is looking backward, and waiting, endless waiting until the momentum is there to perform the changes you knew unavoidable or necessary for so long already". In this respect the openness of a crisis is a blessing in disguise, because it will stimulate awareness among citizens. Policy-makers might even stimulate the open character of a crisis in order to accelerate the growth of awareness in citizens. So far we have only dealt with so-called first-order crises, during which a certain policy system is in jeopardy. In the course of such a crisis second-order learning might lead to major shifts in political preferences. Such shifts might bring about a change of government within the existing institutional framework of the society under consideration.

It has become clear from the above that higher-order learning processes of a constitutional nature might lead to more fundamental institutional crises because citizens have begun to wonder whether the existing institutions can any longer function in a satisfactory manner. There is nothing so contagious as failure, one might say. Whether a shift in citizens attitudes towards their political institutions will easily lead to any real change depends on the degree of firmness, referred to by opponents as stubbornness, of the authorities or the relative repression applied in that society. However crises generally deepen as a consequence of an evolution to higher-order learning processes.

## 2.3.6   Internalisation

Is it fate then that policy systems gradually deteriorate as described above? No, there may be another evolutionary path, that of second-order learning processes which might be such that normative attitudes of citizens move into a policy conforming direction. Citizens may feel that the partially effective policies do improve the quality of their own or others' lives, that the normative assumptions underlying the present policies hold a stronger and more positive intrinsic value than earlier assumed. As a consequence they may "internalise" these assumptions and gradually start to consider them as their own norms. They may produce spontaneous behaviour that corresponds perfectly with the objectives of the implemented policies. An extreme case is one in which the policies become completely superfluous because without any regulation at all citizens would behave in norm conforming ways. One could formulate a law of increasing effectiveness for policies in this case; such a "law" would have some validity in a context in which this type of second-order learning takes place. It is almost unnecessary to add that such learning takes a lot of time, decades rather than years. For instance, merit good provision was accompanied in its first phase of development by many regulations enforcing citizens to consume those goods; the justification for enforcement being found in the supposed latent character of citizens needs: parents without education would underestimate the value of their children's education, therefore it was just that the state enforced parents to send their children to school. Later, this regulation was internalised by almost all, so it became almost redundant. Our concluding observation is that internalisation in general leads to increasing effectiveness of the policy system, and in the extreme case to its redundancy.

## 2.3.7    Life-cycle of policy systems

So far we have defined the characteristics that determines the life-cycle of policy systems. The engine of the dynamics formulated above is the human potential for reflexivity: both policy-makers and citizens, public bodies and private organisations experience learning processes of different orders. The most common case is the one designed by the dynamic interaction of two "laws", the law of diminishing effectiveness and the law of policy accumulation. They bring about crisis as well as the death of the policy system concerned; put in a more constructive way, the crisis at hand opens the window for a change of frame. The exceptional case is one where the gradual redundancy of the policy system is caused by intense second-order learning processes in a policy conforming direction so that no regulation is needed any longer because spontaneous behaviour would produce policy conforming effects. Of course we should not forget that the different types of learning might be operational at the same time, but also in opposite directions. So that the slow change of citizens' normative patterns in a policy norm con-forming direction might be overshadowed by the faster erosion of effective-ness of the policy system as a consequence of first-order learning. The net result of different types of learning processes may even appear paradoxical, with contradictory phenomena being observed: for instance, the people who supported policies wholeheartedly at the start of implementation, show first-order behavioural reactions that then undermine the effectiveness of those policies. Another confusing observation may be found when public support for undoubtedly ineffective policies seems to increase, because citizens have gradually internalised the original norms underlying those policies, but not to a sufficiently strong degree that their spontaneous behav-iour has changed accordingly. Policy-makers need to conduct a thorough analysis concerning the different and maybe contradictory but simultaneously operational learning processes.

## 2.3.8    Inter-active learning

It is clear that policy-makers may utilise specific tools or instruments in order to further learning processes so that their objectives will be met. It is even possible to anticipate future policies by making attempts to bring about second-order learning processes. As Reich points out, public managers might... "stimulate public deliberation over what was good for society rather than to decide specific policy." A public manager might feel ... "that public learning was at least as important a part of his job as policy making, because the public had to understand and decide for itself what value it was to place on certain issues lying within the manager's domain."... "Rather than view debate and controversy as managerial failures that made policy making and implementation more difficult, these managers saw them as natural and desirable aspects of the formation of public values, contributing to society's self-understanding." Reich refers to such public managers as the US Secretary of Education Bennett, who saw it as his business ..." to raise the level of debate, focusing the public's attention where it hasn't been focused before". We consider this type of functionary above a policy-maker. Although it may be clear that management by speech and other tools could have an impact on second-order learning, these effects might be overshadowed by less favourable short-term side-effects. The policy-maker who enters the normative debate explicitly runs the risk of being confronted with very hostile attitudes, because citizens feel very uncomfortable with his approach. They easily feel manipulated by policy-makers in the role of preachers. This hostility can destroy the support a policy-maker needs in the short term in order to be effective at all. Apart from the risk of negative side-effects there is one more major disadvantage of second-order learning oriented approaches: the time-horizon of many policy-makers is so short, while the results of second-order learning can only be expected way beyond that time. In practice of course, it is not only individual policy-makers and individual citizens who are involved in learning but also many organisations. They too may consider it their mission to influence each other's learning processes. They may attempt to anticipate flaws in societal learning, or to correct them. Consequently, quite complex patterns of interactive learning can be observed in today's society, with the outcome being uncertain in principle.

### 2.3.9     Dimensions of policy systems: a closer look

### 2.3.9.1   Degrees of decentralisation

If we observe the usual systems for governance of higher education, we might find six or seven levels of decision-making. There is a visible hierarchical chain from the constitutional level to the formal legislature, to the discretion, "das Freie Ermessen", of the national executive authorities, to regional authorities and/or intermediary organisations, to the central board of a university, then to the faculty, and last but not least to the work floor, where either processes of collective decision-making take place, or the individual professional is his own boss and master of his own professional universe. First assumptions might suggest that the "highest" hierarchical level takes the broad and global decisions, and the "lowest" concentrates on daily operations. That is the model of a "machine bureaucracy" found in many textbooks. If we realise that a university system is more of a professional organisation, we can see that the decisions on professional processes are taken by the professionals themselves, while all "higher" levels abstain from steering on the contents of teaching or research, and concentrate on resource management and/or on the constraints of university activity. Generally theoretical statements on governance focus on the desirability of a considerable degree of decentralisation, however politicians feel the need for accountability on their part as long as the state subsidises higher education. One minister once said: "Any university autonomy ends where the state subsidy is larger than zero". In real life the decision-making hierarchy is not so simplified and is more nuanced. In many cases a decision maker will be dependent on approval of his decision by a "higher" authority, or the decision maker could be called to court by a "lower" actor, or still other parties might be authorised to interfere. In current private sector practice a system with six or seven layers might be judged as extremely immobile. Gradually policy makers in the public domain are gaining the insight that one might aim at flatter, and therefore more flexible systems.

### 2.3.9.2 Subjects for steering: inputs, throughputs and outputs

Respect for professional discretion can lead to the idea that outside governing bodies should concentrate on the steering of university inputs such as resources and perhaps student numbers, leaving the professional practice to the professionals who can take care of steering outputs. In many regulatory systems national legislators have also concentrated on the steering of throughputs, both curricula, exams and degrees, and the internal organisation of the university. Counting the instances in national policy systems for higher education where outside authorities influence university governance brings us to a figure of 200-300. Enormous complexity is the result.

A recent politically enforced trend in a group of countries has been the introduction of concepts of stricter management for universities. In many cases this has meant that policy makers have started to concentrate on the steering of outputs by introducing quality control, performance indicators and output oriented budgeting. Chapter four analyses the consequences of this management trend.

### 2.3.9.3 Instruments: regulation, money and persuasion

Influence is exercised in many ways and with different tools or instruments. We divide the most usual instruments into three broad categories: regulation, money and persuasion. This distinction is of course too basic: a subsidy with certain conditions attached is also a means of persuasion, and allocation schemes in general are also laid down in formal regulations or budget laws. The legal form of regulation is easy to imagine, but generally the steering instrument of persuasion is only indirectly given shape in educational laws, for instance by the legal obligation for the decision maker to deliberate with the parties concerned before a decision is taken, to discuss a draft, etc.. A fully developed legal system for higher education will easily possess 100-200 steering instruments. In western Europe one finds a common tendency to shift from regulation as the most important instrument, to money and persuasion. Chapter four discusses this phenomenon.

2.3.9.4  Complex policy systems

Now that we have looked at the main dimensions of policy systems, we may recognise their enormous diversity and complexity. This recognition is important because we need also to be aware that no single human being can internalise the effects of all that diversity. Policy systems are fruits of nurture and nature, are "Gestalten" with their own specific characteristics and consequences of which nobody has objective knowledge. This is the intellectual landscape of legislators who deal with policy systems.

2.4      Educational policy traditions in Europe

It is not only the obsolescence of human capital theory that causes the trouble or stagnation in the necessary change of educational policies. Even if the need for a new cultural paradigm could be satisfied, we would still remain confronted with a mixture of the four traditions of higher education policy which are visible in the Western hemisphere. They are called the Napoleonic, the Humboldtian, the American and the Newmanian tradition. The following outlines their features and mentions some of their important characteristics:

The Napoleonic tradition fits into the broader centralistic tradition of the French state, with universities in a position of extreme dependence on the state. The main decisions concerning the affairs of a university are all made at the national level, even including the appointments of functionaries and professors. The individual university has hardly any autonomy at all. Such a system has produced universities with a public character, with curricula defined by national government, and the universities' main task being teaching. The most important research is performed in separate institutes outside the universities. Student access to studies in general is free, and is based on the diploma received after the secondary school exam. The student fee is low, and the drop-out rate is considerable. These universities are the opposite of their sister institutions in French higher education, the grandes écoles, where the entrance exam is very serious, and the drop-out rate afterwards is close to zero.

University buildings are a matter of national concern. The universities' internal organisational structure is described in great detail in the national legislation. National committees decide on appointments of professors, and the university leaders are appointed by the national government. The financial regime is much like that of the ministries. The discretion of the university itself is minimal. The principle steering instrument is regulation. Traditionally inputs and throughputs are the main subjects of steering. The whole regime is very centralised, and the standardisation of all official aspects of university life is considerable. Given France's international position this tradition has spread to a number of countries.

The second type refers to the Humboldtian tradition, which developed roughly over the same period as the Napoleonic. It characterises a university with its back to the rest of the world as far as its primary processes are concerned. The research it performs is aiming at pure science, the accumulation of knowledge, and absolutely independent of any outside societal interest. The core expression here is Interessenlosigkeit, the absence of any outside interest. This type of university has much akin with a cloister. The teaching is a derivative of research, and it is characterised by the freedom to teach and the freedom to learn, by Lehr – und Lernfreiheit. The learning process is aiming at an academic, research oriented attitude, the unity of teaching and research is continuously stressed. The curricula are designed inside the university and not decided upon by any external authority The decisions on the presidency and on the professorships are also made inside the university, although a regional authority may have the right of formal appointment. Education is free of charge. Access is open but can also be restricted by a numerus clausus or a numerus fixus. This concept of a research university has been widely disseminated and can be recognised in some shape all over Europe and in other continents.

We speak about the American type, but not by any means suggesting that one single basic model for a higher education system can be found in a country characterised by so much diversity. However there is one specific characteristic of a considerable number of American universities, not found in the Napoleonic and Humboldtian traditions, and which has influenced quite a lot of European policy makers and European universities in the second half of the twentieth century. That characteristic is the idea that a university exists in order to render services to society, its external orientation towards society at large can be considered as the prime reason for its existence. In many ways this type of university is the opposite of the Humboldtian category, in so far as its relation to its environment is concerned. This openness pervades both its primary processes, and teaching and research, which have to be justified as activities serving the broader interests of the society. Such an orientation enables the university to operate both in a public and a private environment, thus combining a rather successful mix of task and market oriented processes. It continuously redefines its mission and its core activities in response to societal change, not in a mechanistic way but through a reflexive process. Its face is directed towards the world, but its own set of values are held in great esteem.

The Newmanian concept, named after Cardinal Newman, concerns aspects of the British university, that is less visible and explicit elsewhere. The central objective of the presence of students at the university is only partially accounted for if one restricts it to the teaching of knowledge and skills, as the preparation of students for later life, and the balanced development of students´ personalities are also considered important. Therefore a university can not only consist of faculties, but also of colleges, and often the most influential teacher is not the professor, but the tutor. It is not by chance that the continental method of standardisation of degrees at Oxbridge was absent until recently. Students were prepared for their future position as the elite of the Empire, and the reproduction of societal values was a very important part of this type of education.

In many European regions two or more of these above-mentioned traditions have, in different periods, influenced university life as well as legislation on higher education. Currently in most European countries one finds a mixture of these traditions although with differing relative weights. However depending on the combinations major tensions may result. The strong introduction of a market oriented approach in a Humboldtian environment will cause much more trouble than the same development in an American tradition. These typologies are discussed in chapter four.

## 2.5    Towards a heuristic scheme in order to deal with societal dynamics concerning legislation for higher education

We have observed so far that it is worthwhile to adapt a contingent approach when analysing the relationships between nation states, legislation and higher education. Firstly, the concept of the nation state is very diversified, as both the concept of democracy and the stage of socio-economic development vary widely, and as a result approaches to policy making are very different. This diversity in turn has major consequences for policy making on higher education.

Secondly, the historical roots of higher education are often much older than the nation state and can be connected to a society's fundamental characteristics which are only partially found in the public domain today.

Thirdly, the concept of law in a particular society may have been given shape according to specific principles that concern the relation between written and unwritten constitutions, the shape of legislation, and the degree to which matters are left to internal university regulations, etc.

So it is necessary to deal with contingent relationships between three interrelated complex issues:
·    the character of the nation state;
·    the structure of higher education;
·    the concept of law.

We have described a view of legislation as connected to policy systems in dynamic terms, and constructed a life cycle concept. We have explained the main dimensions for analysis of policy systems.

We have given an outline of the four great policy traditions that dominate European higher education.

We have sketched a number of macro-trends in western European societies, and have been more modest in our observations of today´s eastern Europe.

These trends provide driving forces which should be met by adequate policies on different levels. The traditional underlying policy concepts are not unchangeable, but one should realise that they are rooted in the environment of the public domain or even society at large.

This heuristic framework, and the preliminary observations in § 1.2.1 help us to analyse the major issues in legislation on higher education in Europe in chapter four, after the comparative overview in chapter three, and in the light of the country reports of chapter five.

# 3

## GUIDELINES TO COMPARISON

### 3.1    Introduction

To quote from Swanson's (1971) categorical terms: "thinking without comparison is unthinkable". But, must we not ask, how we are informed of comparability, and of comparable realities as such, and who informs us? As to the first issue, the comparability of matters, there is no harm in accepting Swanson's premises here, namely that we are simply informed thereof. The second issue, however, of how we are informed of each of the issues we wish to compare, touches upon the chosen method and, therefore, warrants some reflection.

Many of the determinants deemed fundamental to the practical validity of normative systems are shielded from a specifically legal analysis. The question, for instance, why we accept the rule of law in general, and that of a specific provision in particular, may very well be answerable in exacting anthropological terminology. It is, however, well beyond the positive attainments of comparative law. Likewise, to the extent policy-makers are informed directly by their constituents, any comparative analysis becomes more a task of sociology and related sciences, rather than of jurisprudence. We must observe, too, that the combination of different systems of reference is to no avail. While such different systems may be complimentary in fact, they are not so in their methodologies. Any system of reference represents an abstraction in its own right, and one may rightly say, that comparability exists only within the chosen system. This latter contention should be acceptable to all who expect results to benefit a particular practical task.

Higher education legislation is frequently changed by policy makers, who may find changing a highly specific derivative of the law of general applicability relatively easy. Indeed, drafting reforms in a very specific segment of the law involves rather more limited sets of factors than reforms, say, of property rights. It is then against these peculiarities that the grounds of comparison are posited. Neither the constituents inform us of the object of comparison, nor does society at large, because the degree of specificity of the issues involved corresponds to the specialisation of the interlocutor, it is the educational lawyers and policy-makers at the legislator's drafting board.

These drafts men are acutely conscious that specific changes have repercussions through the law of general applicability, and eventually may alter and revise fundamental societal concepts. However, normative systems are complex, and the impact and direction of legal and social repercussions are neither always intended, nor are they easily foreseen. It is, amongst others, the purpose of this analysis to identify the chosen directions, and to trace the concurrent developments.

Identifying directions in legislative change, and doing so by way of comparison, is largely an issue of coping with definitional disparities. There exists no common agenda shared across Europe, not even in eastern Europe (Karcyewski, Witold, 1995). Therefore, as a general problem, which Kazemzadeh and Steube (1995) discuss in more detail, different definitions from different countries can lead quite easily to erroneous conclusions, and also to drawing none where such would be appropriate. However, increased international co-operation has mitigated the problem to some extent. It has contributed to a more uniform usage, and has also increased mutual understanding of the more purposeful deviations.

As to the second objective, to trace the concurrent developments, engendering a bias must be avoided here. While at present, it is seemingly the central and eastern European countries which provide the most rewarding environment, directions in the migration of ideas are themselves plentiful, and continuously subject to change. The fact that the countries in transition have sought inspiration and solutions from western systems is hardly disputable. Nonetheless, even where wholesale imports of such systems occur, one can always observe alterations particular to that host country, which more often than not result in structures not only proper to this country's culture and heritage, but are perhaps even more advanced than those of the imported version. Time will have to testify to the latter, and for this reason, one must closely watch for an eventual re-import of processed aspects of the original system.

Judicious comparison with regard to the central and eastern European countries requires still another word of caution. The focus on legislation is in itself a rather delicate business where power configurations of various extremity may effectively defy a rule of law in the proper sense. It is conceivable that acts of the legislature may be entirely irrelevant to the actual social condition, in which case they do not represent sensitive data; though, such law may nonetheless be meaningful in terms of an eventual reinstatement of legislative authority. It is with these reservations in mind, that the following assessments must be approached.

## 3.2    Organisational principles of change

### 3.2.1    The challenges of choice: academic or vocational drift

Universities are not always the largest institutions of higher education in terms of numbers of students enrolled. In virtually all systems of higher education exists a wide range of vocationally oriented institutions, polytechnic or non-university sector institutions, which may be highly specialised or offer a broad range of subjects, but always combine some elements of theoretical study with those of vocational training. The first basic organisational principle underlying higher education legislation proceeds from this structural distinction, and from there either pursues a policy of co-ordination, or one of strengthening each branch in its own domain. This distinction is not identical with the traditional dichotomy of teaching and research. While research is historically associated with the universities, it is not so intrinsically, and some central and eastern European countries actually retain the Soviet model of conducting research solely in distinct specialised institutes.

A wholesale inter-institutional reshuffling of disciplines currently under way in Europe complicates the issue of situating research within the institutional environment even further (Clark, 1995). It appears, the redistribution of functions among the several institutions has led, especially in some western European countries, to the emergence of highly specialised multi-disciplinary branches, which require entirely new research training systems (Gellert, 1993). The need to overcome the separation of research and teaching, which is felt by virtually all countries formerly member to the Eastern block, does not, however, entail necessarily an abandonment or fusing of the academy's research institutes of the Academies with the appropriate faculties (Šebková, 1994). The German, French and Dutch models of Graduiertenkollegs, Ecolés doctorates or Onderzoeksscholen, for instance, may offer viable alternatives. All countries are witnessing efforts to implement a new diversity, though institutional rigidity generates some noticeable impediments in some places.

The issue of diversity will be discussed in more detail below. However, care should be taken to observe here, that this movement towards increased diversity in Europe is rarely driven by government policy, and is therefore, if for no other reason, largely directed at institutions which are in one form or another segregated from the traditionally university-dominated tertiary education sector.

Bulgaria, for instance, which has been operating its public system under a binary structure now for almost 75 years, has no specific legislation applicable to the proliferating private sector, which in turn appears to inspire much of the recent initiatives taken within the public system. As to the universities, however, these initiatives may be taken to tighten structures within the traditionally university taught disciplines, such as medicine and law. Estonia has established vocational higher education institutions, thereby breaking away from the highly centralised former system, while Latvia exiles what is essentially vocational education, entirely from the tertiary education. Hungary, too, operates a public system of a binary structure composed of universities and colleges which both offer tertiary education. However, other institutions not integrated into the State system provide vocationally oriented education. The hungarian system is currently in transition, but the basic features will abide. In a different way, the Czech Republic pursues a policy of establishing distinct entities which are deemed more responsive to the demands of the economy and also more efficient in their use of resources, at the same time allowing universities to offer higher professional education and thus creating a "spectral" system of higher education. This applies to the creation of college type institutions, as well as to the reintegration of research and teaching in universities.

Germany shields its traditional universities from a too immediate pressure from the community, too. The country's independent Fachhochschulen accomplish much of the vocational work undertaken by the eastern European institutions mentioned earlier. The Netherlands operates an even stricter system consisting of universities and higher professional education institutions and underscores this policy with the laws of 1986 and 1992. A similar development towards, local, autonomous higher vocational establishments can also be witnessed in Slovenia. Norway enacted explicit policy delegating vocational training to regional colleges which are again considered particularly responsive to local demands (Nossom, 1981). Whilst Spain stresses its universities' active role within the communities, the communities themselves directly control so called non-autonomous higher vocational institutions.

Generally, the disciplines referred to as scientific, academic, or are otherwise traditionally taught at universities, continue to draw up their curricula, irrespective of a policy of diversification. Certain exceptions may be seen to come from Turkey, on the one hand, and from United Kingdom and Malta, on the other. Turkey has actually increased the total number of universities from 19 to 57 since its 1981 reforms, by way of creating a uniform system from amalgamated academies, teacher-training and vocational schools. The United Kingdom and Malta equally do not follow the general trend. Since 1992 polytechnics in the United Kingdom have gained university status, and now compete with the universities in what has been termed a "study-market". Malta has created one university engaged in all subjects; the countries' size obviously being an argument.

In most systems, therefore, a clear hierarchical structure is held to exist, still. While the traditional universities continue to maintain and accentuate institutional differentiation, it is highly probable that increased diversification of non-university provenance will eventually eradicate much of the impact of historically cast orders.

3.2.2    The principle of subsidiarity

As the second principle governing the changing relations between the State
and the institutions, the principle of subsidiarity in higher education is
gaining a certain acclaim. Initially promulgated in the social welfare encyclic
Quadragesimo Anno (1931), subsidiarity has become a fundamental principle
of Community Law since, despite numerous problems related to its implementation. In essence, subsidiarity consist of conferring only such responsibilities to a higher superior unit as can not be fulfilled at the lower level.
There are few national legislations acknowledging the principle expressive
verbis, as has Belgium in article 17 of its Constitution. In countries where
federal structures situate educational matters with the confederate members,
e.g. Germany, it is applied implicitly. While the majority of European
countries neither mention subsidiarity in their legal texts, nor evidence a
structural application, increasing conformity to the principle can be observed
as a matter of political necessity.

This mode of operation has profound consequences as concerns the relations
between the State and higher education institutions. First, it delegates to the
institutions tasks formerly performed at the governmental level. Second, this
delegation of tasks affects institutional autonomy, and thereby also the very
exercise of the freedom of education. The following section addresses these
issues, then the interrelations of subsidiarity and diversification will be
examined.

3.3      Institutional autonomy: the decline of a monopoly

One may regard the freedom of education as derived from the freedom of
speech, expression and religion. Historically this may be correct and it may
be defensible legally, as well; though, as is readily apparent in the context
of teaching, it can be a rather questionable foundation (De Groof, 1995).
However, the better view is, treating the freedom of education, including
higher education, as an independent fundamental right, notwithstanding the
Council of Europe having suspended deliberation on proposed Cultural
Rights, which included the freedom of education. Whether it constitutes a
social right in the affirmative sense is debatable, however, it is largely
regarded as such (Nowak, 1993). At any rate, freedom of education is at

the heart of securing an economic, social and cultural life of acceptable standard. Whether it is primary, secondary or tertiary, is a basic service at the very foundations of democratic societies and of the exercise of civil rights within them. In a modern approach to human rights, the freedom of education in general, and of higher education in particular, can no longer be regarded as derivative of other basic rights. Academic freedom, as encompassed by educational freedom, applies to the teaching and research undertaken by individuals, and is in most systems guaranteed by law, sometimes within Constitutions.

The concept of institutional autonomy, on the other hand, does not promulgate a freedom. Rather, the concept presents a historical organisational pattern, and as such, an institutional implementation. It constitutes an institutional and procedural implementation of the educational freedom. Institutional autonomy's conceptual validity is supported, of course, by pragmatic considerations. Higher education institutions, with the exception of military academies perhaps, can not be administered like a police station, nor as closely audited as a financial institution. However, while these considerations are important, it must be kept in mind, that institutional autonomy represents, first of all, only a specific vehicle to educational freedom, namely, a protection vis-à-vis the State. As such, the fundamental right of educational freedom is neither premised by the concept of institutional autonomy, nor is institutional autonomy essential to the right's exercise, which itself may embark on different avenues, employing different means in the course.

Institutional autonomy is one of the issues of the day. Like most safeguards of fundamental rights, however, institutional autonomy should not be valued against disaster – the Inquisition, the revolutionary tribunals and dictators of Europe in their day, all crushed safeguards of quite another calibre – rather, its function must be assessed against day-to-day activities of governments, institutions and market participants under passably civilised conditions, as are ours today. Then, indeed, one must wonder, whether the newly perceived threats to educational freedom and its exercise truly issue with the State, as Russel (1993) believes for instance, rather than with swiftly changing economies and invariably saturated labour markets. It is our contention here, that the increasing delegation of tasks formerly assumed by governments to the institutions and increasing diversity within the national systems, have substantially altered the traditional traits and implications of institutional autonomy.

Government's legitimate interests in diversification and modularisation, in multi-disciplinarity and in consumer protection is indeed shared by higher education institutions who seek to attract students against rising costs and the uncertainties of the labour market. These interests are also shared for the very same reasons by students, and they are certainly championed by other participants of national economies, whose needs seem better accommodated herein, than they are in rigidly canonised systems. Diversification, to be sure, does not by itself mark a departure from the concept of institutional autonomy. It does, however, reflect the erosion at the concept's justificatory foundations, and, to the extent it contributes to the complexity of modern societies – without rendering them less free, therefore – it may eventually vitiate the issue altogether.

Means and points of departure differ from country to country. It is important to discern, however, that the traditional concept is at stake not only in the rare case when an institution's autonomy is infringed upon directly, but also when it is rivalled. For, the practical worth of institutional autonomy is rather a matter of its exclusivity. Breaking this sort of monopoly by admitting rivals, amounts to an indirect infringement on the formally untouched autonomy of the university; as has effectively happened in the Czech and Slovak Republics, where the 1990 Act on Academic Freedom vested – not without precedence – university faculties with legal personality. In Bulgaria the status of non-university tertiary institutions was assimilated with that of the universities, in that these institutions may now create new academic programmes, found new departments and even establish affiliated institutions in other cities. In the German higher education reform, some Ministries propose enhancing the status of the country's non-university and Fachhochschulen.

When measuring institutional autonomy against exclusivity, it may seem sophistic to question the validity of the concept of institutional autonomy once the binary system has been integrated, as instances of which, one may cite again the above-mentioned countries Turkey, United Kingdom and Malta. However, it is one thing to nestle an academic administrator's discretionary powers within institutional autonomy as such, and quite another to view them as a matter of administrative necessity; much current usage of the term appears to refer to the latter, anyhow. In unified systems it is difficult to see how autonomy, as a sort of superstitious category distinct from actual necessity, confers any benefit at all. The fact that today discretionary powers are also legally understood in the latter sense, however, must be regarded as a consequence of proliferation in the private sector, which by definition has no recourse to classic autonomy, what ever the surrounding system may be.

Viewing institutional autonomy in terms of administrative necessity and discretionary powers, or of divisions of responsibilities, as we called it earlier in § 1.2.1.1, demystifies the concept and redirects its function in favour of a realistic assessment of the interests involved. The results are tangible specifications relative to the specific tasks increasing subsidiarity assigns to the institutions. The new relationship between the higher education institutions may be described, thus, as accountable management in Maurice Kogan's (1992) sense of the word. Of course, accountable management as such does not eradicate the structural hiatus of the discipline with its interests, on the one hand, and those of the "enterprise" (Clark, 1983), the institution, on the other. Like autonomy accountable management is not indicative of any rights vested. The concept, as De Groof (1994) notes – with regard to subsidiarity – is only relevant as concerns the exercise of the vested right. As such, however, it maintains a dialogue with, and is directed at the several disciplines, while the former concept of autonomy amounts to a benevolently paternalistic representation vis-à-vis the State. The widespread acceptance of policy concepts such as output-orientation and performance-budgeting calls more and more for managerial rather than purely academic professionals, at any rate. There is no indication that these managerial professionals will safeguard specifically academic liberties any less scrupulously than their academic counterparts have. Even if output-oriented planning eventually amounts to more narrowly defined discretionary powers, this can not be attributed to State interference, but rather, is a consequence of drawing on more accurate and relevant data.

3.4    The private sector: an engine of subsidiarity?

Having or allowing private higher education institutions is a matter not of choice but of principle. The freedom of education posits both the right to educate and the right to receive an education, to freely choose a school or university, and to see to an education which meets the legitimate demands of society. Non-denominational public, semi-public and private educational institutions are not only indispensable, the freedom of education effectively bans any contrary monopoly of the State. The right to educate and the right to freely choose an education requires positive safeguards and encouragement for private education and even, under certain conditions, funding on equal footing with public education.

In countries where the development of a private sector as such is a relatively recent phenomena, it can be observed that private institutions emerge almost instantly, often where the base of the public sector academic supply is limited; in Croatia for instance, the first ten applications received regarded institutions offering programmes in business, economics and law. An academic offering may be narrow not only in terms of the subject matters taught, but also as to the degrees conferred and as to the qualities of admitted students. The ability to respond swiftly to market demands contrasts here with the slower response from the public sector institutions, and may be attributed in part to less entrenched engagements and modes of operation, as well as to the fact that the private institution invests little, if any, funding in research. The public universities will directly or indirectly be subject to the factual standards set by the private sector, and to the ensuing legal implications.

Innovations in this sector include stimulating the growth of external degrees, pioneering the very concept of the assessment of prior learning, and challenging the concept of what merits a degree. It is argued, for that matter, that the nature of a degree for mature adults should be something entirely different as compared to someone who lacks industrial experience and whose achievements are assessed on the basis of successful completion of a number of three-hour examination papers. As a consequence, there has been a rash of new colleges and universities founded specifically to offer non-traditional degrees, based on continuous assessment, cumulative credits and project work in addition to pure academic learning.

While these aspects are of primary importance to the eastern and central European countries and to their adjustment to market economies, the issues in the west are, squarely, parity and consumer protection. The first set of parameters of accountable management as a descriptor of the relations between the institutions and the State emerge in this context.

## 3.5 Parity and quality assurance: situating the intermediaries

### 3.5.1 Intermediaries

The roles of intermediaries are manyfold. They negotiate, advise, co-operate, render services, represent interest groups, make decisions on the basis of attributed or delegated power, or perform a mixture thereof. To a large extent, they are influencing the strands of the judicial networks. Usually situated between the State and the institutions they affect both the ministerial responsibility and the institutional autonomy, thus changing the lines of accountability. The number of intermediaries has grown rapidly over the last decades. This makes the analysis of past, present and future legal respon-sibilities and legal structures highly complicated, especially in the field of education, but also more important when it comes to policy making and legislation. However, operating costs, structural rigidity and questionable added value have been the main reasons to re-examine the phenomena intermediaries in some countries.

Whichever name intermediary bodies answer to, whether "Academy of Education" (Belarus), Hochschulrektorenkonferenz (Germany) "Inter-Univer-sity Council" (Flemish Community of Belgium), Association of Co-operating Dutch Universities (Netherlands), European Network of National Information Centres, or whether they simply represent an "expert body co-ordinating activities in regard to legislative reforms, and budgetary allocations for teaching and research, etc," (which, for example, since 1992 the Bulgarian Rectors' Conference operates), they are effective and powerful instruments not on account of statutory rights, which they often do not posses at all – such is the case with the just cited Bulgarian Rectors Conference – but primarily because of the political weight of their members. Frequently, therefore, national systems comprise several such bodies. In Hungary there operates alongside the Conference of Rectors and Directors, the Hungarian Accreditation Committee and the National Council of Higher Education and Science, all advisory bodies to the State, dealing, for example, with the creation or abolition of new faculties. Romania, too, has several different committees, namely the National Council of Academic Assessment and Accreditation, the National Council of University Scientific Research the National Council for Financing Higher Education and also the Rectors' National Conference, all of which seek to implement performance criteria for higher education. In Estonia the newly established Higher Education Evaluation Council consists of representatives from the higher education institutions and the commercial and cultural sectors. Similarly, the University Council in Spain includes the Rectors of all the public universities, representatives of all the Autonomous Communities and dignitaries from the scientific sector. In the Slovenian Council for Higher Education participates in the preparation of the government's National Plan for Higher Education which determines criteria for the assessment of study programmes.

Relations between the Ministries and the higher education institutions are influenced by other intermediary bodies outside the governmental sector which have a decision-making capacity and which promote the State interest. Good examples of such an intermediary body are the Higher Education Funding Councils in the UK and the Bulgarian National Assessment and Accreditation Agency which takes decisions of even a fundamental kind concerning the creation and abolition of institutions or faculties. An noteworthy example of an international body is the Baltic Higher Education Co-ordination Committee.

### 3.5.2    Parity and quality assurance

Parity amounts to equal recognition of institutions by the State and must be distinguished from parity as in the eyes of the public. There appears to exist a more even-handed generosity in central and eastern Europe. Belarus, for instance, offers equal opportunities of recognition and funding to public and private higher education institutions, while only a few western countries pursue a clear policy of creating parity, namely the Netherlands – where the recognised private institutions are actually listed in an appendix to the Higher Education and Research Act – and Belgium. Flanders, for instance, recognises no private higher education leading to a diploma not officially sanctioned in the strictest sense.

The issue of assuring and evaluating quality is of central concern. Formal accreditation machinery has been set up by Hungary, the Slovak Republic and Croatia. Accreditation has been imported from the United States by central and eastern European countries, and has led to a number of misunderstandings there. This is largely due to the fact, that accreditation as practised in the United States is applicable to a system of private higher education only. Other approaches to quality assurance, sometimes ambiguously termed "quality control", include licensing of institutions and elements of assessment, which may or may not entail a recognition of degrees awarded, and the modes of State-recognition mentioned earlier. One of the most notable effects of quality assessment is quality consciousness, by which management of the higher education institutions itself assures institutional concern for quality. This indicative of a general conviction that the transformation of the culture of higher education is both a result and a necessary condition of quality assessment and improvement. For, self-analysis and self-criticism are premised by an environment of independence and equality.

Quality assurance is a matter of setting and enforcing standards, of course. The more narrowly focused discussion, therefore, centres around the composition, powers and proceedings of bodies to be entrusted with these functions. The particular organisational form of these bodies is secondary, at least in so far, as these institutions are not devised and administrated according to either the competent Ministry's directives or those of the higher education institutions themselves. They enjoy administrative discretion, and the greater their independence the greater their reputation, and thus their influence on the ministries and on higher education institutions.

It is worth noting, that it is not the very nature of research and higher education that necessitates such panels. Of course, how should a Ministry meaningfully advise higher education institutions on what experimental results to present, or to what standard of excellence to hold its students. Nonetheless, such deference could be vested in closely controlled faculties and their appointed chairs, as it was a more or less remote past in virtually every country. The success of these new forums springs rather from an often unbridled conviction of academic pursuit being no longer a liberty apart, but an integral component of a liberal society's economy – which shall directly, then, inform academia of its immediate ends and of the scarcity of resources it employs. Accordingly, these bodies include members from the business community and other stakeholders almost as a matter of course.

Notwithstanding these factors, however, legislative authorities remain keenly concerned with the internal organisational structures of higher education institutions. Internal structures have impact on the contents and quality and they strongly affect checks and balances in the governance of institutions. Especially after 1968 it became clear that new institutional engagements for participation in university decision-making by students, assistants and administrative staff had become a political necessity, although the pendulum seems to have slightly swung back in Denmark and other countries in that region. Legislation governing internal structures and procedures, however, apportions the authority allotted to intermediaries, and, to the degree of its density, limits the impact of their function as mediators; which in turn is not without ramifications as regards subsidiarity. Where university administrators are government appointees, for instance, legislation specifies the entitlements and duties of those functionaries. In this context, it is often provided, that institutions conduct their affairs under the individual leadership of a rector; formal collective leadership, as can be found in the Netherlands, remains an exception. The rector, or sometimes president or director, is elected by a board or by the senate of the higher education institution of which she is a member. However, formal appointment is generally made by State authority, in most cases by the Ministry of Education or Science, sometimes by the Head of State as is the case in the Czech and Slovak Republics. The details of the actual procedures evidence some important differences as to the degree of State influence and of participation granted to various stakeholders. Statutory criteria of eligibility are of particular interest in this context. In Denmark, in certain institutions in Switzerland, and in Spain a rector must be elected from amongst a group of full professors. In other systems, eligibility extends to academics and researchers, as in Slovakia, or to individuals not even members of a higher education or research institution at all, as is the case in Germany.

The introduction of accreditation, in particular, is necessarily accompanied by the instatement of intermediary bodies, which are regarded by some central and eastern European countries as a safeguard against a possible return of the "ancien regime" and its interventionist policy. However, competing methodologies of quality assurance by self-assessment are increasingly welcomed as fear of interventionism is slowly diminishing and self-assess-ment may even protect institutions better against State intervention than accreditation committees. Also, countries often discover accreditation mech-anisms incompatible with their rooted legislative and political traditions and cause systematic disparity.

### 3.5.3    Diversification

The increase in student numbers, and the ensuing movement towards diversi-fication, is attributable for the most part to State policies which positively equate the welfare of society with the level of education of its members. Nearly everywhere diversification of higher education has been introduced as a response to a variety of problems connected with this policy, the issue of equality not being the least. The benefits of diversity are seen in an increase of the range of choices available to learners, in accommodating a very large number of learners, and in matching education to the needs and abilities of individual students (Rasmussen, 1992). Demands of the labour markets and those of students go hand in hand. At the root of diversi-fication, therefore, we find exigencies of national economies and not a thrust of the suppliers of education.

There have been two major and separate diversification philosophies. First, the nineteenth century brought the technical universities – first in Germany and subsequently in most industrialised countries – which aimed at providing industry with engineers and with technological research. Similar specialised institutions have been introduced later in most countries in fields such as business administration, agriculture, medicine, veterinary medicine, sports etc. As a general rule, these institutions differ from universities by maintain-ing stronger ties with the industrial or professional world outside. But like the universities, most of these institutions place strong emphasis on research and on the relationship between research and teaching. Second, we have the post-war development of what has been termed the binary system, as a system for higher education aimed at supplementing traditional university teaching (Bernt, 1994). Diversification may, however, also take place between two or more traditional universities, between non-university institu-tions, and conceivable within a single institution, too.

Diversification within the single institution, is not everywhere as visible an element in the general debate on diversification, as the need for external diversification diminishes to a certain extent the need for universities to establish diversified programmes, courses, or organisational structures within their own system. Horizontal diversification, such as between institutions at the same level, is a generally approved model. There is practically no disagreement that institutions should be encouraged to respond to specific demands and to develop new courses and programmes. And, in many situations the institutions need no special encouragement to pursue this line of diversification. Especially smaller institutions may have better prospects of finding suitable niches. Favourable aspects of vertical diversification in non-university tertiary education have been mentioned earlier, although reinforcing the traits of the traditional universities, which led to such a diversification in the first place, it may indeed be one of the favourable aspects, since it should lead to more diversity.

However, there appear to be uncertainties, whether market mechanisms are likely to create constructive diversification. Sometimes it is suggested, that market mechanisms promote a trend towards conformity. One contention in this context is, that many institutions are presumably more likely to copy the programmes of successful competitors than to develop their own. Alleged incentives are the lower costs of copying, and it being easier to market a local version of an established and successful programme, than to convince potential students and employers of the merits of an entirely new and untested product. Such are generous economics, but they are nonetheless expressive of a distrust in academia embracing the market place; which the institutions themselves do not always appear to share. At the root of such contentions one may suspect the renewed western preoccupation with lasting ethical values which transcend fashions and the fleeting moment, and to which educational institutions are to provide a safe harbour; as noted by Litt in 1927.

To keep with the categories introduced by Goedegebuure et al. (1994), a qualitative description of diversity can be attained in terms of systematic, programmatic and structural diversity. The term systematic diversity refers to differences between institutions with respect to their size and modes of control. Systematic diversity has increased in the central and eastern European countries largely as a consequence of adopting western models to accommodate rapidly changing needs. Programmatic diversity is closely linked with systematic diversity, and refers to institutional differences in the supply of educational, research programmes and service activities. For instance, cross-country comparison shows that certain subjects can be offered at both, university and college level. The issue here is one of determining the criteria of differentiating between the different types of programmes. Also, the borderline between secondary education and higher education is not as rigid as is generally believed. To take nursing education, should it be part of vocational training within the school system or should it belong at a higher level within non-university sector institutions? Of course, there will be different solutions all of which will be acceptable and expressive of the status reserved to a particular profession within a society.

Structural diversity is a result of differences in the legal foundations of institutions in terms of their external structure, as well as in internal aspects of governance. For all practical purposes today, the structural diversity concerns the relations between public and private higher education institutions. The central and eastern European countries, especially, are experiencing an expansion of the private higher education sector. Certain elements characteristic to private higher education, e.g. the paying of tuition fees, resurge even within the public system. For, as long as an institution's budget is directly linked to the number of students the State may limit, then those not admitted will create a demand which, to the extent that it is not satisfied by private institution, may be met by the public sector, however, against fees. At least in the respect, an assimilation of public and private institutions must be acknowledged. The relevance of distinguishing public and private institutions is called into more serious doubt, though, once their budgets are derived from the same sources, and subject to the same conditions. While legal denominations are important, the practical distinctions may be overruled in fact by the intricacies of financing.

## 3.5.4   Budgeting and general accountability

The crisis of public budgets everywhere has also affected the educational system, notwithstanding legislators' ever keener concern for education. Thus, allocations to higher education institutions, in almost all countries have in effect decreased, and work conditions have often deteriorated in recent years.

The educational system has to find other ways out of its financial dilemma, than only bargain for a higher percentage of the State's resources.

Having recognised that efficient decision-making is better accomplished at the institutional level, many State authorities now suspend budget line funding in favour of lump sum funding or budget financing. Changing budgetary policies calls for new criteria, of course, to assess total amounts to be allocated. Many countries espouse the idea that emphasise be given to the notion of "success." Almost uniformly, success in this context is determined by an institutions performance in what is termed a "user's market". The basic assumptions behind the concept are the following. For both the private and the public sector, individual budgets continue to be a function of total student numbers. Therefore, institutions have an incentive to attract as many students as possible. It is worth noting that "as many as possible" does not always mean, "as many needed to meet marginal costs". In principle, only the strictly private institutions, those solely financed by private sources, have to adhere to this stricter standard. "Unit costs", e.g. costs per student graduated or per exam passed, can be indicative per se, of course, where economies of scale are concerned. However, within the educational sector economies of scale can be realised only to a certain extent, and are absorbed quickly (Haywire, 1992).

Where public institutions are permitted to charge "users" fees, as is the practice in parts of eastern and central Europe, continuous budget-cuts may eventually "privatise" these institutions, in the sense that the fee-paying student's interests prevail, and as a consequence free-market standards of efficiency as well. The same effect can be prompted by charging institutions commercial rates for the premises they occupy, or for other public resources they employ (Woodhouse, 1995). Competition between "State students" and "private students" is an issue already, if for no other reason than the latter category paying on time and directly. As not only the American experience tells us, there is little risk of institutions developing an incentive to admit students solely on ability to pay. However, social welfare and equal opportunity standards may be at risk nonetheless. Unlike the United States, which continues to show the highest numbers of tertiary sector graduates world-wide, most European countries does not dispose of an inexpensive and easily accessible third pillar to their mostly binary systems. Furthermore, the European Court for Human Rights and the Brussels Court are hostile to measures within the realm of the American affirmative action programmes, which are aimed at promoting certain disadvantaged groups. These courts' reluctance is not unfounded. It shall suffice here to take note that Regents of the University of California, for their part, recently suspended all such programmes for the entire seven-campus system, and so did other major universities. The impacts of current developments must be watched closely, because in most European countries, the task of advancing social welfare and equal opportunity is deferred to the public institutions, among them the most distinguished universities. Of course, the granting supplementary funds, which as of yet serves as an instrument of interventionist policies in the private sector (Goldschmidt, 1978).

The new relationship between the State and higher education institutions is not restricted to matters of budgeting. In many countries, the State directs the universities and non-university sector institutions to engage in new tasks and to assume new responsibilities within, more often than not, self-determined ambit, which is not without ramifications. As Burton Clark pointed out, "semi-autonomous departments and schools, chairs and faculties act like small sovereign states as they pursue distinctive self-interests and stand over against the authority as a whole" (Clark, 1983). A State policy of only supervising and frame-setting, thus, may produce a more efficient and diverse environment. However, in light of the fragmented structures within the institutions, decision-making may cause unwarranted strain, particularly during periods of transition.

## 3.6    Conclusion

Relations between the State and higher education institutions have taken directions suggestive of increased subsidiarity, an increase that must be attributed to the proliferation in the private sector. As a consequence, institutional autonomy has become a matter of vesting distinct discretionary powers with the institutions. Increased diversification and subsidiarity go hand in hand and mark a trend which directly ameliorates the institution's independence vis-à-vis the State, while subjecting it, no less directly, to the constraints and uncertainties of national economies.

When examining change, however, emphasis is placed on the concerns of the enterprise, almost as a matter of course; and we have done so as well, within the thematic boundaries of this volume. Regulatory schemes are inherently concerned with institutions and their proper specific environments, of course. As mentioned earlier, the specificity of these national environments may be seen to defy any notion of a common agenda as concerns the institutions. The challenges and demands the disciplines face, however, can hardly be said to emanate from within national or European confines. These challenges stem from within scientific pursuits, for neither the pursuit of better engineering, nor that of truth as such, is anything particularly European or western. One common agenda does exists, thus, and it is not a trivial matter.

When legislators make "international standards" a matter of law, as is the case in several countries, they refer to this agenda. These international standards comprise, not a set of unwritten rules, but commitments to substantive achievements in disciplinary specialities, and are therefore directed at the individuals engaged within them. To the extent subsidiarity accommodates this agenda, its actual impact is absorbed by the regulatory systems. Where, however, international standards imply international education, and such education is a matter of individual pursuit, we may expect considerable undercurrents to alter the disciplinary foundations in ways undetectable to national policy makers. Such data points to the limits of subsidiarity in national systems. Future change in higher education legislation may, then, safely be expected to issue with fora of international co-operation. The need of such fora is recognised. Already in 1974 most States member to the Council of Europe deployed National Equivalence Information Centres (NEIC). As a result of the UNESCO Convention of 1979, the Network of Information Bodies on recognition and mobility was established, and in 1984 the National Academic Recognition Information Centres (NARICs) in all the EU and EFTA States. As a result of co-operation between the Council of Europe and UNESCO, these organisations merged their networks and formed the European Network of National Information Centres (ENIC) in 1994.

# 4

# CONCLUSIONS

## 4.1    Introduction

Legislation creates structures and furthers processes. It sets norms and standards. It attempts to guarantee the entitlements of people. It tries to protect valuable cultural quality, and it designs steering instruments for public authorities and university governors and administrators.

The simple view on legislation is that it either ensures the effective impact of already existing values and norms or reshapes, modifies, the existing order by the introduction of new rules: the codification-modification distinction; even dilemma. Thereby the system under governance then is considered as infinitely transparant and open, so that steering itself delivers no problems of its own. This assumption has been both empirically refuted, and theoretically denied. The effectiveness of steering by legislation already is often doubtful from the beginning, and moreover it tends to decrease over time, as we saw in chapter two. The system under governance appears to be reflexive and relies on learning in response to the steering impulses. Closure more than transparency is the main characteristic of the governed system.

Legislation on higher education concentrates on issues where the state desires to penetrate into the institutions and systems of higher education that are characterised by closure, by lack of openness, by resistance to any influence from outside. But it also sometimes aims at the protection of individual or institutional freedom, even against the state itself. In this chapter we analyse some of the main issues in today's European policies on higher education. Of course they all relate to effectiveness and legitimacy. We will utilise the analytical tools offered in chapter two.

We will maintain our, more complex view that legislation may serve other purposes than substantial rationality alone. Its symbolic functions may be as important. Legislation on its own creates a virtual reality of its own, which may only partially correspond with other realities. Following rules is conditional. We may specify the conditions under which it is probable that norms and rules laid down in legislation will be respected and followed.

We will elaborate on an analytical framework in § 4.2, generalise some empirical observations in § 4.3, put forward a number of paradoxes and dilemma's in § 4.4 and digress a little on internal university organisation in § 4.5.


## 4.2    Analytical framework

### 4.2.1    The eternal questions: effectiveness and legitimacy

Legislation may be a product of parliamentary democracy, but other sytems also produce legislation. There may exist a discrepancy between the formal notion of democracy on one side and the material degree of consensus and of representation on the other. In this context the eternal questions of legitimacy and effectiveness hold us in their grip. We have already mentioned that it seems worthwhile to consider both concepts as dynamic notions. That dynamic character refers to more fundamental aspects than the simple problem of successful implementation, than the idea that there may be a gap between formal decisions and implementation in practice.

Norms and standards are easy to formulate in abstract, but are at the same time extremely hard to ensure. Incentive structures are corrupted in due course by intelligent learning processes on the side of the individuals and organisations under governance. Higher education institutons are no exception to this rule.
We described these dynamics already in chapter one and two, referring to the law of diminishing effectiveness, the law of policy accumulation, and different typologies of learning processes – such as first-order and second-order – learning processes. Where first-order learning hollows out the policy system, the second-order type may lead to internalisation. This last category

of learning processes would enhance the legitimacy and effectiveness of the legislation under consideration.

We may look at legislative processes as examples of societal learning. If a draft bill is put forward, the argumentation is often based on either the theoretical conviction, that a certain proposal could "work", that it would be effective, or on comparison of empirical data: this proposal is very successful elsewhere, so why would it be different here? Of course, here the whole problem of comparability is at stake. Cloning or aping may be very dangerous, if we imitate a feature of a system from a very different context. For instance, if somewhere in eastern Europe a new bill on higher education is designed, it is worthwhile looking at the country's history of higher education and the characteristics of its institutions in order to select suitable approaches. If for instance the Humboldtian type of university has been predominant for a long period during the last two centuries, it may be very risky to introduce a Napoleonic legislative system overnight. The role of international consultancy during the 1990s in central and eastern Europe can be criticised in this respect.

Educational institutions are closely linked to more general features of national culture. They have emerged from internal emancipation processes in earlier centuries. They may have served as symbols of specific developments, of civil wars and of liberation movements. Generation after generation may have made considerable emotional and moral investments in those institutions. They may also have been designed in more recent eras as expressions of influential political configurations, such as the polytechnics in Great Britain. So the creation of institutions may be the consequence of an evolutionary process of many centuries, but may also be part of contemporary policy-making. Traditions can be attacked but in many cases they cannot be wiped away as they are deeply rooted in the management culture. If legislation only reflects volatile majority judgements or benevolent dictatorship, it may exercise disastrous influence on the necessary continuity of institutional evolution.

The legiferation of organisational structures in higher education deserves specific attention. Regulation and deregulation are not symmetrical processes. Regulation to a certain degree is irreversible, in particular if the legislation is of a constitutional character and has created decision-making bodies. This is not only true at the central level of the state; decentralisation creates its own problems. The "plea for internal democracy" revolution at the end of the 1960s in western Europe and the USA has tempted legislators to come up with proposals for legislation in order to prescribe very specific and very detailed constitutions and other organisational concepts for universities. The legislative decision-makers considered this type of interventive strategy as effective in order to avoid further societal disruption.The democracy ideal was translated into multi-layered systems of decision-making councils within universities in a number of countries. A couple of decades later the political viewpoints had changed dramatically as well as the internal opinions in universities on the preferable structure of internal governance. The prevailing opinion then considered that it would be better to leave the decisions on the internal organisation to the universities themselves, allowing the legislator to withdraw. But loudly the councils declared that they themselves were indispensable for adequate university governance, and hence it appeared more difficult to convince policy makers that more diversity would be desirable, and that national legislators would be wise to withdraw from the field, as far as the regulation of internal university organisation was con-cerned.

New legislative proposals in many cases did not deregulate but replaced a specific prescribed organisational structure by another one.

Of course the legitimacy question cannot be dealt with by only looking at the legislative process. The authority structure in society at large may be a very influential variable. If the public sector is subject to considerable corruption, then the effects of legislation will be influenced by it. If there is a lot of civil disobedience in a specific national society, then the signifi-cance of legislation will vary accordingly.

## 4.2.2   The analytical tools refined

We may observe that the recent macro-trends in western Europe described in chapter two – erosion of political motives to finance higher education, partial commercialisation of knowledge, revolutionary developments in communication technology, and the gradual introduction of life-long learn-ing – all point at decreasing importance of legislative measures as far as specific legislation on higher education is concerned. General legislation on fair competition will become more important for universities as they enter the market place; civil law will partially replace administrative law. The horizontal world of the private sector will mingle with the hierarchical principles of public authority. Universities will become more and more hybrid organisations. Therefore we need a separate set of specific analytical tools. Legislation should leave sufficient space for the "entrepreneurial" part of university operations.

Also the internal organisation of universities should reflect the possible hybrid character of its operations. We will refer to that aspect in § 4.5.

Legiferation itself produces solidification and, to a certain degree, also irreversibility. Recommendations as well as reflections on legislation therefore should take this into account, as a solidification could hamper later necessary changes.

The subject matters to be covered by legislation can be divided in a number of categories:

- structures and systems;
- the allocation of authority to different decision-making bodies;
- institutions, educational and research institutions, and intermediary institutions;
- outputs and outcomes;
- processes and procedures, and other so called throughputs;
- inputs, among which are productive factors, and also students.

The institutional legislation concerns both institutions that perform in teaching and research, and intermediary institutions. The latter flourish in eastern Europe. In nations with more evolutionary traditions in intermediary institutional life it appears that these institutions can also hamper change.

The regulation of throughputs may concern primary processes such as curricula, but also so called meta-procedures such as quality care.

The autonomy of institutions grows as the legislation becomes less detailed. Chapter two discussed the concept of steering at a distance where accordingly a shift of concentration from inputs to outputs is brought about.

It is very difficult to analyse a regulatory system as a whole. Identifying three dimensions to steering sytems: levels of decision-making, subjects of steering, and instruments does help to order its complex characteristics, but it is of course insufficient to formulate adequate recommendations in forthcoming legislative problems, then the context and political structure play a major role.


4.3     Analysis

4.3.1   Threats and opportunities in the future

It seems feasible to us that the major trends described above will lead to systems of higher education in Europe that are more differentiated than the old ones in many respects. The monotype university will disappear; educational programmes will become more varified. National systems will split up into public and private parts, but also hybrid shapes will be visible. The post-initial phases of higher education will be subject to a price mechanism more than the initial ones, but the latter will also become more self sufficient financially than today. Basic research inevitably will remain a collective good and therefore will be financed from public sources. It is very uncertain how far the global conglomerates in the communications industry will penetrate higher education. It is not hard to formulate a number of major threats to future higher education. If legislation leads to very inflexible institutions and processes, the diminishing political support for the financial responsibility of the state in higher education will cause stagnation. If, on the other hand, universities become too dependent on commercial sources, their development will become very one-sided. It is maybe unnecessary to point out that the very important position of universities as critics of societal events would disappear as they become completely dependent on commercial sources. Legislation protects the most precious functions of societal institutions. So legislation on higher education in the future as often in the past will function as a counterbalance to undesirable developments threatened by the evolution of higher education context, in order to protect its nucleus of independent spiritual and intellectual activity. Although it is quite uncertain how European societies will evolve, and so it is equally uncertain how the shape of future legislation will be, this function of legislation remains the same.

Society probably will become more and more reflexive. The insight gained from the consequences of legislation will increase, and work out on future legislative activity. It is my firm belief – but not more than a belief – that a mix of the American type of university and the Newman approach to students' personal development will be one of the very vital future shapes of higher education. The legislation should however allow as much variety of institutional forms and categories of higher education as the future labour market will demand. Monotype higher education appears to be obsolete.

If the attention to effectiveness remains the same, inevitably the legislation will be much less detailed than in many present situations. A more global type of regulation will leave more choice available at the institutional level, and will enable more flexibility.

Maybe it will become usual in the future for higher order legislation to forbid the emergence of norms and rules on a decentralised intermediary level in order to protect the liberties of the decision-makers at the basic level. The attribution of authority to the basic level, such as the recognition of academic freedom has not been too effective in many countries as intermediary deci-sion-makers have not abstained from regulatory activity in those domains. So it is a major challenge to produce legislative systems and techniques that will meet this demand.

In so far as the symbolic policy view predominates, the legislation in itself – as well as the processes in order to change it – will be at least partially symbolic, but will also create symbols.

To actors with another orientation symbolic legislation will seem to be the creation of the emperor's clothes.

## 4.3.2 Output-orientation

In educational policies in western Europe the 1970s were devoted to the improvement of strategic planning and budgeting, while the 1980s brought the predominance of output orientation, quality control and steering at a distance. It became clear then that the traditional type of steering by regula-tion was not effective any longer for a number of reasons ( the general culture in society changed as well as the internal dynamics of the educational domain; the calculating individual and the calculating institution had appeared). Within the framework of several concepts of "new public management" new ideas on steering emerged. Their common denominator was, that the national central governance of higher education should step back somewhat and concentrate from then on on broad guidelines, be concerned with the performance and outputs of institutions, and utilise smart incentive systems as additional instruments for steering instead of regulation. Performance budgeting and indicators took their place together with more intensive quality control systems. Clear indications or even proof could subsequently be shown of the increasing output per unit of inputs. This has led to the ongoing popularity of this type of steering concepts for more than a decade now. There was and is no public sign of awareness that maybe the increase of measured outputs in essence was and is independent of the amount of resources, and that therefore decreasing budgets were and are not necessarily followed by decreasing outputs).

The concepts were sold under headings such as the enlargement of university autonomy, and deregulation. As we saw above, the deregulatory aspect became visible at the central level. But it was compensated or even overcompensated for by regulation at a decentralised level in many instances. And moreover quality control demanded byelaws very often.

A decade or so after the introduction of these types of concepts it seems worthwhile to evaluate the real consequences.

Steering by incentives – stimuli within allocation schemes or stimuli pointed at other tangible resources – differs from steering by regulation because no norm is formulated explicitly, no central "command" is presented on desirable actions, but a reward or compensation is promised if, and only if, a certain increase in ( to the opinion of the allocator, the governing body) desirable units of performance are reached. The norm may be present, but it remains hidden within the allocation algorithms. The imperative power of an incentive system has proven to be as great as that of a regulatory system. However, the governing body can hide the norms and values underlying the steering within the subtle characteristics of a budgeting system, or a related system like the student loans and grants system. Democratic control will be weak. The allocator does not account for those characteristics in public generally. For instance, if a government restricts the entitlements for student loans and grants to a certain number of years, it provides strong incentives for educational institutions to limit the length of studies accordingly. Or, if the government relates the continuation of student grants to a certain expression of performance or success, it produces strong stimuli to adapt to those expressions. Another type of stimuli is produced if the government, for instance, rewards the completion of PhDs within the calculating formula of block grants to universities, but not to any other successful product of graduate education. Then it provides a strong bias in the direction of a single type of graduate education.

People and organisations have gradually found themselves trapped by incentive systems; they have experienced strong uneasiness and a feeling of being manipulated which remains from then on. So the hidden hostility towards incentive systems delivers a serious problem in some cases.

The unwritten or hidden regulation may accumulate the disadvantages of a written regulation and those resulting from the uncertainty surrounding the absence of explicit rules.

The second observation is that – like all steering systems – incentive structures are due to diminishing effectiveness. As a consequence of the learning capacities of the governed institutions and the individuals concerned, the perverse effects of the incentives gradually tend to dominate. Actors adapt, succeed better and better in avoiding the unfavourable effects of the stimuli, and in immunising their actions. For instance, the incentive of rewarding research output in any form, either by counting publications or by measuring impact through the number of quotations, will lead to behavioural reactions. In due course it will seem as if scientific productivity has increased considerably, but apart from behavioural adaptations nothing has happened. In other terms, the life cycle of these systems is limited. That means that we have to build new information systems with new performance indicators from time to time. The investment in those new systems may prove to be too costly.

As has already been mentioned, the modernisation of steering systems has been accompanied by a continuous decline of available resources per "unit" of production, both the production of graduates and the number of PhDs, in the vast majority of OECD countries. Statistically the visible increase of efficiency is overwhelming. What is overlooked here is that critical thresholds may be passed quite easily. The pretention of an output-oriented budgeting system is that the available resources for each actor depend on effectiveness and efficiency. In the Netherlands, for instance, such a system was in operation during the major part of the 1980s, later also in Great Britain. The number of graduates and the number of PhDs rose dramatically. The net result was that each actor – however successful – had to face decreasing resources in absolute terms as well as in terms of resources per unit of production. The total budget did not increase in accordance with total production, but it decreased slightly and the "price" per unit of performance has as a consequence decreased sharply.

This trap – a classic case of prisoners' dilemma – has become visible during the first half of the 1990s, and this has led to the replacement of this system by less expicitly output-oriented systems in some cases.

The main conclusion must be that "steering at a distance" has produced a number of negative side-effects, but the main aim of increasing university autonomy with the use of incentive structures has not yet been abandoned.

The output-oriented concepts have shifted attention from inputs to outputs. However in many instances it has appeared very difficult to identify outputs in a trustworthy manner. Sometimes therefore the net result has been a shift from inputs to throughputs. Processes and procedures had been prescribed in the regulatory systems instead of outputs or outcomes. Often the regulatory "density" did not decrease at all, but only shifted.

### 4.3.3   Management group thinking

The above mentioned concepts introduced a new kind of management thinking in higher education. The role of management became much more explicit. The "integral manager" was introduced; programme and resource management being combined. Accountability and control became fashionable terms. The concepts were marketed, in many instances, under the name of decentralisation or at least deconcentration. In the domain of higher education the motto was: increasing the degree of university autonomy.

The net result has been that university administrators have gained influence: vice-chancellors, rectors and deans, but also directors of institutes are now more important in Europe than a decade ago. The similarity with the longer established situation in the USA has grown. On the other hand, the individual university teacher and researcher have certainly lost part of their freedom or discretionary choice; individual autonomy has decreased. Standardisation or even bureaucratisation of teaching and research prevail. We do not reveal a value judgement on that development, but the observation is clear. Some argue that, particularly in the field of scientific research, this development will lead to increasing risk-avoidance, so that risk-bearing research will not be undertaken any longer.

If that assumption proves right, that might be a major disadvantage in the long run. Studies in other fields suggest a broader observation, that maybe the general practice of national authorities in coping with professional elites, is to discipline them gradually through the introduction of professional management combined with considerable decentralisation at the institutional level.

Major progress has been made in many countries in the domain of quality care around teaching and research. The awareness that also here the methods used are subject to deterioration and the laws of diminishing effectiveness, leads to periodical change, and in particular more attempts at improvement. We observe that the legitimacy of intermediary institutions between the state and the universities has been strengthened considerably where they have succeeded in playing a role in quality care procedures. By comparison the position of Academies of Science in central and eastern Europe has been controversial as they have been identified with some of the disagreeable characteristics of their former regimes. A clear role identification of these Academies with generally accepted quality care systems could be a means to overcoming this type of controversy.

The relationships between the outcomes of the quality care systems and allocation schemes in many countries are vague. Judicial guarantees against wrong or corrupted quality judgements are generally not very successful. When the power structure penetrates the peer review part of quality care, nothing helps any longer.

The trust in the integrity of quality care or discretionary decisions on grants and subsidies is a vital condition for legitimacy of the system of governance. This trust can be furthered by adequate global legislation, but of course never ensured.

The predominance of thinking in terms of quality has enabled us with concepts of discriminatory decision-making. The former overwhelming stress on distributive justice in left-wing European ideological thought has been replaced by an even more imperative accent on quality. One may observe a shift from block grants to universities to more project-oriented funding.

The legal basis for the latter is in most cases restricted to procedural guarantees.


4.4     Paradoxes and dilemmas

In general it must be clear by now, that the previously espoused concept of integral planning, based on the orthodox plannning theory with its top-down character, is obsolete. Legislation promoting or referring to that concept for that reason is obsolete too. More dynamic and modern planning theories now only allow for process-oriented legislation. This tye of legislation always provokes the question whether it is necessary to regulate the planning process at all.

When considering and reviewing the existing legislation on higher education in Europe, one might wonder whether the paradox of legislation is not that the issues dealt with are symbolic in many respects, but that they are so ineffective in an era that is obsessed by effectiveness. The tragedy of legislation in a democratic context may be that it can bring about only piecemeal change, and then only with sufficient support and momentum. Farreaching ambitions in legislation therefore inevitably lead to major gaps between pretention and reality.

Legislation itself is a solidifying phenomenon, which means that it can only ameliorate flexibilty inside higher education. Overregulation is a continuous threat, but it cannot be judged independently from its context. Underregulation leads to decentralising struggles for power, or even decentralised dictatorship.

Any legislation destroys variety to some degree, although the main objective may be to elicit variety on the level of the primary processes inside higher education. But regulation in general is unfit to maximise creativity in itself. It may only be able to get rid of some of the hindrances of maximum creativity.

If intermediary institutions are created by law, they will look for a useful domain to work in as long as they exist. They will be very difficult to get rid of, and this could only be achieved by law. Their natural behaviour will be to develop themselves as regulating authorities; there will be an extra amount of regulation as a consequence of their creation.

With regard to the three dimensions of the steering networks created by law there are a number of paradoxes:

· as far as the level of decision-making is concerned, the recognition of the professional character of universities leads to a firm degree of decentralisation. As long as the allocation of resources is a centralised process, it demands criteria which will necessarily concern outputs and outcomes as long as the objective of effectiveness is predominant. The preocccupation of the central executive authorities with outputs and outcomes threatens the heart of professional autonomy;

· the shift from inputs as the main subject of steering to outputs and outcomes will increase the managerial autonomy of the decentralised university managers. However they are not able to influence in an effective manner the subtle nucleus of the primary processes, that is the quality of teaching and research. Therefore they, in their turn, agree to install systems of quality care. So the centre of gravity of regulation will – at a lower level – shift to throughputs, the procedures concerning quality care and its consequences;

· the shift from the regulatory instrument to others like incentive systems will provoke a lot of hidden regulation – without the clear guarantees of democratic control – and again enlarge the influence of the decentralised management at the expense of the individual members of the academic staff.

The main dilemma legislators find themselves confronted is the following:

In anticipation of the learning capacity of the system under governance it seems worthwhile by moving from substantial norms and rules to so called meta-legislation that concentrates on quality care systems and incentive systems. But in the long run these systems will also be subjected to deterioration as a consequence of the laws of diminishing effectiveness and policy accumulation. Moreover, it is doubtful whether central legislation is apt to prohibit decentralised bueaucratisation and the decentralised accumulation of substantial regulation. The lead-time of a change in central legislation may be too long, so that the harmful effects of the just described developments can not be anticipated or otherwise avoided.


## 4.5    Guidelines to the future

### 4.5.1  Problems within universities

Chapter two puts into order a number of the exogeneous vectors influencing the future development of universities and university management. In this chapter we have analysed some of the recent shifts in the relations between the state and higher education. The internal development of universities thus is determined by amongst others:

·    the evolution of steering concepts

     National government is subject to "political business cycles"; periods calling for decentralisation and increasing autonomy of universities are followed by calls for increasing accountability, etc.
     A more structural trend may be that professional in advanced societies are "disciplined" through the introduction of managerial thinking and the "integral manager".

·    the above mentioned macro-trends described in chapter two.

Declining public resources put a major stimulus on universities to find new financial sources; some national governments have created "policy prisons" by the intense relationships between the system for financial support to students on the one hand and the subsidies to institutions on the other. In this case a government cannot allow universities to set their own prices because the financial consequences of an increase in prices would "return" to government, as an increase in loans and grants.
The intensity of the societal demand for higher education is frustrated by the "policy prison". Uncoupling is a necessary but not sufficient condition for escape from the "policy prison".

In order to cope with the imperialism of communications-technology conglomerates universities should cooperate among themselves and with national governments in order to maintain a sufficiently strong position.

The hybrid character of many European universities will necessitate university administrations to design or to reveal values and attitudes towards hybridity. The centrifugal properties of hybridity have to be eliminated. The societal driving forces moreover will create continueous turbulence in the university environment. In past centuries universities reacted to external impulses with *"dynamic conservatism"*, and a consequently lost a considerable market share in post-experience teaching and applied research. This approach cannot be continued because the core tasks of the university – initial education and fundamental research – will not be financed by future national public authorities in an adequate manner. So the future strategies of universities have to be directed towards agressive approaches in order to grasp a larger share of expanding educational and research markets.

Internally the management of universities has to gain speed, flexibility and the potential for strategic change.
An all-encompassing model for university organisation is not presented, because that would neglect the *contingent* characteristics of different situations in different countries and in different corners of the educational domain.

However, what is presented is an hypothetical example of a proposal for university reorganisation in a country where the tradition is a mix of Napoleonic, Humboldtian and American characteristics, where public resources are declining and where all the above mentioned macro-trends are present.

The present university organisation is characterised by
· depth;
· relative immobility;
· top-down administration by a mainly allocating and facilitating body.

The depth – the number of partially vertically ordered layers of decision-making – is a consequence of the bureaucratisation of the classical concept of the university, its faculties, departments, Fachgruppen, etc. The relative immobility may also be a consequence either of too complex legislation or of bureaucratisation. A number of administrative layers have gradually been constructed between the top and the workplace. All impact is indirect and partial. Although all theoretical concepts concerning advanced professional organisations point towards the necessity for a flat organisation, many university organisations have evoluated as "machine bureaucracies". The complexity of internal decision-making in universities is considerable, partially as a consequence of the introduction of formal democracy at the end of the 1960s.

The lead times between design of innovation and implementation therefore are long. In a competitive environment this kind of immobility may prove to be too long. According to the traditional mainstream of theoretical developments the leadership in pure professional organisations will and should be restricted to resource allocation and facility management. This principle has been laid down in a number of countries in the notion of a "duplex ordo" where the presidency or the board are separated from the senate or faculty. The board allocates and facilitates, while the senate is concerned with primary processes. Of course a "duplex ordo" is quite hostile to the notion of integral management.

In Europe one may observe a considerable number of university leaders who evolve into integral managers and who have a major impact on teaching and research. There are also many university board members who like to concentrate on facility management. At the departemental level there are deans, faculty boards, etc. which combine a number of functions. They govern primary processes more or less as well as facilities and human resources. A lack of transparancy is the main consequence. Our design concentrates on flexibility and self-control; we stipulate that traditional university organisation patterns and structures could be replaced by a design where internal markets are crucial and where functional differentiation predominates. In other words, we criticise the concept of the integral leader inside the university, because this concept is based on an unrealistic assumption, of either the available qualities of men or women, or of the possibilities of collective leadership.

The design is as follows:

A university consists of a presidency and of two types of organisational components:
· primary processes, education and research, and maybe also other societal services;
· treasure chambers, which house all the academic personnel.

The presidency has the following main functions:

· the installment and discontinuation of primary processes and treasure chambers;
· the appointment of primary processmanagers and treasure chamber managers;
· the allocation of resources to primary processes;
· the monitoring of primary processes and treasure chambers.

A primary process can be a teaching programme or a related set of research activities. A primary process is led by a manager, the primary process manager, who takes the main decisions on the shape and character of the primary processes under his control. The primary process manager reports to the presidency, and takes responsibility for the primary process. A primary process has no personnel.

A treasure chamber is a – partly virtual – organisation comprising all the university staff, and it has no activities. The treasure chamber is managed by a treasure chamber manager, who bears responsibility for optimalising the human resources within the chamber. The treasure chamber manager reports to the presidency.

All money streams lead to the primary process managers. The presidency allocates public money, and the market income, earned by contracts, is also added to the resources that the primary process manager may dispose of. The treasure chamber does not receive any regular income from the presidency.

The dynamics within the institution are channeled through the most central mechanism, an internal marketplace, where primary processmanagers and treasure chamber managers agree on contracts to hire human talent for a certain period of time according to the primary process framework. The primary process manager will try to hire the most able experts, and the treasure chamber manager will try to "sell" all available manpower. If the income of a treasure chamber is insufficient to cover the costs of human resources, the treasure chamber manager envisages problems. If a primary process manager does not succeed in hiring adequate manpower from one of the existing treasure chambers, he too then has a problem. If the primary process manager is allowed to shop outside the university, a financial deficit will follow, unless some of the treasure chamber managers are able to sell part of the manpower in an outside market too. A mutual insurance fund will cover the risks that treasure chambers run in the short term. If a treasure chamber is confronted with permanent deficits, it will have to downsize.

Can such an organisation function in reality?

At first sight the disadvantages seem enormous:

·   the transaction costs of the functioning of the internal markets may be considerable;
·   the primary process manager lacks legitimacy to decide on the contents of a primary process; therefore he needs to receive advice from many experts – internally and externally – in order to make sensible decisions on the scope of a curriculum or the shape of a research programme;
·   the internal hierarchy inside a treasure chamber does not motivate professionals in an optimal manner, but will possibly alienate them;
·   there may be major discrepancies between supply and demand for specific manpower; relative prices therefore will widely differ;
·   the span of control of the presidency could be insufficient to monitor adequately all primary processes and treasure chambers.

On reflection the advantages of the model become visible:

·   the internal markets do not only allocate scarce resources, but can be considered as very effective information systems too, revealing judgements on the relative quality of manpower in a transparent way;
·   the organisation of the university is quite simple and clear, as well as the division of responsibilities;

- the primary processes can be managed consistently as the primary process manager receives all income; so the centrifugal consequences of a mixed task-market-orientation are less harmful; hybridity does not hurt any longer; an analogous observation is valid for the treasure chambers;
- the demands of the primary process manager and the treasure chamber manager for management skills are more modest than the demands put to an integral manager;
- the flexibility of this type of organisational dynamic seems considerable.

Of course we do not argue that this type of university organisation should be introduced overnight. But the scheme may prove to have heuristic value. One might wonder how the responsibilities of the primary process manager and the treasure chamber manager are distributed in a real university, whether they are sufficiently clear, etcetera. One might discover – as we did in some earlier studies for instance – that in a certain university the management responsible for basic education is dispersed over a number of functionaries, or that the responsibilities of the treasure chamber manager are altogether diffuse. So the scheme enables us to focus on the crucial bottle-necks of real universities with a fresh viewpoint.


## 4.5.2   Self-control within sensible public environments

In the previous paragraph we have described a number of crucial variables in the evolution of the environments for higher education, we have sketched some of the ongoing transformation processes, and we have pointed at some necessary changes in paradigms underlying government policies for higher education. We have designed a new type of internal university organisation as a starting point for reflection on the organisational changes to be made in real universities.

Uncoupling of financial systems at the governmental level, flexible management with an acceptable degree of hybridity at the university level, and self-control at the level of primary processes appear crucial. The university as an institution "where competence counts a little bit more" could survive.

We have concentrated on formal conditions for vitality. In this way we have necessarily not paid sufficient attention to the "sense making processes" inside universities: leadership often shows more in value patterns, in inspiration than in utilisation of formal authority. Mass higher education in effective universities demands the intimacy of an active scolarly learning environment on the one hand and the large group on the other. The management of large educational programmes asks for well-planned and executed activities, not for the benign chaos that is so characteristic of traditional dreams about university life.

Legislation should utilise the self-regulating potential of professional organisations more than in the past. Selfsteering of universities necessitates leadership by inspiration besides the use of methods for pricing and costing, planning and evaluation. The governance of universities in the next century will be characterised by hybridity and diversity, and new cultural patterns will emerge to ensure that universities remain the most attractive organisations in the world.

# 5

## COUNTRY REPORTS

# 5.1

## ALBANIA

### *Ilia Prifti*

5.1.1    Current situation in higher education; Institutional diversification

Higher education is relatively new in Albania. The first Higher Pedagogical Institute was established in 1948 and the first university in 1957. Until the end of the 1990-91 academic year the University of Tirana was the only university in Albania, consisting of 11 faculties, covering the natural sciences, medicine, social sciences and engineering. There were also seven institutes, three of them situated in Tirana, the rest in regional towns: Shkoder, Elbasan, Gjirokaster and Korçe. In 1991, the University of Tirana was subdivided into two parts:
·    the University of Tirana, with seven faculties;
·    the Polytechnic University of Tirana, comprising four engineering faculties.

There have also been changes in the status of some of the institutes. The Agricultural Institute of Tirana and those institutes located in Shkoder, Elbasan, Gjirokaster and Korçe have gained university status, the Institute of Fine Arts has become an Academy of Arts, while the Institute of Physical Education has preserved its old status. In 1994 the newest university was established in Vlora. Albania now has eight universities and two higher non-university schools under the authority of the Ministry of Education. There are also two Military Higher Schools, which, however, do not come under this Ministry's authority. All of these are public institutions and are financed by the State. In total there are 35 faculties and 126 departments able to confer university and post-university diplomas and degrees in more than 70 subjects. There are nearly 2200 teachers (1680 full-time) teaching in the different kinds of higher education institutions, of these 160 are professors, 260 are assistant professors and 285 "doctoral" degree holders.

### 5.1.2    Higher educational system and research institutes

The controlling bodies within the higher education system are the Committee for Science and Technology, the Commission of Scientific Qualifications, the Consultative Group of Higher Education, the National Office of TEM-PUS-Programs, and the Academy of Science. The Committee for Science and Technology is a governmental institution dealing with problems of design and implementation of scientific research and applied new technologies. Joining with the universities it works through the Ministry of Education. The Commission of Scientific Qualification is a national board dealing with issues of post-university scientific qualification, and in particular with the organisation and supervision of post-graduate education. This Commission, attached to the Council of Ministers, has decision-making powers concerning post-graduate affairs. The Academy of Science is an institution embracing the whole system of scientific research organisations and research institutes.

The Higher Education Law of 1994 specifies that scientific research is one of the most important objectives of higher education. Despite the institutions' fine research tradition, current budgetary and other constraints are making this goal rather difficult to attain. The new legislation also envisions cooperation and coordination between universities, the Committee for Science and Technology and the Academy of Science.

The Consultative Group of Higher Education is a national board which advises the Minister of Education on important problems on higher education strategy and policy. The head of the board is the Minister of Education and its other members are some of Albania's most respected professors. In the near future this board will be replaced by the National Council of Higher Schools, which will carry out the same functions.

5.1.3    The higher education budget

The higher education institutes are public and are financed by the State with allocations established under the "Budget Law". Each university is granted its own budget; in addition they and other higher education institutes receive public funding for research activities made available by the Committee for Science and Technology and by other ministries. This is done with a view to establishing national research programmes. Within the framework of the higher education law there are other possibilities of obtaining funding through joint activities with "third parties" such as private enterprises or state institutions.

The higher education budget takes low priority, and constituted only 0.43% of GDP in 1994. Of the total budget for the education sector, only 11% is designated to higher education, approximately 7 million US dollars in 1994. For 1995 the situation was similar, with the total budget for higher education at approximately 7.34 million US dollars. Allocations within the higher education budget for 1995 are as follows:
·    58% on personnel (salaries and social insurance);
·    17.5% for scholarships;
·    11% for investments;
·    13.5% for building new laboratories, staff training and other services.

5.1.4    Enrolment structure

Since 1991 the universities have administered their own entrance examinations. Admission is restricted to a "numerus clausus". In the 1994-95 academic year almost 28,300 students (17,800 full-time and 10,500 part-time) were admitted to 10 higher education institutions, i.e. 0.8% of the total population. Table I presents the rate of admittance 1990-95, and the number of students enrolled in higher education institutions 1990-95. It should be noted that between 1991-93 there was a great increase in the admittance of young people from families persecuted under the old communist regime. They were accepted by the universities without having to sit entrance examinations, and made up 35%-40% of the total number of new enrolments.

Table I

| Year | 1989-90 | 90-91 | 91-92 | 92-93 | 93-94 | 94-95 |
|---|---|---|---|---|---|---|
| Rate of acceptance (%) | 16.6 | 17.1 | 21.1 | 32.8 | 19.4 | 22.4 |
| admitted (in thousands) | | | | | | |
| total | 5.5 | 6.0 | 6.7 | 10.0 | 5.0 | 4.6 |
| full-time | 4.9 | 5.4 | 5.4 | 6.0 | 3.6 | 3.1 |
| part-time | 0.6 | 0.6 | 1.3 | 4.0 | 1.4 | 1.5 |
| Number of students (in thousands) | | | | | | |
| full-time | – | 22.0 | 22.7 | 22.8 | 20.2 | 17.8 |
| part-time | – | 5.0 | 5.3 | 9.8 | 10.0 | 10.5 |

These figures reflect the admission policy during the transition period which has been orientated at "market demands", meaning, the distribution of students across subjects is related to the current employment situation in Albania. Currently the majority of university graduates especially in engineering and agriculture are unemployed. The government accordingly continues to limit the total number of students, and allocates them to disciplines in ways deemed more responsive to student aspirations and the demands of the labour market.

## 5.1.5    Reform in higher education: strategy and policy

Forty-five years of indoctrination and isolation from the rest of Europe has left the higher education sector gravely underdeveloped, particularly as regards teaching methodology and scientific research. However, the democratic changes which have taken place during the last three years and the introduction of a market economy brings bright prospects for higher education. Many changes have already been accomplished, but more needs to be done to entirely restructure higher education and eradicate the worst aspects of the former communist regime; notably the isolation, indoctrination, extreme centralisation and limited intellectual scope which have collectively resulted in backwardness and poverty.

The successful implementation of higher education reform requires a clear strategy aimed at the creation of a democratic system, up to European standards, supported by high professional qualifications, well-directed research and competitive technological progress. Under the new law higher education reform is developing in three main directions:

- improving curricula, syllabuses, academic staff training, as well as developing interuniversity cooperation;
- building a new academic structure with the department as the basic academic unit of teaching and research;
- establishing quality assurance and academic accreditation of higher education institutions.

The second and third points are only now being addressed. To realise these goals, higher education needs support in two important areas. In the formulation of a contemporary European outlook, and in securing adequate financial support from the State and third parties. In more detail, the principle lines of higher education reform consist of the following:

- to increase previously absent academic freedom and autonomy of universities in academic, financial and administrative matters;
- democratisation of the governing academic bodies, including the student body;
- reform of the qualification and of the post-graduate system;
- implementation of new admission criteria;
- raising the level of aptitude in teaching and research, by training academic staff, either in Albania or abroad;
- extending collaboration with foreign universities through European projects.

The main aspects of this strategy are determined in new legislation based on progressive European standards supported by, and implemented with the help of, the Council of Europe. The new legislation lays down the democratic determination of Albanian higher education, both internally and externally. Internally, it vests academic freedom and autonomy in the higher education institutions. Externally, it sets forth rules relative to the establishment of higher education institutions, to academic cooperation and to the opening of Albanian institutions to the world.

So far, international organisations, as well as companies and foundations have been very helpful.

The most progressive developments over the last three years have been contacts with universities abroad, as well as membership in higher education associations such as the Mediterranean University Community. Still, higher education policy pursues long term goals and their gradual implementation requires extensive material and human investments. With this in mind, the above mentioned private and public efforts must be continued and intensified.

# 5.2

## BELARUS

### *Boris Kopissky & Nikolai Listopad*

5.2.1    The Constitution of the Republic of Belarus provides in:

Art. 49: Everybody has the right to education. Access to free general secondary and vocational and technical education is guaranteed. Specialised secondary and higher education is accessible to everybody in accordance with his/her abilities. Everybody can get appropriate education on a competitive basis, free of charge in state educational institutions.

Art. 50: Everybody has the right to use their mother tongue and to choose the languages of interaction. The State guarantees according to the law the free choice of education and the language of training.

Art. 51 of the Constitution promulgates freedom of scientific, artistic and technical research, as well as of instruction, and not least, the protection of intellectual property.

5.2.2    The current legislative situation

As stated in the Law of Education of the Republic of Belarus, state policy in the field of education must be based on certain principles, the most paramount of which are the following:

· the priority of humanistic values ought to be preserved;
· the national-cultural basis of education shall be observed;
· higher education shall be scientific in character;

- it shall adhere to internationally recognised standards of research and instruction;
- it shall be connected to social practice;
- it shall exercise due regard to ecological, social and democratic constituents;
- it shall pursue unity of spiritual and physical achievement;
- it shall encourage and promote the gifted;
- and finally, 9 years of schooling shall be compulsory.

Based on these principles educational policy in the Republic of Belarus aims at creating favourable conditions for versatile personality development, the full realisation of creative potential, and the forming and re-informing of national consciousness of the citizens, as well as of their respect for other countries and peoples of the world. Some particular aims may be highlighted as follows:

- ensuring command of the State language as the main means of communication between the citizens of the Republic of Belarus;
- preserving and enlarging the intellectual potential and cultural values of the Belorussian people and other national groups in the republic;
- forming ecological consciousness;
- fostering respect for family life;
- achieving a reasonable correspondence between a person's experience and knowledge;
- developing scientific technical and cultural activities in accord with the rate of development of the Republic;
- bringing up conscious respect for democracy as a form of governance and organisation allowing, for the benefit of society, every person to take part in decision-making processes;
- bringing up conscious respect for a world order based on the recognition of political, economic, and social rights of all peoples of the world.

In the educational establishments of the Republic no activities of political parties or other social groups pursuing political goals are permitted. The same applies to children, students or youth organisations which depend on such parties or groups.

All citizens of the Republic of Belarus, and also foreigners and those without citizenship who permanently reside on the territory of the Republic, have a right to equal access to the national education system. This right to education is available through state and other educational institutions of various forms, and through their teaching methods. Free education is provided at state basic schools and other state educational establishments for all who fulfil the entry requirements or who are subject to the privileges stated in the legal code of the Republic of Belarus.

## 5.2.3    Higher education

The objective of higher education is to prepare students for specialised tasks in the creative and public spheres of life which require scientific or otherwise specialised knowledge. Higher education is provided on the basis of secondary schools, in specialized comprehensive educational establishments or professionally orientated educational establishments, and in universities, academies, or at institutes. Higher education establishments may operate preparatory departments and courses, lyceums and colleges, as well as professionally orientated schools and other educational platforms for the training of the most talented youth.

Teaching in higher education establishments must be carried out on the basis of the latest data on scientific and technical progress and closely integrate scientific and practical activities. Studies at any higher education institution are completed either upon passing the specific state examination, or upon presentation of a specific scientific project, or upon successful completion of course work. In the latter case a bachelor's degree may be awarded, and the in the former, a master's degree.

## 5.2.4    State and intermediate leadership in the education system

Leadership in the education system in the Republic of Belarus is a domain both of the State and of intermediate bodies. Functions carried out by the Council of Ministers of the Republic of Belarus are as follows:

·   the establishment of state requirements for education, and the control over their implementation;

·   the promulgation of rules concerning formation, reorganisation and abolishment of higher education institutions, and of charter registration in the educational bodies;

·   the approval of samples of educational documents and of their publication;

·   the promulgation of rules governing financing, material and technical security, the salaries, and the social security of pupils, students and of others under training.

The Ministry of Education of the Republic of Belarus ensures implementation of the state policy, and approves standard academic plans and requirements.

The management of institutions is governed by the institution's bye-laws, and by the principles of participation of teachers, pupils, students, employees, parents, and of public representatives. Higher education institutions are in their decision making on educational, financial and other issues independent – while held to preserve state interests and requirements, such as guaranteeing rights of pupils, students, teachers and other stakeholders.

State organs may interfere with the autonomous activities of higher education institutions only in the event of a violation of the Law of the Republic. Persons managing higher education institutions are, in their official capacities, subject to the Law only, and may not be influenced by political parties and other politically interested organisations.

Content of education and form of control are determined by educational plans and curricula worked out according to the provisions concerning educational institutions, taking into consideration regional and national exigencies. Education may be carried out full-time, part-time or by correspondence, as well as according to individual programmes. It is permitted to obtain certificates of comprehensive and special education in the humanities by pursuing external degrees. Admission into state educational institutions, apart from basic school, is carried out in accordance with the rules laid down by the educational institutions and in state educational requirements and provisions. Admission into non-state educational institutions is carried out in accordance with rules, determined only by these institutions.

Organisation of the educational process is determined by the bye-laws of the institutions. However, employment of pupils and students in services unrelated to their education requires the approval of the Council of the Educational Institutions, notwithstanding legal provisions of the Republic of Belarus. In such cases prolongation of an educational term is permitted, and enterprises or organisations benefiting from an employment often compensate for additional educational expenses.

Non-state educational institutions can carry out education on any level and of any kind. To be valid such institutions must receive a permit from the Ministry of Education of the Republic of Belarus and comply with the rules of this Law. In case of successful fulfilment of educational targets they can receive state subsidies. The Ministry of Education of the Republic of Belarus must give such a permit on the condition that non-state educational institutions are ready to meet the following requirements:

· they must carry out their activity in accordance with the rules of Article 4 of the Law;
  keep to the plans and programmes within the minimum framework as determined by the Ministry of Education;
· assure a professional staff;
· fulfil the educational process on premises sufficiently equipped and in compliance with sanitary and pedagogical standards;
· help in maintaining control in the sphere of education carried out by the state-bodies having the powers on it;
· financing of the educational system.

State educational establishments are financed by the State from its budget. Actually, no less than 10% of the national income of Belarus is spent on education. Other financing sources of educational establishments are incomes from contractual revenues for educational background, payments of businessmen, owners and citizens. These resources may be pooled in governmental and local funds, distribution being effectuated in accordance with the regulations determined by the Council of Ministers and the local Soviet of People's Deputies. It is prohibited for state educational establishments to accept money in return for education, optional courses exempted. Tuition fees are obligatory, however, for the repetition of a course, for foreigners and in second programmes of study. Fundamental and other scientific research, is financed on the basis of contests.

The legislative basis for educational development in the Republic of Belarus is the Constitution, adopted by the Supreme Soviet in 1994, and the Education in the Republic of Belarus Act of 1991.

The Education in the Republic of Belarus Act provides, that the Ministry of Education and Science shall elaborate general principles of enrolment and that it monitors their functioning. At the same time the Law invests the HEI with the power to administer entrance examinations, to determine their number and the grading system. The Law furthermore addresses the possibility of a private education sector, as well as tuition fees for state HEIs. Private higher education institutions, being a part of the educational system of the State, are guided in their activities by the Education in the Republic of Belarus Act, as well as by the decisions of the Ministry of Education and Science, and have a sufficiently wide scope for freedom in defining enrolment scales, principles of enlisting the entrants, contents of curricula and the amount of tuition fee. State higher education institutions are obliged to enrol the number of students set by the Ministry of Education and Science. They have a right, however, to enrol more students, but in this case a student must pay for education.

The legal texts regulating higher education include a large number of orders issued by the Ministry of Education and Science governing particular matters.

Despite its comprehensive scope, legislation on higher education in Belarus falls short of defining, with meaningful precision, the economic and proprietary rights of higher education institutions. This concerns first of all the issue of ownership of lands, but also the rights to buildings and constructions, to royalties and other results of research.

## 5.2.5   The current situation

Nowadays there are 40 state and 17 private higher education institutions in Belarus. The main type of educational institution is the university (academy). All higher education institutions, irrespective of the form of ownership, pass state attestation to have the right to get state license to perform educational activities and to train specialists in established fields. State higher education institutions are subject to the Ministry responsible for the discipline in question (Ministry of Education and Science, Ministry of Public Health, Ministry of Culture, Ministry of Agriculture, Ministry of Transport). Furthermore, all higher education institutions are considered by the State as a part of the educational sphere, which is why they must abide by decisions of the Ministry of Education and Science. The Ministries finance respective higher education institutions and monitor their financial and administrative activity. The Ministry of Education and Science is entitled also to control the organisation of the teaching process in all higher education institutions of the Republic, including teaching content and the level of preparation of school-leavers.

State higher education institutions have no intermediate bodies between them and state authorities, though laws currently in force permit formulation of such an intermediate link.

Private higher education institutions in Belarus are combined in an association, the objective of which it is to protect their interests and to co-ordinate their activities. The Ministry of Education and Science informs private higher education institutions of its decisions and of new legal provisions through this association. However, state educational authorities have no right to interfere with financial and personnel policies of the private higher education institutions.

As of recently, all higher education institutions of the Republic have the right to appeal decisions by Ministries in a Court of Law.

Analysis of the normative foundations of higher education indicates that some aspects of higher education remain unsettled. This is due to Belarus having changed significantly following the collapse of the USSR. Some already adopted Laws are not in force yet and the law-making process in the educational sphere is progressing very slowly.

# 5.3

## THE FLEMISH COMMUNITY OF BELGIUM

### Jan Fiers & Joan Lesseliers

### 5.3.1    The current legislative situation

There are no provisions in the Constitution relating specifically to higher education, Art. 24 of the Constitution relates to education in general. However, as Art. 4 of the Flemish Decree on Universities specifies:

"The activities of the universities are spread, in the interest of the collectivity, simultaneously over academic education, scientific research and scientific services.
They can exert all legal actions and in particular close contracts with this aim with all legal persons of private or public nature".

Art.3 of the Decree pertaining to the colleges for higher education in the Flemish Community:

"The activities of the higher education colleges are spread, in the interest of the collectivity, simultaneously over higher education, services rendered to society and, in particular cases, over thematic scientific research in the framework of cooperation with Belgian or foreign universities or third parties. In addition, development and practice of art is a part of the mission of these higher education colleges that organise education in one of the following area's: audiovisual arts, painting and sculpture, music and drama".

5.3.2    Main features of the higher education system

Since 1970, Belgium has had a unique threefold system of higher education: university education, higher education of the long type (HOLT) and higher education of the short type (HOKT). Since the Decree of 1994 on the non-university higher education institutions, a distinction is made between short courses undertaken within a single cycle and long courses undertaken within two cycles.

Until recently, the authority concerning education, including academic higher education, was almost exclusively in the hands of the national government. The state reform of 1988 entrusted the organisation of education to the Communities, exempting only regulation relative to duration of compulsory education, minimal conditions for the granting of diplomas, and pension plans, that stay under federal (national) competence.

> The relation as of now between the State and the Higher Education Institutions is still quite different depending on the legal quality of the institution (State-operated, public or private), whatever changes the current legislation may have provoked. Higher Education in Belgium can largely be divided into three different kinds of institutions: those that are immediately operated by the state, those that are run by provincial or local authorities, and the private ones.

> The tendency towards equality of status among the institutions is achieved to the extent that in the function of control from the State on the institutions the system is entirely the same. Since the State-operated and other public institutions (operated by provincial or local authorities) are largely subject to public law, whereas the private institutions are subject to private law, this equality is far from being completed.

> As a side remark or an example can be said that legislation is always directly applicable to the public education sector, but that it can be enforced only to the private education sector only if (constitutional) freedom of education is guaranteed. This often implies that the Minister of Education can only impose something by virtue of making subsidies dependent of voluntary changes by the institutions.

Universities, as defined by decree, are engaged in scientific research, teaching and scientific service. Their research activities are supposed to be fundamental and serve as a foundation to teaching. Scientific service, as the third pillar, is directed at the community as a whole. There are eight universities in the Flemish Community, which accommodate a total of 62.840 students (1993-1994). These are, in order of the number of enrolments (1993-1994):

| | | |
|---|---|---|
| · | Catholic University of Leuven | (25.591) |
| · | University of Ghent | (17.576) |
| · | Free University of Brussels | (8.087) |
| · | University Faculties St.-Ignatius of Antwerp | (3.522) |
| · | University Institute of Antwerp | (2.738) |
| · | University Centre of Limburg | (2.304) |
| · | University Centre of Antwerp | (2.267) |
| · | Catholic University of Brussels | (755) |

As for non-university higher education institutions, there exist colleges in the Flemish Community. Colleges offer non-university curricula, primarily in the fine arts. Colleges are also engaged in social service and offer thematic-scientific research opportunities in co-operation with universities or third parties. 157 colleges offer higher non-university education in Flanders today. This situation is about to change drastically as a result of the far reaching reforms initiated by the 1994 law. The largely dispersed, mainly small-scale institutions are currently being merged to create larger, more manageable units. Although the law doesn't explicitly compel the colleges to participate, its revised subsidising system, which favours the larger units, effectively eliminates viable alternatives. Schools of 600 students are supposed to be the critical balancing point.

At the university level the educational structure is subdivided into academic courses, advanced courses and post-academic courses. Colleges have a similar educational structure consisting of basic courses, advanced courses and post-college training.

Higher education is regarded as education for responsible persons, over 18, after their secondary education. They participate voluntarily, in a study or professional training programme, a choice which they make more consciously and independently than their orientation during secondary education. In some study areas of the university, such as applied sciences, an entrance examination is required. The training in the maritime sector of the colleges requires a preceding ability test. An artistic entrance examination is required for artistic training in colleges. Per academic year only two examination sessions are possible for the same year of the same course. In order to succeed in a certain year, one has to take all examinations of that year, with the exception of certain exemptions on the basis of previous studies. A transfer of certain examination results from the first examination session to the second examination session is possible within one and the same academic year and, on special conditions, from one academic year to the next, for instance if one failed.

As well as the traditional contact education, institutes of higher education can also offer training in the form of open education. The possibility also exists to be educated on a part-time basis instead of a full-time basis.

In principle, Dutch is the educational and administrative language for all educational activities of higher education. There are some limitative exceptions to this principle, in order to allow Flemish higher education the benefit of joining the internationalisation of higher education, and in order to create the conditions to encourage the Flemish students to enter an increasingly international labour market of highly educated people. Despite this tendency towards internationalisation, entrance to higher education in Flanders, generally, is made dependant on a Dutch language ability test.

### 5.3.3    Finance and governance

The University Decree of 1991 and the College Decree of 1994 set forth a new philosophy on governance, particularly on the distribution of powers between the government and the institutions of higher education: the traditional centralist view was abandoned in favour of a deregulation concept in which the government defines general policies, and leaves their implementation to the institutions. This implies that for their legal protection the higher education institutions can no longer depend on the Ministry of Education, but have to defend their interests themselves in court, as independent legal persons. Depending on the problem and on the institution either the common or the administrative courts are competent.

Universities in Flanders are financially dependent on public funds. Contributions from the private sector whether through contracts or donations are negligible, they amount to not even 10% of their budgets. Within limits and according to specific terms, the Flemish Community contributes an annual allowances to cover the ordinary expenses of academic education, scientific research, scientific service and administration. The Flemish Community also contributes with an annual allowance to the college-budgets.

The most striking change of policy over the last decennium concerning the financing of the higher education institutions is that the allowances are now mainly distributed according to a (from the government's point of view) fixed budget, allocated according to an institutional scale, in so called 'envelopes', whereas they used to be closely related to the number of students. It should be noted that the systems for the universities and the colleges are somewhat different, and that they have separate budgets.

There is a new embargo on the financing of advanced courses, as a result of an unprecedented explosion in their supply, unjustified by any natural cause, and merely induced by the easy access to financing. Thus institutions are free to organise these courses, but exclusively at their own risk. A corollary to this increased responsibility of institutions is the relatively new system of quality control and assessment of education and research. It seems only logical that the government demands this in exchange for the competencies it has transferred. The quality assessment system is based on self-assessment, peer review and site visit.

As to the management of personnel, the university administration must state every year the global formation of the personnel paid by the Flemish Community, which provides the money for the wages. Personnel administration is carried out by the universities themselves. The management of the college personnel is now, due to the recent legislation, subject to great change, of which the consequences are as yet extremely hard to calculate. As the scaling-up operation proceeds, the colleges will become increasingly able to conduct a real policy towards their personnel. This must lead to a revalorisation of the personnel in the non-university sector. Owing to the new legislation, the college administrations now have the possibility of creating new career opportunities, better or extra remuneration and so on for their staff. Quality of personnel has replaced to a large extent the former standard for wage raises, which was seniority. Although the colleges thus have obtained more autonomy, the principal regulation will still be done on the level of the Flemish Community, not on the level of the (almost) autonomous schools. This is to avoid random treatment of the personnel throughout the Community. For both the university and the non-university sector, an important role in the management of the institutions is reserved for personnel. They are legally entitled to participate in the governance of the institutions, as are, by the way, the students, and other interested groups. The extent of the participation however depends on the legal quality of the institution, e.g. whether it is state-operated, public, or private.

### 5.3.4    Conclusion

The decrees of 12/6/1991 on the universities and 13/7/1994 on the non-university higher education institutions have fundamentally revised the higher education system. The main feature of this change is the scaling-up operation in the non-university sector, amounting to more autonomy for the institutions in higher education and more flexibility in management in the context of personnel and financial policy.

# 5.4

## THE FRENCH COMMUNITY OF BELGIUM

### *Chantal Kaufmann*

### 5.4.1 Constitutional provisions

The Belgian Constitution does not contain any provision specifically concerning higher education. Article 24, however, sets forth the general principles applicable to education:

1. There shall be freedom of education; any measures to prevent it are forbidden; the punishment of contraventions is a matter which shall be regulated by law or decree only.

    The Community shall guarantee parental freedom of choice. The Community shall provide neutral instruction. Neutrality implies, in particular, respect for the philosophical, ideological and religious views of parents and pupils.

    Up to the end of compulsory schooling the schools provided by the public authorities shall offer a choice between instruction in one of the recognised religions and instruction in non-denominational morality.

2. If a Community wishes to delegate to one or more autonomous entities its authority to dispense instruction, it may do so only by a decree adopted by a two-thirds majority.

3. Every person has a right to instruction which respects fundamental rights and liberties. Instruction shall be free of charge up to the end of compulsory schooling.

    All pupils of compulsory-school age shall have the right, at Community expense, to moral or religious education.

4. All pupils, students, parents, staff members and educational institutions shall be equal before statute or decree law. Laws and decrees shall take

into account objective differences, such as characteristics specific to each education-providing authority, which justify appropriate treatment.

5   The Community's organisation, recognition or subsidy of instruction shall be governed by law or decree.

In addition, in setting out the Community's fields of responsibility, Article 127 (1) states that the Communities are to regulate by decree and that the matters regulated include education with the exception of:

a   setting the beginning and end of compulsory schooling;
b   minimum conditions of award of diplomas;
c   the pension scheme.

The main legislation on university education is contained in:

·   the law of 11 September 1933 on the protection of academic awards in highereducation (Moniteur Belge (M.B.) of 27 September 1933);
·   the co-ordinated laws of 31 December 1949 on the award of academic degrees and the university examination programme (M.B. of 1 March 1950), as amended by the decree of 5 September 1994 on the regulations governing university education and academic degrees (M.B. of 8 November 1994);
·   the law of 28 April 1953 on state organisation of university education (M.B. of 1 May 1953);
·   the law of 27 July 1971 on the financing and supervision of institutions with university status (M.B. of 17 September 1971).

The main provision on non-university higher education is to be found in:

·   the law of 7 July 1970 on the overall structure of higher education (M.B. of 12 September 1970);
·   the law of 18 February 1977 on the organisation of higher education, in particular advanced technological and agricultural education of long duration (M.B. of 12 March 1977);
·   the decree of 5 August 1995 laying down general arrangements for higher education at hautes écoles (advanced colleges) (M.B. of 1 September 1995).

5.4.2   The current situation in higher education

The basic distinctions are between university education and non-university higher education and between education provided by the public authorities and private education.

Non-university higher education if in turn divided into long-duration and short-duration higher education, while public or official education is divided into education provided by Belgium's French Community and education provided by the provinces and municipalities. Long-duration higher education is regarded as university education.

Depending on the particular organisational authority and the method of financing, there are three recognised networks:

·   education provided and financed by the French Community;
·   education provided by provinces and municipalities and subsidised by the French Community as subsidised official education;
·   education provided by private bodies and subsidised by the French Community as independent education, which in many cases is denomina- tional or Catholic.

In addition to these categories there are further institutions of higher educa- tion which are either unclassified or classified in categories that are no longer conventional or which come under conventional categories but have a status of their own (the main examples are military, theology and art schools).

The purpose of university education is to train high-level managers and professionals capable of taking responsibility in fundamental and applied research and in the planning and application of scientific research with a view to the development of new technologies.

The purpose of long-duration higher education is to impart scientific and technological training with practical focus.

Short duration education is aimed at producing middle management capable of performing and supervising scientific or technical work. It has a practical emphasis and relates directly to a particular occupation.

Those wishing to enter higher education may enter any type of institution provided they hold a certificate of advanced secondary education ("certificat d'enseignement secondaire supérieur") (CESS) and pay within a specified time a registration fee, the amount which is set by law or, in the independent sector, by decree. For students who do not possess the required certificates, special admission examinations may be held.

Loans and grants are available for the needy. Non-European students may be required to pay an additional registration fee. Apart from this, Belgians and foreigners have the same rights.

Virtually the sole exception to the qualification requirement is, that applicants for university courses in the applied sciences must sit an entrance examination. If they pass the examination they may be admitted to any course offered by the institution.
So far no numerus clausus or numerus fixus has been introduced, but institutions may withhold registration on grounds of intake capacity.

The purpose of university education is to train high-level managers and professionals capable of taking responsibility in fundamental and applied research and in the planning and application of scientific research with a view to development of new technologies.

The purpose of long-duration higher education is to dispense scientific and technological education with a practical focus. It trains highly qualified management for transposition functions and applied research.

Short-duration education is aimed at producing middle management capable of performing and supervising highly scientific or technical work. It has a practical emphasis and relates directly to a particular occupation.


5.4.3   Educational structures and quality assurance

While the overall structure of higher education is laid down in the 1970 Act, the types are governed by special regulation.

Short-duration higher education comprises a single three-year or four-year in the case of certain types of paramedical training-cycle of study leading to a final qualification and giving immediate access to an occupation. This type of higher education leads to a range of qualifications, such as technician. nurse, primary school teacher and lower-secondary school teacher.

Long-duration higher education is divided into two cycles which in all last four or five years: a first cycle of two or three years, depending on the course, and a second cycle of another two or three years, which leads, after submission of an end-of-course dissertation and an oral examination, to the degree of "licencié", or a specialized degree.

University education is divided into three cycles. The first lasts two years, three in the case of medicine and veterinary medicine and leads to a "candidat" qualification, equipping the student with the essential basic knowledge for going on to further study. The second cycle lasts two or three years, four in the case of medicine and leads, generally after submission of a dissertation, to the degree of "licencié", "maître" or doctor of medicine or veterinary medicine or to the pharmacist and engineering qualifications.

The upper-secondary school teaching qualification is obtained in the second cycle and may be awarded upon completion of the "licence". The holder is qualified to teach in secondary schools or at institutions of short-duration higher education. The third cycle, consists of one years' or two years,' (or, in medicine, of up to six years') advanced study or specialisation. This cycle includes the degree of doctorate, which requires a minimum of three to five years' research.

There are alternative study arrangements, whether by law or provided by individual institutions, to enable in particular people with professional or occupational commitments to study certain fields. Provisions include the "panels" introduced by the French Community, "out-of-hours" and social-advancement programmes. There is no exemption from length-of-length study requirements, or from the requirement to obtain intermediate qualifications, when more than one cycle exists.

Although no one type of higher education is subordinate to another, each having its own worth and its own specific aims, over the years has emerged a marked tendency to decompartmentalise the system. For instance, there are arrangements whereby students who have gained a qualification in long-duration or short-duration higher education can enter a university and be given partial credit for their previous studies. There are also special regulations governing examinations. Among other matters, there is a rule that, in each type of higher education, no one may sit the same examination more than four times, unless the Minister for Education and Research grants an exception. On the other hand, institutions can now allow students, particularly first-time examinees, to spread a year's study over more than one academic year.

As regards subjects offered and syllabuses, the decree of 5 September 1994 lays down the 22 fields divided into three sectors in which institutions with university status are authorised to offer courses. These institutions are allowed to set forth syllabuses and examinations as they see fit, provided that the syllabuses cover the main parts or branches of the discipline or disciplines of the particular degree, and include subjects that further the student's general education.

The law lays down minimum hours of study, and of syllabuses which form the framework within which institutions of short-duration or long-duration higher education are authorised to offer courses under the decree of 5 August 1995.

Until recently universities awarded three types of degree:

·   Statutory degrees ("grades légaux") are awarded for successful completion of courses where the entry requirements, the syllabus and the length of the course are laid down by law. In practice such courses correspond to the traditional cycles of study offered in the 5 basic faculties (philosophy and arts, law, medicine, science and applied science).

·   "Scientific" degrees ("grades scientifiques") are awarded for successful completion of courses of which are determined by the university, as are the entry requirements, the syllabus and the duration of study. The courses concerned are mainly offered by schools, institutes or faculties of non-traditional type and are designed to meet new needs.

- Statutory degrees awarded for academic purposes are degrees awarded to students (foreign students in particular) who do not fully meet the legal requirements for admission to a university, or who do not wish to practise a profession in Belgium.

From the strictly academic standpoint, there is no difference between statutory degrees, academic degrees and statutory degrees awarded for scientific purposes. Academic degrees, however, do not confer the entitlements conferred by statutory degrees, except where special legislation so provides: an academic degree, for example, is not recognised as a qualification for official posts, unless it is awarded for studies in which no statutory degree exists.

These distinctions were abolished by the decree of 5 September 1994, where the sole term used is "academic degree" and which entered into force in academic year 1995-96.

There is no legal requirement here concerning the universities, The new decree on hautes écoles introduces machinery for the supervision of teaching standards and of compliance with the educational, social and cultural plan.

### 5.4.4 Management bodies

The law of 28 April 1953 sets forth the governing bodies at the French Community's universities , these are, the rector ("recteur"), the academic council ("conseil académique"), the administrative council ("conseil d'administration") and the standing office ("bureau permanent") the terms of appointment and their powers, are specified in a regulatory order of 23 October 1967.

The rector chairs the various bodies, represents the university for external purposes, and is the executing authority in all academic matters. The academic council is an advisory body in all matters concerning the university. The administrative council, assisted by the standing office is a decision-making body, in particular as regards appointments, allocation of funds and design of syllabuses.

In non-university higher education, the decree of 5 August 1995 requires that both the French Community's hautes écoles and the subsidised hautes écoles have an administrative body, a managing board, an educational council and a social council.

The managing board is responsible for carrying out the administrative council's decisions, and exercises powers vested in directors and deputy directors of institutions of higher-education.
The educational council is consulted by the administrative council or managing board on any matter concerning the use of teaching resources or allocation of human resources.
The social council consults with the administrative council or the managing board on any matter relating to students' material and social circumstances.


5.4.5   Teaching and research staff and financing

In the case of universities the law lays down the recognised categories of staff. The universities are allowed to create other categories and pay them out of their own finances. There is an order laying down the staff categories in non-university higher education. The law of 7 July 1970 and an implementing order, lay down the qualifications required at both levels, while two recent decrees and a Crown order respectively lay down the rights and duties of staff in short-duration higher education in the 3 networks, including recruitment and appointment arrangements. The Community makes an annual financial allocation to help cover universities' ordinary administrative teaching and research expenditure.

The allocation made to the individual institution for the financial year is equal, in each branch of study, to the standard cost per student multiplied by the number of students legally registered for that branch of study at 1 February the previous year. The Government annually fixes the standard cost per student.

The law also lays down, depending on the branch of study – minimum numbers and maximum numbers for teaching staff and research staff as well as the proportion of each (teaching staff 40%, research staff 60%, the 60% breaking down into 24% temporary and 36% permanent).

Legislation and regulations on the financing of long-duration and short-duration higher education are at least as complex as those governing the universities, and calculations are again based on the number of students legally registered at 1 February the previous academic year.

## 5.4.6 Research

Freedom of action in this field has been complete since the special law of 8 August 1988, which made two innovations:

· firstly its provisions relate to all research, and not just, as previously, applied research;
· secondly, each authority (whether national, Community or regional) is now responsible for research in all fields.

Under these provisions, and the special law of 16 January 1989, central government transferred to the French Community large of funds earmarked for research, of any, kind provided it falls within the Community's field of responsibility (broadly speaking, education).

Appreciable amounts of research funding have, of course, long been included in the allocations made to the universities to cover their operational expenditures. Fundamental research and research-associated activities (publications, associations, conferences, cooperation, etc.) receive special support (more especially since 1965) from the Directorate of Higher Education and Research.

Hitherto the preserve of the universities, applied research is now also one of the functions of the hautes écoles.

## 5.4.7 Political authority and intermediate bodies

Although it is the Minister for Higher Education and Research who lays down general policy in higher education, the minister is assisted by various administrative bodies and advisory bodies which perform specific educational or administrative tasks:

The Ministry for Education, Research and Training, which is:

- the legislative body responsible for grants, organisation of teaching, teachers' rights and duties, and inspection in higher education;
- in charge of overall supervision of compliance with legislation;
- responsible for appointment of teaching staff;
- responsible for approval of non-university academic awards in higher education and statutory university degrees (its responsibility will shortly extend to approval of all university degrees);
- responsible for recognition of foreign certificates and degrees.

The Education and Training Council of the French Community, co-operates with the business community and industry to work out policy meeting education's needs, as well as those of the employment market.

The Francophone Inter-University Council (CIUF), an advisory body on matters of university education makes arrangements for consultation between the French-speaking universities.

The Sectoral Councils ("Conseils supérieurs sectoriels"): scrutinises proposals for educational reform, syllabus content,etc.

The Standing Council for Higher Education, has an advisory role on matters relating to two or more categories of higher education.

The Hautes Ecoles General Council (Conseil Général des Hautes Ecoles), the successor to the Standing Council, acts as a think-tank, delivers opinions and arranges consultation between the hautes écoles and the different categories and types of higher education.

The Education Committee of the French Community, delivers opinions on the educational, social and cultural plans as submitted by the hautes écoles.

The Educational Developments Unit (Cellule de prospective pédagogique), investigates educational innovations, assesses them and centralises information on research and experiments conducted by the hautes écoles.

### 5.4.8   Conclusion

The many advisory bodies, and the fact that the various stakeholders (staff, students, industry, business, the trade unions, etc) are well represented in the various administrative bodies, are curbs on highhanded use of powers, whether in education itself, or in relations between education and the central authority.

Besides the civil courts, there exist two supreme bodies, one administrative, the other judicial, to protect institutions and their members against misuses of authority:

·   the Conseil d'Etat, which can set aside any decision for procedural irregularity and for abuse of authority;
·   the Cour d'Arbitrage (Arbitration Court), which is empowered to quash laws or decrees, in particular, for contravention of Articles 10, 11 or 24 of the Constitution, (which deal with equality before the law, freedom of thought, and education).

Recent higher-education measures by the French Community both simplified the system (doing away with distinctions between statutory and "scientific" degrees and by standardising third-cycle university diplomas and degrees they remove barriers between levels and networks not only by grouping official and independent institutions offering short-duration or long-duration education but also by introducing features into the "hautes écoles" which had previously been the sole preserve of the universities (eg research and student participation). Above all, they give extensive recognition to the principle of institutional autonomy, autonomy which institutions have long pressed for. The French Community can no longer balance its budget if it continues to finance institutions directly on the basis of the number of students enrolled. Student numbers have been rising sharply every year, especially in the short-duration sector. This has forced the Community increasingly to restrict the number of students eligible for grants (through the rule laying down a maximum of two times two examination sessions per year of study) as well as the standard cost per student. For instance, the Community has introduced various measures – including allowing students to spread the first year's study over two years – to combat the rate of student failure, with the ultimate objective of granting each institution a relatively fixed sum of money.

The present tendency towards privatisation likewise has to be seen in the context of budgetary stringency. Universities, for instance, are mainly developing the sector which is genuinely specific to them – the third cycle – and research contracts with firms.

As to the introduction of hautes écoles, although there was some resistance to the idea it is generally agreed that the French Community had too many higher-education institutions (some 110, not counting the universities and institutions with university status, of which there is also a considerable number in a sector which has greatly expanded more particularly since the law of 9 April 1965).

# 5.5

## BULGARIA

### *Tsvetomir Georgiev*

5.5.1    The Constitution of the Republic of Bulgaria, as adopted by the
         Grand National Assembly in July, 1991:

Art.53 (3) In circumstances established by a law, the higher education
institutions shall provide education free of charge.

Art.53 (4) Higher education establishments shall enjoy academic autonomy.

Art.53 (6) The State shall promote education by opening and financing
schools, by supporting capable school and university students, and by
providing opportunities for occupational training and retraining. It shall
exercise control over all kinds and levels of schooling, including universities
to a certain extent. One should bear in mind the fact that this Act of 1990
was passed a year before the adoption of the Bulgarian Consultation, at a
time when there were no private universities in Bulgaria.

5.5.2    The current legislative situation

The Academic Autonomy of the Higher Education Establishments Act, as
adopted by the National Assembly on 25 January 1990, provides in pertinent
part:

·    Art.1 (1) The State concedes autonomy to the higher education establish-
     ments in the processes of teaching and research, as well as in other
     activities carried out at the institutions of higher learning.

- Art.1 (2) This Law regulates the relations of higher education establishments with the State, state agencies and other social communities and structures on the basis of institutional autonomy.
- Art.2 (1) Higher education establishments realise their activities in conjunction with institutional autonomy and with accountability before society and the State, which implements unified policy in the higher education sector.
- Art.2 (2) The rights of higher education institutions given by both this Law and the Higher Education Act can not be changed or restricted by any state agencies and other organisations except for the cases specified in the Constitution.
- Art.14 (1) The State governance of higher education is realised by the National Assembly and the Council of Ministers.

The Higher Education Act, as adopted in February 1958 and amended subsequently many times, provides in Art.2 that establishments of higher education and centres for teaching and research (academies) are set up by the National Assembly.

For almost 75 years Bulgaria has had a hierarchical binary structure of tertiary education involving establishments of higher learning, the universities and higher institutes/academies, and the so-called semi-higher institutions which are comparable to the German Fachhochschulen or some British colleges. Up to 1991, all the institutions of tertiary education were public (state-owned), but during the past four years some private universities and colleges were founded on an initiative of non-profit legal establishment.

The presently operative Higher Education Act defines the mission of the Bulgarian institutions of higher learning in terms which include:

- the training of professionals and specialists capable of developing or applying academic knowledge in various areas of human activity;
- the pursuit of post-graduate training;
- the promotion of science and culture;
- the pursuit of fundamental and applied research, as well as of artistic and creative activities.

Following the recent political changes in the country, the Academic Autonomy Act was passed in 1990. Through the provisions of this Law, higher education institutions have acquired considerable rights of self-governance, and in particular, they have become responsible for the contents and organisation of their studies in matters of curricula and syllabi, examinations, as well as in research and the transfer of knowledge. Institutions can now also open new academic programmes, new departments, as well as branches in other cities, without prior approval by the State.

The admission of students to establishments of tertiary education is carried out in strict observance of general state requirements, the principles of equal opportunity and additional institutional criteria. For every academic year, the State designates to the public universities and institutes a number of students whose education is entirely financed by the governmental budget. Students enrolled within this quota are eligible to receive monthly non-repayable bursaries for the duration of their studies, provided they maintain good academic progress. Private educational institutions rely primarily on tuition fees. Most of the public tertiary education establishments have also started offering full- or part-time courses against tuition fees, the recommended levels of which are determined annually by the Ministry of Education, Science & Technology (MES&T).

Bulgarian legislation for higher education assigns the following responsibilities to the Ministry:

- to develop and co-ordinate the national strategy on higher education, science and technology;
- to create and propose to the National Assembly bills intended to modernise the structures of higher education and science;
- to develop state requirements for receiving higher national diplomas and professional qualifications;
- to determine the number of students per academic course, in cases when the education of these students is financed by the State;
- to legalise certificates and diplomas.

The MES&T co-ordinates the relationships between the system of higher education and science and other ministries and institutions. It also develops draft legislation, standards, proposals concerning the opening/closure of tertiary education schools, and submits these suggestions for endorsement to the National Assembly or the Council of Ministers. The MES&T is also entitled to define priorities and formulate science and technology strategies, while the higher education institutions are entitled to plan their scientific research. During the past couple of months state criteria for receiving Higher National Diplomas in law, medicine and for teaching credentials have been developed by the MES&T and adopted by the Council of Ministers. The standards specify minimum requirements concerning the minimum number of fundamental disciplines taught, personnel qualification, teaching loads, etc., which must be met by every institution offering these courses. The development of similar criteria in economics, engineering and other subjects is in progress.

Some establishments of higher learning have separate organisations engaged in research activities only. These organisations, or centres, also provide technological services. However, due to the difficult economic situation in Bulgaria, the traditional link between institutions of higher education and the business community have weakened. For all practical purposes, the State therefore remains the principle source of research funding for higher education institutions.

The educational process at tertiary education establishments is now carried out in compliance with teaching-documentations, which encompass qualification requirements for higher education diploma holders, matters of curricula and syllabi, as well annual timetables and schedules of studies. As mentioned above, through the Law for Academic Autonomy, institutions were given the right to open new courses, and to determine their curricula. As a result of the demand of the market economy, a considerable number of new academic programmes (business administration, marketing, etc.) have been offered lately. In order to attract more and more students against tuition fees, many institutions have also started offering some of the more popular courses, such as law and economics.

The revenues of the public universities and higher institutes are now predominantly linked to the number of students whose education is ordered by the State. Each institution negotiates its annual budget directly with the Ministry of Finance. The establishments of higher education have responsibility over their internal financing and extended flexibility in the use of investment budgets. Significant investments for research projects at higher institutes are granted by the National Science Fund established in July 1990. This Fund is administrated by the MES&T but receives its reserves directly from the national budget, and is therefore relatively independent of the Ministry's policy and expenditures. The main function of the Funds for Structural & Technological Development is to finance the R&D activities and to stimulate collaboration between industrial enterprises and higher education and research institutions. The trend in percentage of GNP, devoted to entire education, higher education and science (R&D) expenditure, respectively, is shown in the following table.

| Expenditure for (in % of GNP) | 1988 | 1989 | 1990 | 1991 | 1992 | 1993 | 1994 |
|---|---|---|---|---|---|---|---|
| Entire Education | 4.60 | 4.67 | 5.07 | 5.25 | 6.25 | 5.26 | 4.50 |
| Higher Education | 0.65 | 0.30 | 0.70 | 0.72 | 0.78 | 0.77 | 0.64 |
| Science (R&D) | 2.46 | 2.35 | 2.25 | 1.22 | 1.20 | 1.15 | 0.87 |

The salaries of academic staff have in effect been reduced due to incompletely compensated inflation. As a result, the motivation for high quality teaching and research has decreased, a number of skilled specialists have left the system, and young graduates are decreasingly interested in academic careers. As can be seen from Table 1, scientific research has also been hampered by financial restrictions.

All premises on which the public education institutions conduct their activities are state-owned property. Through the Academic Autonomy Act, establishments of higher learning were given the right to manage the property in accordance with the purposes for which it was acquired.

With the Scientific Degrees & Titles Act of 1972 a State Higher Certifying Commission was created to develop criteria and to control the procedures related to the conferring of scientific titles and degrees. This Commission is directly subordinated to the Council of Ministers and its decisions are final, allowing no complaints from the academic community. The major ranks in higher institutions are in the following descending order: professor, associated professor, chief assistant professor, senior assistant professor, assistant professor and lecturer. The total number of the faculty involved in Bulgarian higher education is about 23,700, with 15,350 of them as full-time employees. The average student-to-academic staff ratio is 13.3, whilst the number of higher education students per 10,000 population is approximately 245. The absolute number of students currently at establishments of tertiary education is approximately 220,000.

Bulgarian establishments of tertiary education use a range of teaching methods that include lectures, seminars, tutorials and practical activities. Institutions tend to require class attendance and participation. In general, teaching methods giving the students a passive role in learning still predominate, but some private universities are changing the way in which their courses are structured, and offer new modular schemes and correspondence courses. Students' work may be assessed in several different ways. Most institutions use some combination of written and oral examinations, and employ a 2-6 grading system with 6 (excellent) being the highest mark awarded. Higher education programmes are completed upon passing a state final certification examination. Passing this examination allows students to receive a Higher National Diploma, and gives them the right to exercise their profession.

### 5.5.3    Legislative principles and policy objectives

The principle of broadening participation in Bulgarian higher education and ensuring equity of access has been provided by General State Requirements for Admission of Students endorsed by the MES&T in 1994. Other legislative principles, included in the new draft of the Higher Education Act, are related to the fostering of relevance and quality of higher education. The future role of higher education has to be based on a judicious balance between the preservation of those features that should remain part of the educational and cultural heritage and the political and socio-economic developments currently taking place. Bulgaria is now facing a period of transition, and higher education is an important tool that can be used to master these challenges. Higher education institutions should be given a leading role in the process of democratisation of the Bulgarian society, as well as in the renovation of the entire education system. All conceptual frameworks aimed at development and enhancement of higher education are based on the principles of academic freedom and institutional autonomy. Adherence to these two principles is a prerequisite for the normal functioning of higher education institutions and for the accomplishment of reform. Quality assurance is also an important issue and is now seen as a high priority for the successful transformation of the Bulgarian higher education system.

In the draft of the new Higher Education Act, special attention was paid to the area of quality assurance, assessment and accreditation. Internationalisation is also one of the principle features, which has received considerable attention during the past couple of years. International co-operation has helped to ameliorate the qualifications of academic staff, particularly in areas of knowledge neglected during the time of totalitarian rule. A number of international programmes were directed at encouraging research and teaching activities through the exchange of personnel and students. Other projects have been prepared with the assistance of international experts. These will require combined funding from the national budget and a World Bank loan, and their realisation will promote interaction between universities, research institutions and the business community. Bilateral and multilateral agreements between governments, higher education establishments and research organisations have also contributed to the mobility of lecturers and students, as well as to the adjustment of curricula to market requirements.

The most important objectives of the intended reforms may be summarised as follows:

- institutional changes aimed at improving operation of the system, the quality of education and research activities;
- infra-structural modernisation, including consolidation of some higher education institutions;
- increased institutional autonomy, accompanied with enhanced social responsibility;
- re-orientation of higher education to the requirements of the market economy, which includes the introduction of new academic programmes, the redrafting of curricula and teaching methods, such as modular courses, education through correspondence courses, etc.;
- increased democratic participation of students and the communities in the educational sector.

These policy objectives can be achieved through concrete and mutual programmes enacted by the State and higher education institutions. The reform can be assisted significantly by international co-operation, especially through projects co-ordinated by the Council of Europe, the EC, OECD, UNESCO, the World Bank and the European Bank for Co-operation and Developments.

### 5.5.4    The balance of power between the State

The overall administration of Bulgarian higher education is accomplished by the National Assembly and the Council of Ministers. The former institution can open, transform or close schools of higher education, as well as also determine their status and approve the annual budget of public establishments of higher learning. The Council of Ministers sets up general guidelines of state formulated policy in the sphere of higher education and science, opens, transforms or closes faculties that operate as public legal entities, orders to public higher institutions the number of students whose education will be financed by the State for every academic year, and adopts state requirements for receiving higher national diplomas. Since 1992 the Conference of Rectors has operated as an expert body co-ordinating activity in regard to legislative reforms, and budgetary allocations for teaching and research, etc.

The Ministry of Finance is the actual distributor of the national budget among the state-owned establishments of higher learning. Traditionally, the Fund for Structural Reform and Technological Development is controlled by the Ministry of Industry. Many foundations, such as the Open Society Fund, the National Academic Foundation, etc., help higher education institutions to expand their capacity and improve their facilities by providing them with significant support for teaching and research equipment. According to the new Higher Education Act the accreditation of establishments of higher education will be realised by a National Assessment and Accreditation Agency (NA&AA), which ensures:

·    the observance of academic autonomy at the institutions of higher educa-
     tion;

· the application of uniform requirements and criteria to all autonomous institutions;
· the independence of its assessments and decisions, which will be publicly disseminated.

The NA&AA will be a legal entity subsidised by the governmental budget. It will consist of an Accreditation Council (AC) and expert commissions. The AC will be the governing body of the NA&AA, and its composition will include representatives of higher education establishments, and members of science and research organisations. Along with the AC, the governance of the NA&AA will be exercised by an executive director appointed by the prime minister. The decisions of the AC will be taken by simple majority vote.

5.5.5    Legal protection of institutions for higher education against State decisions

Autonomy of establishments of higher education was legally recognised in 1990 and subsequently guaranteed by the Constitution of 1991. Institutional autonomy is conceived as embodying:

· academic rights and freedoms;
· self-organisation and self-regulation of teaching and research.

The former components include independent and unconstrained creation and implementation of course curricula and syllabi (in accordance with state criteria), of research projects, as well as pluralism and academic tolerance in the pursuit of scientific truth. The principle of self-governance is accomplished through the adoption of individual bye-laws for the organisation and functioning of each respective higher education institution, through elective systems and mandatory terms of office for all academic governing bodies, and independent appointment of both teaching and research faculty in compliance with the promotion regulations provided by Scientific Degrees & Titles Act. In addition to State admission requirements, establishments of higher learning can now formulate their own conditions of enrolment. Institutions are free to define the forms of teaching and training provided to undergraduate, graduate and post-graduates students.

The State has no role in the appointment of rectors, governing bodies or academic staff. The Academic Autonomy Act vests the institutions with the right to be fully responsible for financial policy, investments in buildings and equipment, as well as for the terms and conditions of employment, though general regulations (Labour Law) must be observed. As legal entities, establishments of higher education can also decide upon the terms of co-operation with other institutes and seek membership of international or-ganisations. Higher institutions can enter into contractual relations with the State, business companies and other consumers by signing agreements for training specialists or accomplishing fundamental and applied research. Establishments of higher learning may appeal to the Supreme Court against State decisions which infringe upon their rights related to the institutional autonomy. However, the Academic Autonomy Act contains no guarantee of inviolability of university and institute premises as such.

5.5.6    Conclusion

There has been an urgent need for more governance in Bulgarian higher education recently, and for this reason, the new draft of the Higher Education Act has been developed. In this draft, autonomy and delegation of power are of great importance to the relations between the State and the institutions. The draft bill confers upon the Government the right to levy financial sanctions against institutions which fail to comply with minimum standards. The sanctions include the withdrawal of all financial support for an incum-bent faculty, department or study programme.

The new Higher Education Act was finally passed by the Parliament on 12 December 1995. Eleven chapters are included in the new Act, and they are as follows: Chapter 1 General Provisions; Chapter 2 State Administration and Governance of Higher Education; Chapter 3 Types of Higher Educational Establishments, Opening, Transformation, and Closure; Chapter 4 Academic Autonomy; Chapter 5 Structure and Organisation of Studies at Higher Educational Establishments; Teaching, Research-and-Teaching, and Research Faculty at Higher Educational Establishment; Chapter 7 Honarary Titles; Chapter 8 Organisation of Research at Higher Educational Establishments; Chapter 9 Under- and Post-Graduate Students, and Specialising Students;

Chapter 10 Accreditation of Higher Education Establishments; Chapter 11 Property and Finance of Higher Education Establishments.

When the Law becomes effective, which is expected to happen by the end of 1996, both still operative Higher Education Act and the Academic Autonomy of the Higher education Establishments Act are automatically abrogated. Some amendments in the Scientific Degrees & Titles act of 1972 are also envisaged through the provisions of the latest Law. Moreover, new higher educational and qualification degrees, equivalent to those used in the Anglo-Saxon system; are introduced: "bachelor", "master" and "doctor", which requires changes of the present curricular and syllabi of the higher education institutions. The semi-higher institutes will be transformed in colleges conferring on the higher educational degree "specialist", and each of them could either be within the structure of a given establishment of higher learning or an independent and self-governing college. The main features of the newest Bulgarian legislation for higher education will be described in more details in some of the following series' volumes of Council of Europe's Legislative Reform Programme.

During the past few years, Bulgarian higher education has undergone significant changes. Some positive steps have been taken in the right direction, but much work remains to be done. Institutions of higher learning have to adapt the structure and form of their operation to the dramatic social and economic changes. The implementation of a system of quality assurance becomes a fundamental prerequisite as a means to improve education and research activities. New forms of teaching and learning must be introduced and assessed, a flexible financing system for higher education is to be designed as well. These trends should be accompanied by additional programmes of international co-operation in the fields of education and science. The legislative principles, upon which all the improvements in the Bulgarian higher education system could be made, are already established in the draft Higher Education Act. Its final adoption by the Parliament is eagerly expected, not only by the academic community.

# 5.6

## CZECH REPUBLIC

*Emanuel Ondráček, Helena Šebková & Stanislav Hanzl*

5.6.1   Two constitutional texts exist in the Czech Republic, the Constitution of 1993, and the List of Basic Rights and Freedoms of 1993 which in Article 33 states:

1   Every person has the right to education. School attendance is mandatory for the period stipulated by law.
2   The citizens have the right to a free elementary and secondary education and, based on the individual's abilities and society's possibilities, also to higher education.
3   Schools other than state schools may be established and teaching at them provided only under the conditions stipulated by law: at such schools, education may be provided for a fee.
4   The law stipulates the conditions under which the citizens have the right to assistance during their period of study.

5.6.2   The current legislative situation in higher education

The current legislation on higher education must be seen as a reaction to legislative developments prior to 1989, in particular to the Acts Concerning Institutions of Higher Education of 1950, 1966 and 1980. These developments were issued under the centralised state control of the higher education institutions, and significantly limited their autonomy and academic freedoms. The freedom of research was restricted, basic research was concentrated at the Academy of Sciences. The social sciences experienced detrimental political influence. It is important to note, however, that the State's intrusion was not confined to qualitative measures, rather, it encompassed quantitative perpetrations as well. Thus, the State determined the number of students the institutions had to admit. It also denied the institutions their right to establish their own teaching staff.

The 1990 Act on Institutions of Higher Education primarily re-established the traditional position of higher education institution and their academic freedoms and significantly restricted the state's influence at the institutions of higher education. The first step toward the diversification of the higher education had been made: the act introduced short-time professional oriented study, so-called bachelor type of study. The other necessary institutional steps, however, were not carried out. The act maintained the state monopoly in the establishment of higher institutions as well as in providing the university type of study.

The five years of experience with the 1990 higher education act confirmed the act's undisputed priorities. It has been shown that in order to achieve further steps in the democratisation of the higher education system and its management, certain new problems have to be legislatively resolved. Therefore the draft of the new act has been prepared, approved by the government and – at the present time-debated by the parliament of the Czech republic.

The proposed act clearly delimits the relationship between the necessary degree of autonomy for the educational institutions in the higher education system (without, they cannot fulfil their objectives educational, scientific, artistic and generally spiritual area) and the state. It has decisive share in its financing, provides a guarantee for the quality of the higher education system and of its accessibility. The rights and obligation of the Accrediting Collegium, which guarantees the quality of higher education system, are newly defined.

The study programme is considered as the basic structural unit of the higher education teaching/learning process. The term "study programme" is understood as a project encompassing a wide spectrum of curricula divided into several fields of study. Increasing the freedom of institution with regard to programming is expected to lead to a greater diversity of study programmes. In order to ensure the appropriate quality of the study programmes realised by the higher education institutions and other legal entities, it is required that they be accredited and registered by the ministry.

The bill distinguishes three basic types of study programme. The bachelor study programme, which has a minimal duration of three years, oriented primarily at the professions. The master study programme, which lasts from four up to six years, and represents the classic type of university programme. Finally the doctoral study programme, which is aimed at preparing the student for research activities. The educational institutions determine contents and structure of these study programmes, however, the bill assigns expert deliberation to an institutional scientific council as the authorized body.

A higher education institution could be established providing only bachelor study programmes; the bill terms such an institution a higher education institute. Accredited study programmes could also be realised by any legal entity (in doctoral programmes, these can be research institutions, for example those of the Academy of Sciences of the Czech Republic), called external educational institutions. These institutions have to conclude an agreement with a university to award academic titles because only universities and higher education institutes have the right to award them. All education institutions mentioned above (universities, higher education institutes and external education institutions) encompass the higher education system.

As opposed to the current situation, the founder of a higher education institution may be the State, as well as some other legal entity. The state universities are generally established by act of parliament, and the state higher education institutes are incorporated by way of a government decree. Non-state universities or higher education institutions may obtain a position similar to that of a state institution by obtaining authorization from the Ministry, which basically requires the consent of the Accreditation Collegium.

Certain modifications in the structure of the universities are also proposed as well as to the authority of their academic bodies and officials. These modifications aim at strengthening the universities' autonomy, balancing the powers of the academic senate and the scientific council, and at ensuring greater openness to the public. As far as the higher education institutes are concerned, their structure and management system are to be determined only in the form of a framework.

A key problem for further developments in higher education is the reform of university research, however. The restoration of the traditional link between teaching and research is a long term process which needs, besides proposed higher education act, another legislative prerequisites. It is the policy behind the bill to vest the university institutes, which are units of universities primarily oriented towards scientific activity, with rights similar to those of the faculties.

It is expected that the diversification of study programmes and the establishing of professional oriented bachelor study and of the non-state sector of higher education institutions, proposed in the bill, help also to solve some problems of admission to higher education studies. At present demands for higher education studies exceed significantly the contemporary capability of places in higher education institutions. The establishment of state and non-state higher education institutions will increase the offer of study opportunities. In 1994/95 year there were 98,777 enrolled students in short-cycle professional study programmes (bachelor study) and 6,760 students in doctoral study programmes, total approximately 133,000 students.

The major portion of the financial costs will continue to be borne by the state. It is proposed to introduce tuition fees also at the state higher education institutions and to prescribe its limited range by the act. The tuition fees at non-state education institutions is considered as self-evident and its amount does not have to be regulated. The aim of tuition fees is to strengthen students' personal responsibilities for the study programme and to raise their interest in its quality, to support the development of fields of study which enjoy greater popularity, and, last but not least, to limit unjustified prolongation of study periods.
However, since tuition may not act as a social deterrent to acquiring an education, the state guarantees tuition loans to students.

5.6.3    The balance of power

The proposal of the new Higher Education Act seeks to ensure the balance of power primarily by way of implementing the following legal principles:

·    autonomy of the higher education institutions;
·    democratic Governance within the higher education institutions;
·    accreditation as a form of State guarantee of quality;
·    State participation in the financing of higher education institutions, also as a means of steering.

First, the bill confirms the full scope of academic rights and freedoms set forth in the 1990 Act. They establish statutory bodies and elected higher education institution bodies vested with rights and responsibilities, and thereby respect the internal democracy of these institutions as being free and fully autonomous.

Secondly, the bill specifically name the Accreditation Collegium as an integral part of the higher education system. They conceptualise the Accreditation Collegium as an expert advisory body. The members of the Accreditation Collegium are nominated by members of the government, the University Rectors Conference, the university academic senates. Research and Development Council of the Government of the Czech Republic, the higher education institute directors and the statutory bodies of external educational institutions. Actual appointments are within the authority of the minister. The Accreditation Collegium develops expert assessments of the proposals for accreditation, or to revoke accreditation, and also states its position on other key issues in the area of the higher education quality assurance. On the basis of the expert assessment, the ministry subsequently makes a particular decision, including decisions to award state authorization to newly created non-state universities and non-state higher education institutes. Through this assessment process, the State assumes part of the responsibility for the quality of the higher education system.

In the area of financing of the higher education system, the bill specifically confirms the right of state higher education institutions to a contribution from the state budget. The ministry has the authority to allocate the financial resources to the educational institutions, and to check on the legality and the economic application of the financial and material resources it provides. As a result, in addition to ensuring operation of the higher education institutions, the State's decisive share in financing is a significant form of steering the system's strategic development, and thereby the development of society as a whole.

The allocation of the state financial assistance is in principle oriented on the number of enrolled students, but, allocation norms and procedures take in account also another indicator concerning scientific activity, such as quality of research, staff qualification and specific demands of the providing of various programmes (medicine, engineering, music etc.).

The appointments of the universities' rectors by the President of the Republic on the basis of recommendations issued by the academic senates, may be considered as a partial concession to the balance of powers vested in the higher education system, and those retained by the State.

The bill does not contain explicit language on the rights and responsibilities of organisations representing the higher education system as a whole. Such organisations are the Czech Rectors Conference and the Council of Higher Education Institutions. Nevertheless, due to their nature and informal authority, these entities are significant partners in the dialogue between the ministry, Government and the Parliament on the one hand, and the institutions on the other. Until now, they have commented on all important matters, including the distribution of the state budget. It can be realistically expected that the natural authority of these entities will contribute towards maintaining the balanced relationship between the State and the higher education system.

### 5.6.4    Conclusion

On the basis of five years of restoring democracy in the Czech Republic, a new higher education strategy is being prepared. It seeks to define accurately the functions and relationships between higher education institutions and the State, while fully respecting academic rights and freedoms. The intended diversification of higher education is undertaken by way of clearly specifying the types of degrees and programmes, and by developing a plurality of institutions providing higher education. The quality of educational activities will be ensured by an accreditation body, which will issue assessments on the basis of individual criteria. According to the new concept, the State as well as the students will participate in the financing of higher education. Non-state higher education institutions will have the opportunity to obtain contributions from the state budget for their teaching activities. The proposal of the Higher Education Act is intended to be compatible with the legislation of developed countries, namely with higher education regulation within Europe.

# 5.7

## DENMARK

### Jane Planck

5.7.1    The current legislative situation

The Constitution in Denmark has no specific provisions regarding higher
education. This report treats research-based education at universities and
other institutions. The non-research based higher education institutions
offering vocational training are governed by specific and widely dispersed
legislation, which the Ministry for similar institutions is presently casting
into framework laws similar to university Act but adjusted to their specific
situation.

In the Act on Universities and Other Institutions of Higher Education the
following provisions are the most important concerning the relations between
the State and higher education:

1(3)    Each institution of higher education decides on the study programmes
it wishes to offer and the intake of students always subject to section
2(4) and section 9(5). The offered programmes shall be approved
by the Minister of Education.

1(4)    An institution of higher education decides on the research it wants
to conduct.

9(2)    The institution shall have free disposal of approbations, grants and
income on the condition that it abides by the premises on which the
grants were founded and by the rules of disposal and that it carries
out the tasks for which the approbation has been made in pursuance
of.

The University Act has created an actual autonomy for the institutions. The Minister of Education cannot on his own initiative intervene in decisions made by the institutions in accordance with the Act. The Minister of Education can only make decisions on institutional matters to the extent laid down by the Act. According to the Act, the Minister of Education lays down general regulations pertaining to:

· quality control, including the role of external examiners,

· the award of doctoral degrees,

· the appointment of teachers and other academic staff,

· complaints to the institution from students, including deadlines for complaints in connection with examinations and tests, grants and premises for student organisations. grants shall be awarded on the basis of the respective student groups' share of the total number of student votes given at elections for the Senate.

In these areas, the Minister will thus be able to issue both general (circular letters) and concrete orders. All other areas are pursuant to the University Act protected against decisions made at government level. The institutions are thus by the Act legally protected against state-decisions.

5.7.2    The balance of power

On 1 January 1993 the new University Act became effective. It applies to all higher education institutions in Denmark that are assigned the task of conducting research and offering education to the highest scientific level. As a consequence of the decentralisation which took place in the 1980s, the Act is a framework act aimed at enabling the universities to adapt themselves most appropriately according to their respective needs and traditions.

The reform was prompted in part by the universities' role having changed, during the 1980s, from educating an elite to serving the public as institutions of mass education. From relative isolation they initiated increased cooperation with circles outside the universities. And last but not least, the financial situation of the universities, which initially was entirely State-funded, was changed as income streams from other quarters, e.g private and public funds or income as a result of contracts drawn up with private business enterprises.

To be better prepared for their new role, the universities were given, with the University Act, greater economic and academic autonomy and at the same time the Act laid down a clear division of power and responsibility between the rector and the collegiate bodies of the University. This should all together make the institutions more effective and energetic.

The division of power between the rector and the collegiate bodies within the institutions clearly appears from the Act.
The collegiate bodies are only assigned with the powers mentioned directly in the Act and stated below. All other decisions are at the discretion of the rector, who though naturally will delegate some of these to his subordinates.

3(1) The senate is the supreme collegiate body of the institution. The senate safe-guards the interests of the institutions with respect to teaching and research and establishes the guidelines for its long-term activities and development.

3(2)   The senate shall approve:
1       The organisation of the institution, including the faculty and departmental structure.
        The budget of the institution,
3       Proposals for statues.

5(2)   The faculty council has the following tasks:
1       Approval of curricula,
2       The appointments of assessments committees for work submitted for PhD and senior doctoral degrees,
3       The award of PhD and doctoral degrees,
4       Submission to the rector of composition of expert committees which are to assess applicants for academic posts.

Besides that the faculty council shall approve the development plan and budget for the faculty.

7(2)    The executive committee for the department shall lay down general
        guidelines for the activities and the development of the department
        and shall approve the budget of the department.

8(4)    The study committee shall approve teaching plans, including the
        assignment of teaching resources and shall draw up proposals for
        the curricula.

8(6)    The study committee may within general guidelines make exceptions
        from the provisions of the ministerial order according to the rules
        laid down herein and from the provisions of the curricula within the
        framework of the order.

The Act has now been in force for 2,5 years, and all higher education
institutions have, within the framework of the Act, laid down their own rules
regarding the internal structure and management of their institution.

In Denmark there exists intermediate bodies between the State and the higher
education institutions. These are committees advising the Minister, but
without further competencies.

The higher education institutions have a long historical tradition of independence and autonomy in academic and economic matters. In the 1980s, the
autonomy was, however, undermined on essential points. The aim of the
new University Act was therefore to restore the universities' extensive
autonomy. This has been done particularly in the financial area where the
institutions have been given full freedom to dispose of the total grant
(research and teaching) under one budget line. It provides them with a
greater freedom vis-à-vis the Ministry which previously allocated grants for
many separate objectives. The stage has also been set for greater self-deter-
mination in educational matters, i.e. in relation to which courses they can
offer (shall be approved of the Minister) and which students they can admit.
The institutions have full freedom of research as well as full self-deter-
mination in academic matters such as the awarding of PhD and doctoral
degrees.

### 5.7.3    Conclusion

With the new University Act, the autonomy of higher education institutions has been maintained and extended as a natural consequence of the comprehensive decentralisation of important decision-making powers from the Ministry to institutions. This applies especially to economic and academic areas.

# 5.8

## REPUBLIC OF ESTONIA

### Voldemar Tomusk

5.8.1    Section 38 of the Constitution provides:

Science and the arts, and their instruction shall be able to exist freely. Universities and research institutions shall be autonomous, within the limits established by law.

5.8.2    The current legislative situation in higher education

The Estonian Law on Universities provides that:
- the decision to establish, merge and partition a university, or terminate its operation, shall be made by the State Assembly on proposal by the Government of the Republic;
- a university shall be a legal entity of public law, which shall operate on the basis of the present law, other legal acts and its own statutes;
- it is permitted to expropriate fixed assets belonging to a university with the permission of the Government of the Republic.

Estonian higher education has undergone radical changes since the 1988 movement for national independence and liberalisation. Higher education institutions were forerunners in this movement as they claimed academic autonomy and freedom of research and instruction. Following the recovery of the Estonian nation state in 1992 developments gained further momentum. Prior to 1992, Estonian higher education was an internal part of the highly uniform and centralised higher education system of the former Soviet Union. When political power shifted to the Estonian government, educational matters had often to yield to more pressing concerns. Eventually, however, powers in higher education accumulated at the institutional level.

During this time, when the Soviet legal system was being abolished, and the Estonian system had not yet been established, institutional activities dominated policy, and State authorities had little more than nominal say in higher education matters. Having passed some legislation on higher education the State Assembly sought to centralise more functions. These continuing efforts have been complicated by the institutions' refusal to delegate newly acquired powers to a central agency, and by the State having missed the opportunity to define its role vis-à-vis the higher education system.

Since the dissolution of the Soviet system – in which universities were the only higher education institutions – four types of higher education institutions have emerged in Estonia:

- public universities which enrol 80% of the student population;
- public vocational higher education institutions, accounting for 8% of enrolments;
- private vocational higher education institutions, attended by 12% of the students;
- non-recognised higher education institutions, accommodating an unknown number of students.

Of these four groups, only the public universities are governed by a comprehensive legal text, the University Act of 1995. The public vocational higher institutions operate under a temporary ministerial decree, but a separate law is currently being prepared. Merely a few provisions of the Private Educational Institutions Act apply to the proliferating sector of private higher vocational institutions.

To a considerable extent, higher education in Estonia is still dominated by the dated behavioural patterns of the former Soviet Union: free of charge higher education, low student per faculty member ratio, a relatively long nominal duration of study programmes which are overloaded with relatively irrelevant subject courses. The patriotic movement in public higher education institutions has been strong. This has led to a decrease of study programmes offered in Russian; however courses offered in Russian have increased at private higher education institutions and non-recognised institutions. Among these, several are affiliates of higher education institutions of the Russian Federation.

Establishing its own higher education legislation, Estonia sought a new start on the basis of a framework addressing specific sectors. The 1992 Education Act reflects this approach. However, it was gradually understood, that importing foreign legal innovations would not obviate the need to define the several specific actors on the legal stage in Estonia. The University Act of 1995 did confer upon the universities the status of legal entities of public law. However, legislation passed during this first period does not necessarily reflect a uniform policy, and its provisions are not always compatible.

Thus, while the legal status of the universities has been settled in principle, the actual meaning of the terms remains disputed. Not all government agencies are willing or ready to accept the extent of institutional autonomy granted in application of the law. Attempts are made to construe the law as investing the universities with some limited authority, while retaining state ownership and control.

The public vocational higher education institutions operate as state institutions exercising limited power over certain financial transactions, however subject they are to ministerial control. It is highly probable that the Vocational Higher Education Institutions Act currently under deliberation will abide by this logic.

The rapid structural and ideological changes in Estonian higher education have not yet been followed-up by a sufficiently lasting period of stabilisation. Although the University Act was passed in early 1995, the distribution of responsibilities set forth therein has not been implemented so far. The same may be said for academic mission. Indeed, if it was the strategy of the early 1990s – when the secondary vocational sector was established – to institutionally separate applied and higher academic education, then, more integrating forces have now begun to prevail. The university sector is looking for additional activities in order to maintain its relatively large size under conditions of economic constraints. Some universities have now begun issuing diplomas commonly understood as degrees of vocational higher learning. Concurrently, some of the vocational higher education institutions, which so far operate without a clear legal framework, are now claiming university status. The questions surrounding private higher education are even more complicated. Established as private vocational higher institutions, some offer master and doctoral programmes. However, the field for study programmes offered in the private sector is limited mainly to business and to theology.

In the meantime, Estonia acknowledges the need for comprehensive quality assurance. The mechanism set up by the University Act still awaits full implementation by the Higher Education Evaluation Council. According to the Law, all study programmes in public universities must be evaluated and accredited once every seven years. In the event of a less than satisfactory assessment, diplomas and qualifications may be denied official recognition. Furthermore, such programmes may in principle be shut down by ministerial decree, and, in the event of more than one third of the curriculum failing to meet the criteria, an institution may be shut down entirely. By January 1999, all study programmes at all of the six universities must have passed accreditation. However, once this process was started up, many hidden obstacles became apparent, and amendments to the University Act towards a smoother and less costly quality assurance system are highly probable in the near future.

No quality assurance system has been established in vocational higher education, whether public or private. The only way to ensure their quality is to intervene at their inception, where certain conditions – set forth in the Licensing Standards for Higher Education Institutions – must be satisfied. However, the impact of these standards is limited. They are repeatedly circumvented by way of political intervention and interpersonal connections.

In the former Soviet Union only one higher education qualification existed – the so called higher education diploma, which was issued after successful completion of a five-year programme of university level studies. Currently in Estonia, there are diplomas, too, but they have acquired the meaning of vocational higher degrees, as was mentioned above. Universities now issue bachelor's, master's, and doctoral degrees following completion of four, six or ten year programmes respectively. The relative weight of the new degrees and qualifications has not yet been legally assessed. It is assumed, however, that the former diplomas are roughly equivalent to the new master's degrees, and that the former Candidate of Sciences degrees are comparable to the new doctoral degrees. There is no equivalent to the former Doctor of Sciences in the new system.

## 5.8.3    The balance of power

Determining the delimitations of power between different levels has been a major problem for Estonian higher education since the dissolution of the former Soviet Union. In principle, the Soviet higher education system had been extremely centralised, and the institutions had no authority to modify curricula or to define admission and recruitment criteria. These and other matters belonged to the competence of the central government. Of course, it may safely be assumed, that for lack of capacity to manage the system at the central level, unidentified bodies and persons had retained a great share of the power for themselves.

Following dissolution of this former central level, its functions are now exercised by the Ministry of Culture and Education, which requires all higher education institutions to accommodate certain numbers of qualified students in their programmes. Although this system resembles the Soviet pattern, institutions have found ways to admit additional students, and to charge them, while higher education in public institutions is in principle free of charge. This practice creates tensions between the higher education institutions and the Ministry of Culture and Education. However, to promote an entrepreneurial approach in higher education and to mobilise additional funds, further amendments to the law seem unavoidable.

According to the University Act, principles of organisation and governance of a university are set down in bye-laws (the university's constitution). Generally, the institution is governed by its rector or president, who acts under the authority of the institution's council or board of trustees. A rector is responsible for the development of the institution and its overall management. He is accountable to the Council and the Ministry of Culture and Education. He is elected every five years by the council in a procedure provided for in the bye-laws.

In public universities rectors elected by the university are put under contract by the Ministry of Culture and Education for a five year term. The rector may be removed from office for a term of at least three years in the event of more than 1/3 of the curricula receiving an unfavourable evaluation. A rector may also be dismissed if the Council of the university passes a no-confidence resolution by a majority vote of two-thirds of its members. Provisions of the employment laws remain unaffected, too.

A rector has the authority to:

1   implement the highest administrative and disciplinary power in the university,
2   approve internal regulations,
4   approve official administrative regulations,
5   give binding orders to faculty and staff,
5   determine the number of vice rectors, and their duties,
6   appoint vice rectors,
7   ensure compliance with ordinances and decisions by the council,
8   veto decisions of the council, which may be re-passed,
9   form a university government, and determine the bases and procedures for its operation,
10  organise teaching and research activity,
11  ensure that the budget of the university is executed,
12  represent the university and to carry out transactions in the name of the university, to the extent of the authority given to him by law and the bye-laws of the university,
13  resolve all other issues arising under the law or the bye-laws of the university.

The highest collective body of a higher education institution is the council. The constitution of the council is determined by the institution itself. The council will include the rector, vice-rectors, representatives of the faculty and research staff, representatives of the students body – who should comprise at least half of the membership of the council, and any other persons prescribed by the university bye-laws. The council issues general regulations concerning the administration and the academic programme of the institution. The council is empowered to:

1 approve and amend the bye-laws,
2 approve the bye-laws of the structural units of the university,
3 adopt development plans for the university and present them to the Minister of Culture and Education for approval,
4 approve the curricula of the university,
5 determine the procedures and conditions for defending degrees,
6 determine the conditions and procedures of admission of students,
7 make recommendations to the Minister of Culture and Education regarding fields of study and admission quotas,
8 determine the areas, forms, and procedures for further study,
9 approve the application compiled by the rector for financing the university from the state budget and to submit this to the Ministry of Culture and Education,
10 approve the budget of the university and the report for its execution,
11 determine general regulation regarding the management of the university and its teaching and research activities,
12 decide general issues regarding teaching and research activity involving at least two structural units,
13 determine the procedures for employing tenured teaching staff and research workers,
14 elect tenured professors,
15 accord the title professor emeritus,
16 decide issues relating to university property,
17 receive the reports of the rector, vice-rectors and heads of the structural units,
18 express no-confidence in the rector,
19 decide entry of the university into international organisations,
20 decide other issues presented by the rector, or by members of the board, in accordance with its by-laws.

Originally, intermediate bodies did not exist in Estonia. In accordance with the Universities Act the Higher Education Evaluation Council was established in 1995, consisting of representatives of higher education institutions, and of the commercial and cultural sectors. However, implementing quality assurance after the extensive de facto decentralisation of higher education amounts to a painful procedure, and only the future can show, how independently from institutional interests and political power the Council will be able to act. Reviewing all the existing universities by their study programmes, and accrediting them all in four years, as stipulated by the University Act, will be an extremely complicated issue.

Establishing universities as legal entities of public law has drastically changed the status of university property. Until recently universities did not own their premises as the state was the ultimate proprietor. Following the new law, the State must assign the property rights to the universities, however some restrictions will continue to apply to some transactions.

### 5.8.4    Conclusion

The Estonian higher education system is undergoing radical changes and is not yet entirely stabilised. The first reason for this is that the legal framework for the system is not yet complete. Following the changes, most of the power concentrated at the institutional level for lack of an authoritative legal system and the inability of the newly established state to exercise its functions in the educational sector as a whole. Recent developments can be described as re-centralisation of certain functions, however, the institutions tend to resist this infringement upon their recently acquired powers.

An important share of the higher education system, the newly established vocational higher education is not yet governed by regulation of any sort, several new legal acts may be expected therefore. Also, the existing legal acts are not always fully compatible. As the system has not stabilised at this point, it may be susceptible to further drastic revisions.

# 5.9

## FINLAND

### *Eila Rekilä*

5.9.1   The Act amending the Constitutional Act

In 1993 the Finnish Government submitted a bill to parliament amending the constitutional catalogue of fundamental rights. The incumbent provisions dated for the most part from 1919 and had therefore become inadequate, particularly in view of international human rights covenants, and of constitutional developments in Europe. The amendments extend the scope of fundamental rights to cover economic, social and cultural rights, rights relating to the legal protection of the individual, the right to vote and to be elected, and the right to social participation, and rights concerning the environment. In addition, the subjective scope of protection was extended, conditions restricting fundamental rights were elaborated and the applicability of fundamental rights and their surveillance were improved.

The Act amending the Constitutional Act was passed by parliament in 1995, and the amendments came into force on 1 August 1995. The fundamental rights are recorded in Chapter II of the Constitution Act. Several new fundamental rights were added. The most important economic, social and cultural rights are therefore now guaranteed constitutionally.

Section 13 of the Constitution Act which concerns the right to free primary, secondary and higher education now reads:

·   Everyone shall have the right to primary education free of charge. Provisions on compulsory education shall be enacted in an Act of Parliament.

·   The various public authorities shall ensure all persons equal opportunities
    for post-primary education and for personal development according to
    their abilities and particular needs without being prevented by the lack
    of means.
·   The freedom of sciences, arts and higher education shall be protected.

Individual rights are protected against interference by public authorities. The
fundamental rights bind public authorities, who must implement fundamental
rights and human rights. The fundamental rights will particularly influence
legislation. The reform will also improve the application of fundamental
rights in courts of law and other official organs.


5.9.2    The current legislative situation in higher education

All of Finland's 20 universities are state operated and subordinate to the
Ministry of Education. There is a separate statute on the administration of
each university. University degrees and teacher training are also governed
by specific legislation. However, rapid growth of the higher education system
has necessitated changes in the economic and administrative status of universities and in their internal administration. Universities now have considerable
autonomy with respect to decisions on instruction and research, and in recent
years, their authority in economic and other internal matters has also
increased. The position of rectors and deans, in particular, has been
strengthened, and participation of all faculty members in administration is
encouraged.

Up to the mid 1980s, the administration of the Finnish higher education
system was centralised. Universities' internal organisation and decision-
making were regulated by administrative orders and decrees. The university
budget determined the allocation of funds in strict detail. Decrees on studies
and degrees dictated curricula and the provision of instruction. Teachers'
duties were laid down in detail in collective agreements.

In the late 1980s, the State began to relax its grip on university administration. Some universities now have quite an extensive freedom of
action, even by international standards. The Ministry's new strategy for

steering universities is based on coordination and on academic, state and market regulation. The following changes in steering systems will be made:

- The aim is to unify legislation on state universities. The separate acts and decrees on each university will be replaced by one act governing all universities.
- In this connection, the aim is to further strengthen institutional autonomy. For instance, universities will be given more latitude to decide independently on their internal administration within the general legislative limits.
- As a result of the increasing importance of cooperation with business and industry, it has been suggested that representatives of outside interest groups should be included in the administrative bodies, as they are indeed already at some universities.

## 5.9.3    The balance of power

Government decisions concerning state-run universities usually concern legislative and budget questions. These decisions cannot be appealed. University legislation provides that the university in question must be heard in the drafting of legislation concerning it. As regards budget preparations, the Ministry of Education consults each university annually.

In the consultations, the parties make a joint analysis of the results obtained by the university, coordinate institutional and general policy aims, and define the resources required to meet the targets agreed on. The outcome is recorded in an agreement on target outcome signed by both parties. The objectives agreed on are entered into the state budget. Before consultations begin, each university indicates the subjects on which it is prepared to agree with the Ministry.

Since the vocationally oriented non-university higher education institutions are not run by the state, it is possible for an organisation running such an institution to appeal certain administrative decisions concerning them.

# 5.10

## FRANCE

### Claudine Bachy

5.10.1   Current situation in higher education

The Higher Education Policy Act adopted in 1968 gave universities legal personality and administrative, financial and educational independence.

Law No. 84-52 of 26 January 1984 on higher education defines a higher education public service bringing together all the post-secondary training dealt with by different ministerial departments.

Universities are multi-disciplinary: each is made up of a number of training and research units (UFRs) dealing with the different academic subjects, run by an elected board and headed by the chair of the board who is elected by its members for a five-year term. Universities can also incorporate institutes and schools set up by order (décret), and departments, laboratories and research units established by a decision of the administrative council of the university. Universities perform the following tasks:

· initial and further training;
· scientific and technological research and utilisation of its results;
· dissemination of culture and scientific and technical knowledge;
· international co-operation.

This Act establishes the fundamental principles to be applied in higher education courses falling within the competence of the minister (responsible for higher education). It also lays down the principles governing the organisation and functioning of all higher education establishments including universities, non-university colleges and institutes, écoles normales supérieures (higher teacher training colleges), French colleges abroad or the grandes écoles (higher professional training colleges). It encourages them both to broaden the scope of their activities to include training of a predominantly vocational kind and to increase further training and research. It set up a national assessment committee responsible for monitoring and evaluating all the activities of higher education establishments.

The state still has major responsibilities as regards higher education: it is in charge of drawing up curricula, certifying national diplomas, allocating teaching and research posts, assessing research programmes with the increasing assistance of foreign experts, particularly European ones, and, finally, co-ordinating the university map.

In keeping with the spirit of the Act of 1984, a new form of relationship with the higher education establishments was introduced in 1989 in the form of four-year contracts between the state and the universities. The aim was to give new and tangible substance to the independence of universities while enabling the state to perform its role as the instigator and co-ordinator of higher education policy to the full. Each university has to devise a development project which meets training needs both at national and at local level. This project covers the whole range of the university's activities.

Higher education in France is characterised by a wide variety of establishments whose organisation and admission requirements vary according to the type of establishment and the purposes of the courses they run.

5.10.2   Universities

For admission to a French university a candidate must have the French baccalauréat (secondary school leaving certificate) or an equivalent qualification or have obtained the higher education entrance certificate (DAEU) which is a national certificate issued by authorised universities.

Admission to the various levels of post-secondary education provided by an establishment which falls within the competence of the ministry responsible for higher education, whether it be a university, an institute or a state college – may also be authorised through the recognition of qualifications, professional experience and personal achievements, under the conditions laid down in order No. 85-906 of 23 August 1985 and order No. 93-538 of 27 March 1993. Such recognition may open the way directly to courses run by the establishment leading to a national diploma or a qualification whose acquisition is regulated by the state, or it may entitle the candidate to sit the entrance examination for a particular establishment, or it may exempt the person concerned from some of the qualifying examinations. Holders of foreign certificates or diplomas in particular may request recognition of their qualifications. The decision concerning recognition is *taken by the vice-*chancellor of the university or the head of the establishment on the advice of an academic committee.

1) Long university courses

The regulations governing the first and second "cycles" (ie. the first 3 or 4 years) of university studies are set out in the order of the Ministry of National Education and Culture of 26 May 1992 (published in the Official Gazette of 30 May 1992) relating to the general certificate of university education (or DEUG), the licence (bachelor's degree), and the maîtrise (master's degree).

The first cycle takes the education provided at secondary level further and prepares students for continued study in the second cycle or for work. It comprises two years of study and leads to the DEUG (general certificate of university education).

Under the educational reform which has gradually been implemented since 1992, courses are arranged in the form of unit modules (i.e. groupings of related courses) designed to make it easier to change subjects, take up studies again or study part time. At least one modern language is taught as a part of all courses.

In the particular case of courses in the medical sciences (medicine, dentistry, pharmacy and human biology), there is a process of selection based on the first year results and the number of candidates to be admitted to the second year is set annually by a joint order of the Minister responsible for Higher Education and the Minister of Health.

The second cycle is a period of more detailed study and high level general, scientific and technical training designed to prepare students for the exercise of professional responsibilities. It comprises two or three years of study. There are a number of different types of course:

- basic, professional and/or specialised courses leading to a licence or bachelor's degree (DEUG plus 1) and a maîtrise or master's degree (licence plus 1);
- two-year vocational leading to the maîtrise (master's degree) in science and technology (DEUG plus 2) or the maîtrise (master's degree) in computing applied to management (DEUG plus 2);
- courses leading to an engineering qualification. State engineering colleges recruit their students via competitive examinations or on the basis of qualifications either at secondary school-leaving age or after 2 years of higher education (in the preparatory classes for the Grandes Ecoles, the first two years of university, a university institute of technology (IUT) or a section for higher technical studies (STS). The length of the course varies between 3 and 5 years depending on the college. At the end of the course the student is awarded an engineering certificate.

Authorisation for colleges to issue this certificate is granted by the relevant minister in charge after consultation with the French Committee on Engineering Qualifications.

The courses offered in the professionalised university institutes (IUP) are a response to the major concern to match training more closely to the needs of employers by creating new qualifications recognising skills required in the economic sectors in question, namely those which have difficulty in finding the managers and engineers they need. The professionalised university institutes offer students who have completed one year of further studies (the 1st year of a DEUG or the preparatory classes for the grandes écoles) a university-level, vocational course lasting three years and leading to a master's qualification (BAC plus 4). The title of master of engineering is awarded by an examining board in the light of the student's whole university career. IUPs also offer continuing education courses.

Courses are taught both by the teaching staff and by professionals from the relevant economic sector. They can be arranged as sandwich courses and include a compulsory period of practical training with a company.

The courses run by university teacher training institutes (IUFM) provide for students who have studied at university for 3 years post-BAC prepare them for the competitive examination to enter the teaching profession and then, for those who pass the competitive examination, vocational training to prepare them for their chosen profession.

The third cycle (post-master's) is a period of highly specialised study and training in research. Admission to the third cycle is subject to a selection process among those who have obtained a maîtrise an engineering qualification or a recognised equivalent qualification.

The regulations governing third cycle studies are set out in the joint ministerial order of 30 March 1992, published in the Official Gazette of 3 April 1992.

There are two types of course:

· a one-year vocational course combined with a compulsory training period with a company, leading to a diplôme d'etudes supérieures spécialisés (certificate of specialised higher studies, DESS);
· a research course, leading to the diplôme d'études approfondies (certificate of advanced studies, DEA), at the end of the first year and preparing the ground for three or four years' work on a doctorate (with a view to preparing and defending a thesis or presenting a series of research projects).

Following acquisition of a doctorate, it is possible to enrol for a research director *certificate to* direct research which testifies to the ability of the holder to carry out an original high-level scientific research project and take charge of young research workers. The main purpose of this certificate is to enable the holder to be admitted to the university teaching staff.

Apart from this, masters of engineering and students in their last year in an engineering college can study for the certificate in technological research

(DRT) which is a post-master's qualification issued following a course in innovation through technological research in the industrial or service sectors.


### 5.10.3   Two-year technology courses

The university institutes of technology (IUTs) are attached to universities. The courses lead to a university diploma in technology (DUT) designed to enable holders rapidly to take up positions of responsibility in industry or the service sector. Admission to the IUTs is subject to selection.

Short courses are also taught in general and technical upper secondary schools in sections for advanced technical studies (STS). These courses, which last 2 years differ from those taught in the IUTs in that they are more specialised and highly geared towards particular jobs; they lead to a certificate of higher education, the brevet de technicien supérieur (higher technical studies certificate) (BTS). Admission to a BTS class is decided on the basis of the candidate's qualifications.

For 1995-96 some establishments are organising classes on an experimental basis for DUT or BTS-holders in preparation for a new specialised diploma in technology, introduced under an order of 4 November 1994. Teaching will be organised on a sandwich-course basis.

University students can also study for two years to prepare a university diploma in science and technology (DEUST), which enables students to take up a career straight away.


### 5.10.4   Institutes and colleges

*State engineering colleges*
There are 233 state engineering colleges, 120 of them under the control of the Ministry of Education. Of these, 31 are independent and 89 are university colleges. They recruit students by competition or on the basis of qualifications (see above).

*Business and management schools*

Many business and management schools offer higher education courses, in particular:

- the Ecole des hautes études commerciales (School for Higher Business Studies) or HEC;
- the Ecole supérieure des sciences économiques et commerciales (Higher College of Economic and Business Science) or ESSEC;
- the Ecole supérieure de commerce de Paris (Paris Higher Business College);
- the Ecole supérieure de commerce de Lyon (Lyon Higher Business College);
- the Ecoles supérieures de commerce et d'administration des entreprises (Higher Business and Company Management Schools) or ESCAEs, of which there are 18;
- the Ecoles or Instituts supérieures de sciences commerciales (Higher Colleges or Institutes of Business Science), numbering 17;
- the Ecoles Normales Supérieures.

The 4 Ecoles normales supérieures (Higher Teacher Training Colleges) or ENS (in Paris, Fontenay/St. Cloud, Lyon and Cachan) have a highly selective admissions procedure for which two years of post-secondary study are necessary in preparatory science classes (particularly, in "advanced maths" and then "applied maths") or arts classes (in "advanced arts" and then "upper advanced arts"). They lead to the state degrees and to the teacher recruitment competitions (the certificat d'aptitude au professorat de l'enseignement secondaire (Diploma of Secondary Education) or CAPES, and the agrégation (Diploma of Upper Secondary and University Education).

*Paramedical and social work colleges*

Students are admitted once they have passed the BAC (secondary school leaving examination), either directly or following a competitive examination, test or interview. Courses can last for up to four years.

*Private higher education*

Private higher education is governed by the principle of freedom of education. This means that the opening of private colleges is subject to official declaration but no prior approval is required.

Private higher education establishments can be divided into two main categories, in terms both of the courses they provide and of their legal status:

·    Free private higher education establishments
These establishments offer generalist courses and are governed by the provisions of the law of 12 July 1875 on freedom of higher education, which does not provide for possible links with the state. This type of establishment can enter into an agreement with a university to prepare students for state degrees.

·    Private technical colleges
Private technical colleges exist for vocational purposes (for the most part they are engineering colleges and business and management colleges), and are governed by the legislative provisions and regulations of the technical education code. They may be recognised by the state and their diplomas may be certified by the relevant ministry, this being the only legal means by which an establishment can issue an official diploma.

·    Under special regulations, private engineering colleges are authorised to award an engineering diploma subject not to state approval but to that of the Committee on Engineering Qualifications.

5.10.5   Administrative organisation

The Law of 26 January 1984 on Higher Education defines universities as public institutions of a scientific, cultural or vocational nature. The law gives them administrative, financial, educational and scientific independence:

·    administrative independence: the university is run via the decisions of the président (vice-chancellor), the deliberations of the administrative council, and the proposals, opinions and wishes of the scientific commit-tee and the committee on studies and university life;
·    financial independence: the university manages the funds allocated to it by the state together with its own resources;
·    educational and scientific independence: in compliance with the national guidelines established by ministerial order for each subject, the university

makes its own decisions on the curricula, course content, teaching methods and materials and arrangement for testing students' knowledge.

Under the Act of 1984, the statutory organs of universities are as follows:

- the administrative council, which takes policy decisions, votes on the university budget, decides on the allocation of posts and approves agreements and conventions signed by the vice-chancellor;
- the scientific committee, which makes proposals to the administrative council regarding the thrust of research policy and advises on initial and further training courses, on research programmes and contracts, and on projects to create or modify university degrees;
- the committee on studies and university life, which makes proposals to the administrative council regarding the content of initial and further training courses, examines requests for authority to teach university courses and proposals for new courses, and makes arrangements to provide students with careers advice, help them adapt to working life and improve their working and living conditions.

These three bodies are made up of elected representatives of the teaching body, research workers, students and management, technical, manual and administrative staff as well as representatives from outside the university.

The vice-chancellor of the university is elected for five years by the entire membership of the three bodies, sitting in plenary assembly: he runs the university, chairs council/committee meetings, and prepares and implements their decisions; he manages the budget of receipts and expenditure, has authority over the entire staff, appoints the various examining boards and is responsible for keeping order.

# 5.11

## FEDERAL REPUBLIC OF GERMANY

### Wolfgang Mönikes & Cornelia Haugg

5.11.1   Legal provisions

1   Constitution (Basic Law)

Article 5 (3) (Freedom of expression): "Art and science, research and teaching, shall be free. Freedom of teaching shall not absolve from loyalty to the constitution."

Article 30 (Functions of the Länder): "The exercise of governmental power and the discharge of governmental functions shall be incumbent on the Länder in so far as this Basic Law does not otherwise prescribe or permit."

Article 91 a (Federal participation in Länder responsibilities): "The Federation shall participate in the discharge of the following responsibilities of the Länder, provided that such responsibilities are important to society as a whole and that federal participation is necessary for the improvement of living conditions (joint tasks)":
1. extension and constructions of institutions of higher education including university clinics;

Article 91 b "The Federation and the Länder may pursuant to agreements co-operate in educational planning and in the promotion of institutions and projects of scientific research of supra-regional importance. The apportionment of cost shall be regulated in the pertinent agreements."

2    Framework for higher education (Hochschulrahmengesetz, 1976), for
     Higher Education Acts on the level of the Länder, Civil Service Law
     for university teachers.


5.11.2   The current legislative situation in higher education

The Federal Republic of Germany is a Bundesstaat (federation) consisting
now of 16 Länder. The unification of the two German states on 3 October
1990 was the most far-reaching event in the post-war history of Germany.
For forty years two German states had existed side by side, looking back
on the same historical traditions but taking diametrically opposed paths. The
West was democratic, federalist, and oriented to a market economy, the East
was socialist, centralist, and operated a planned economy. This contrast was
also reflected in the higher education and research system. During the process
of reunification, the system of higher education in the five new Länder
changed fundamentally. Steps were taken to incorporate the system into the
supra-regional institutions and promotional programmes of the Federal
Government, of the Länder and of the universities. A good part of the
developments of the past forty years was adapted by the new Länder, such
as the principle rule of combining research and teaching, on a par, at higher
education institutions in Germany. The traditional eastern system of Academies of Science was abolished.

Responsibility for educational policy and planning is distributed according
to the principle of federalism. The Länder have what one might call the
"general power" for this sector, as opposed to the Federal Government,
which has only limited powers and may participate in educational planning.
In principle higher education is free of charge.

Efficient higher education institutions are absolutely essential for an
industrialised nation. For this reason, it is in the interest of a uniformly high
living standard to provide framework specific to each of the individual
Länder, and to safeguard equivalence within the higher education system,
at large, as well as mobility within the federal area. As a result, a system
has been gradually devised which enables the Federal Government to exert
influence on the higher education system, without unsettling the federative
patterns of political responsibility.

The Länder, co-operate themselves in the Standing Conference of the Ministers of Education and Cultural Affairs of the Länder (KMK). The KMK is responsible for co-ordinating the individual systems Länder, particularly with regard to structures, institutions and final certificates.

There are several institutions in Germany in which the Federal Government and the Länder develop higher education policy matters jointly. The Bund-Länder-Commission for Educational Planning and Research Promotion (BLK) is composed of government representatives, and is also responsible for all educational sectors. In this context, jointly financed schemes, such as developing distance study are of particular importance; upon successful completion, distance study is included in the standard programmes at higher education institutions as a basis for study reform measures.

## 5.11.3 Science Council

The Science Council (Wissenschaftsrat), which was set up by the Federal Government and the Länder in 1957, is a very important forum dealing with basic higher education policy matters. The Science Council's mandate is to elaborate recommendations on the development of higher education, science and research – in terms of content and structure to accommodate social, cultural and economic exigencies. The fact that the Science Council comprises of representatives of the Federal Government, the Länder, members of higher education and research institutions, and representatives of industry has produced a highly effective co-operation.

## 5.11.4 Extension and construction of institutions of higher education: a joint task

The dual competence structure set forth in the Basic Law of the Federal Republic of Germany was loosened up in 1969 by a constitutional amendment which introduced "joint tasks" as a new form of co-operation between the Federal Government and the Länder; one of these joint tasks is the extension and construction of higher education institutions.

The point of departure for the creation of "joint task" was to take cognisance of supra-regional aspects, as well as of costs exceeding in most cases the Länder resources. Since that time, investments in higher education institutions and university hospitals have been planned jointly by the Federal Government and the Länder via a Planning Committee for Higher Education Construction on the basis of recommendations made by the Science Council.

The current discussion in Germany is focused on national and international challenges. The Federal Government and the Länder unanimously agree that German higher education is in need of structural reforms. The requisite structural adaptations include the following:

a)  higher education studies must distinguish between occupation-related basic studies, on the one hand, and the training scientists and scholars on the other hand. Studies at universities must be designed in such a way as to enable students to complete studies within a fixed period, of four to five years, depending on the subject.

b)  The further extension of Fachhochschulen including the transfer of some university resources to the Fachhochschulsector must increase the latter's share in the total number of study places by at least 40%. This physical extension must be accompanied by an enhancement of study provision including the transfer of university study courses to this sector.

c)  In addition to the reform of basic studies, increased attention is given to graduate studies as the crucial phase of preparing scientists and scholars for research inside and outside higher education institutions.

d)  Higher education institutions are to take the necessary measures on their own, and marge de manoeuvre to do so. The Federal Government and the Länder restrict themselves to legislative and administrative measures, and to giving incentives.

Particularly important are:

·   strengthening the higher education institutions' financial autonomy by globalising their budgets and by giving them greater flexibility.

- assignment of a basic pool of posts and funds for equipment for teaching in accordance with the teaching quality of the higher education institutions (e.g. by making assignments on the basis of the number of graduates, average study times, etc);
- supporting higher education institutions in the selection of suitable candidates;
- updating civil service law for university teachers on performance criteria;
- requiring higher education institutions to submit to report on the quality of their teaching.

### 5.11.5 The balance of power between the State, intermediate organisations and institutions of higher education

The balance of power is one of the basic principles of the German Constitution. This principle is also reflected in the higher education system.

With a few exceptions, such as the colleges of public administration, all institutions of higher education in Germany are corporations under public law and, at the same time, state institutions of the individual Länder. They enjoy autonomy within the legislative framework. Their autonomy is limited by the supervisory rights of the Länder ministry concerned. Thus, by-laws adapted by the higher education institutions, require official approval. The same applies to examination regulations. The management of a higher education institution is the responsibility of an elected full-time principal (Rektor or Präsident). The former procedure of electing a principal from within the professional body for one year – on a part-time basis – has been abandoned. The principal, who is elected by the higher education institutions concerned, is officially appointed by the responsible Länders ministry.

Following fierce arguments about the democratisation of higher education and the participation of assistants and students in the 1960's, the Framework Act for Higher Education eventually codified the principle of graduated participation in line with the function; taking into account previous rulings by the Federal Constitutional Court, Accordingly, all members of a higher education institution are entitled, to participate in self-administration in line with their qualifications, function, responsibility and the degree to which they are directly affected. In the main collegiate bodies at higher education institutions (Konzil/Konvent, Senat, Fachbereichsräte), all member groups – professors, students, academic assistants and other staff members – are entitled to a seat and a vote. In the bodies concerned with matters relating to teaching, research and the appointment of professors, the latter enjoy an absolute majority on the committee responsible for electing a principal. The current system is no-the-less undisputed. Several political groups call for an extension of the rights of participation by academic staff and students.

The organisation of students for the purposes of safeguarding their interests is provided for in different ways in the individual higher education institutions in the Länder. In the majority of the Länder exists a student body corporate (verasste Studentenschaft) represented by the General Student Committee (Allgemeiner Studentenausschuss - AStA).

In order to tackle questions of common concern, the higher education institutions in Germany co-operate on a permanent basis via the Conference of the Rectors and Presidents of Higher Education Institutions (HRK). In many cases, the HRK collaborates closely with state offices and other scientific organisations.

Within the framework of allocation of federal responsibilities, the Länder and their responsible bodies, and numerous institutions and organisations exert an influence on higher education and other academic establishments. All in all, this results in a complex network of many and diverse inter-relations with direct and indirect influences on higher education developments.

5.11.6   A brief conclusion

Germany has a very long tradition in the field of higher education – dating back to the medieval times, when some of the first European universities were founded, and most importantly the early nineteenth century neo-humanist and reform of the university system in Prussia after associated with the name of Wilhelm von Humboldt. There is no need felt for fundamental changes of the system at present. The principal provisions of the system are:

- the German Constitution guarantees that science, research and the arts are able to exist freely. Institutions of higher education are autonomous bodies within a legal framework.
- Research and teaching are combined at higher education institutions;
- universities are incorporated in the federative structure of Germany;

There is, however, an acknowledged need to increase the efficiency of higher education institutions. This includes changing the legal framework to give higher education institutions more autonomy and to allow for more competition between them.

# 5.12

## GREECE

*Roy Hourdakis*

### 5.12.1   The current legislative situation

According to Article 16 paragraph 5 of the Constitution, higher education is assured exclusively by fully self-government institutions, legal entities to public law. These institutions are supervised and financed by the State.

Article 1 of the Law L.1268/1982 defines the assignment of higher education institutions. In order to guarantee the academic freedom, the unrestricted mobility of ideas and scientific research, Article 2 paragraph 5 of the same article forbids the intrusion of any representatives of public order into the premises of the universities without being invited by the competent academic body.

Higher education institutions comprise of schools. Each division consists of faculties. The faculty is the basic functional academic unit which covers the subject of one science. More faculties of related scientific areas compose a school. The curriculum offered with the function of a faculty leads to the diploma which is called "Ptychio".

The bodies of the higher education institutions according to Article 2 of L. 2083/1992, which have replaced Article 11 of L. 1268/82 are the senate, the rectorate and the rector. The senate constitutes the executive. It directs, manages, regulates, supervises and controls the university procedures. The rectorate is a smaller body of representative composition intended to function flexibly. According to Article 2 paragraph 3a of L. 2083/1992, it is composed of the rector, the two vice-rectors, a representative of the students delegates to the Senate and the head of the general secretariat of the institution. The body has the right to vote on administrative, financial, technical and personnel matters.

The rector is the highest rank person of the institution. He represents the institution and exercises managerial duties. His executive authority has recently been enforced by Article 3 paragraph 1 of L. 2083/92, so that certain functional obstacles arising from the reluctance of the institution's officials to take decisions, may be overcome. The rector is assisted by two vice-rectors. One on academic issues and personnel and the other on financial planning and development (article 3 paragraph 1f, VIII L.2083/92). The competence of each vice-rector is decided by the rectorate.

According to Article 10 of L.2083/92 the bodies of a school are: the general assembly, the deanery and the dean. These bodies have limited authority over co-ordinating activities, which is also justified by the reasons of the school's establishment. The general assembly is the most numerous body among all bodies of representative composition. It is composed of all the general assemblies of faculties that constitute the school. The deanery is composed of the dean, the presidents of the faculties and a representative of the students, from each faculty. Its competence is to fulfil advisory functions. The bodies of the faculty according to Article 8 of L. 1268/82 reformed by the Article of 4 of L. 2083/92 are the general assembly, the administrative council and the president. The general assembly is composed of the members of the teaching and research staff, students equal to 50% and representatives of the post-graduate equal to 15% of the teaching and research staff members of the faculty.

The administrative council is composed of the president, the vice-president of the faculty, the directors of the departments, two students and one representative of the post-graduate students. whenever issues related to assistant-supervisors or scientific collaborators or EEP are discussed, a representative of them participates. The general assembly is composed of the members of the teaching and research department, two representatives from the students and one post-graduate student. Its competence is of a co-ordinating, suggestive as well as decision-making character.

The Council of Higher Education (CHE) has been established as a collective body of an advisory nature. The basic function of this body is to make recommendations to the government concerning the establishment, abolition, merge, organisation and function of the institutions, schools and faculties.

The teaching-research staff is composed of professors, associate professors, assistant professors and lecturers. The appointment in a position is accomplished though elections and/or promotions, which are initiated by open proclamation. (Article 6 paragraph 2 L.2083/92). The professors and the associate professors have status of permanence, while assistant professors and lecturers are elected for a three-year service which can be renewed for another term of four years.

The proclamation of positions, is performed by the general assembly of the faculty following the suggestion of the general assembly of the relevant department. Besides the teaching-research staff, the main body of educational and research tasks, the law also provides other specific categories of personnel. This personnel is temporarily or permanently occupied with the educational task, and either renders specific technical, administrative or educational services. Post-graduate studies constitute a crucial part of the educational and research process within the function of the higher education institutions. According to Article 10 and 11 of L. 2083/92 programmes of post-graduate studies (P.P.G.S.) can be organised either by each academic faculty individually or with the cooperation of more faculties of the same or different universities or universities abroad.

In order to promote the research within the university process, Article 17 of L. 2083/92 provided the establishment of the university research iInstitutes which are legal entities to private law. These institutes are established by a presidential decree after the proposition of one or more faculties of an institution of higher education or in collaboration with different institutions. The university research institutes may cooperate either with the public or the private sector.

5.12.2   The balance of power

The balance of power between the State and the institutions is based upon
financial interaction. While the State is the exclusive sponsor of the
institutions, its power is decisive in matters related to the establishment of
new faculties and personnel positions, where the appropriate funds must
be assured. The institutions on the other hand have unlimited authority in
questions of academic procedures and activities where the State without
interfering plays the role of legislator, following the introduction made up
by the relevant iInstitution(s). The present above mentioned situation is still
subjected to further discussion between the competent authorities of the State
and the relevant institutions of higher education for taking all necessary
measures and making the appropriate reforms in order to respond to social
and international needs in accordance with a contemporary higher education
system.

# 5.13

## HUNGARY

*Anna Imre & Janos Setényi*

### 5.13.1   The current legislative situation

There is no reference to higher education in the Hungarian Constitution.

Hungarian higher education consists of a mainly public system with a binary structure. There are two main types of higher education institutions: universities (egyetem) and colleges (foiskola). Other institutions not integrated into the State system also offer post-secondary education, such as managerial and business programmes, or non-traditional adult education. There also exists regional retraining centres. Establishments of the latter kind are not accredited and their programmes are officially not considered part of higher education. Higher education is offered at various universities and colleges. At present there are 59 state, 29 church and 4 private institutions of higher education. Degree programmes are offered at 20 universities, 9 university level colleges and 63 specialised colleges. Although the whole system is currently in transition, both vertically and horizontally, the basic features remain unchallenged. Apart from a few exceptions, all institutions of higher education are state institutions in the sense, that they are created by an act of parliament. The non-state institutions are owned and operated by churches, local governments and private foundations.

In Hungary 19% of the 18 year old age group are enrolled at higher education institutions. Although enrolment ratios are increasing rapidly now, Hungarian higher education has preserved many elitist characteristics. The fact that adult education and the whole post-secondary sector (and sometimes even post-graduate education) were, until very recently, not considered part of tertiary education creates not only terminological problems, but also accounts for misleading statistics and problematic conclusions.

With the Higher Education Act a decisive step was taken towards democratisation and expansion of higher education. Act LXXX, passed by Parliament on 13 July 1993, is Hungary's first piece of legislation dealing specifically with higher education. While the Act continues to define higher education in terms of the binary system of universities and colleges, the new ministerial staff, which were appointed at the last stage of educational legislating, has already begun preparatory work on the legal integration of the post-secondary sector. Over and above its own law, higher education is affected by regulations concerning vocational training, too. Rights, terms and conditions of employment of staff are dealt with by the Public Employees Law of 1992.

It is one of the policies of the new law to increase the number of students in higher education by means of developing a market oriented system, and to increase institutional autonomy. Among the most important changes initiated by the new law are the following:

· the earlier system of higher education, in which governance was shared among various ministries, was abolished. The new steering system vests all supervisory power, except for military and police academies, in the Ministry of Education and Culture;
· for purposes of consultation the Hungarian Rectors' Conference received legal status, and the College Directors' Conference and the Chair of Arts Colleges were established and received legal status. Likewise, for professional decision-making, the National Accreditation Committee and the Higher Education and Scientific Council have been set up;
· the autonomy of higher education institutions was guaranteed, the powers to create post-graduate programmes, to award doctoral degrees and to establish habilitation mechanisms were restored to the institutions. A new, three tier, system of degrees was established introducing B.A., M.A. and PhD degrees;
· the earlier incremental financing was abolished and a more performance-related funding system was developed providing expressly for three channels of financing; also the introduction of tuition fees was made possible;

- the practice of fixed-term appointments has been introduced for junior and assistant lecturers;
- the power of regulating university and college admission procedures was restored to the institutions;
- a deadline was set for the creation of a separate Higher Education Development Bill.

The purpose of an Higher Education Development Bill is to establish the guiding principles of future developments in higher eduction, restructuring and improving institutional autonomy. The bill is furthermore intended to stimulate the integration of different higher education institutions, as well as the delimitation of the binary system. Among the policies of the bill is the introduction of the credit-system into higher education. These measures became effective in the form of a parliament decree in the spring of 1995. The decree makes provisions concerning the development of curricula, the capacity of institutions, and the development of the training, research and student welfare infrastructure of higher education. The decree also imposes regulation upon the internal control and organisation of institutions, as well as upon their financing.

### 5.13.2 The balance of power between the State, intermediaries and the institutions

State responsibility for higher education was previously shared among various bodies. Supervision was carried out by six ministries, but the 1993 Law transferred authority over all institutions except military and police academies to the Ministry of Education and Culture. The first unified higher education budget became effective January 1, 1995. The Ministry exercises its legal supervisory role, conducts strategic planning and preparatory work on educational policy, approves the creation and abolition of new faculties on the advice of the National Accreditation Committee together with the Higher Education and Scientific Council. Last but not least, the Ministry monitors the efficient use of central resources. An important role is also assigned to the Ministry of Finance, which prepares the guidelines of the annual state budget. Aside from allocating resources to the higher education institutions according to the state budget, the government determines general educational requirements, sets the conditions of creating PhD programmes, lays down the regulations for the National Accreditation Committee and the Higher Education and Scientific Council, and sets the regulations governing the establishment, licensing and termination of higher education institutions, as well as for the recognition of foreign degrees.

Academic freedom and the autonomy of higher education institutions has been gradually developed since the 1980s and is now guaranteed by the 1993 law. Accordingly, higher education institutions are free to implement policy governing their organisation and operation, their staff, admission requirements, and academic programmes. New study programmes require the approval of the minister; new disciplines the approval of the government. The institutions manage their budgets and their revenues according to framework regulations themselves. To protect their autonomy, they may appeal to the Constitutional Court. The autonomy of higher education institutions is complemented by assigning to self-governing student organisations, representative, advisory and evaluative responsibilities.

According to the 1993 Higher Education Law, institutions are headed by university rectors or college directors elected by the council of the institution for a three year term at the maximum. Councils, too, are elected for a period of three years. Increasing demand for social accountability and stable institutional leadership has encouraged some university and college managers to establish external advisory boards and to professionalise the administration.

Important bodies, representing interest groups, are the Hungarian Rectors' Conference, the College Directors' Conference and the Chair of Arts College Directors. These bodies emerged in the late 1980s. Currently, private or Church higher education institutions have no institutionalised representation. These three intermediaries play an important role in the process of policy development and have formed a single umbrella organisation to which, however, the new Law does not refer specifically.

In recent years, important changes have altered the access and selection system of higher education, and the profile of certain higher education institutions. Earlier, admission to higher education institutions was granted on the basis of secondary education results and on the results of pre-selective entrance examinations. With the emergence of competition in higher education, less popular institutions have been forced to partially abandon entrance examinations and to resort to internal selection criteria. Some elite institutions have began requiring certificates of foreign language proficiency and other additional items of admission. While 43 % of all candidates did not have to pass a full entrance examination in 1992, the figure increased to 50 % in 1993. The current diversification of admission procedures has already led to increased flexibility. Some inherited problems, however, like the lack of a standardised secondary education examination, and unsatisfactory national co-ordination of admission policies continue to limit students' actual choices. Deregulation of the entrance examination system is continuing in on-going consultations with the Ministry, the Hungarian Rectors' Conference and the College Directors' Conference.

### 5.13.3 Conclusion

The structure of educational programmes in the except and 1960s was characterised by the dominant role of teacher education and technical training, this situation lasted until the late 1970s. As new labour market sensitive and highly popular study fields have often emerged outside and independently of the state system, the need for a profile change and for restructuring became a serious challenge for state universities and colleges. Presently, efforts are directed at developing non-traditional modes of learning as an alternative to universities and colleges.

In Hungary, new legal developments in higher education have led to revived academic independence in the sectors of academic freedom, and institutional and financial autonomy. While academic freedom poses few problems, legal or practical, institutional autonomy is still riddled by uncertainties and on-going debates, the resolution of which would require increased involvement of stakeholders outside the immediate sphere of higher education. Not yet attained is the full implementation of financial autonomy. In this context, the lack of a formula-based financing of public higher education institutions must be regarded as a major short-coming, along with financial management being determined in many respects by the State or the ad hoc situation

# 5.14

## LATVIA

### Andrejs Rauhvargers & Janis Čakste

5.14.1   The Satversme, the Constitution of the Republic of Latvia

The Satversme, the Constitution of the Republic of Latvia, makes no mention of higher education, since at the time of its adoption in 1919, only one institution of higher education – the University of Latvia – existed. The parliament of Latvia, the Saeima, formally approved of the University's by-laws in 1923, promulgating thereby the first Higher Education Act of the Republic of Latvia.

5.14.2   The current legislative situation in higher education

On 19 June 1991 the Saeima passed the Education Act of the Republic of Latvia, Article 38 of which sets out to define higher education as comprising higher professional education and higher academic education. Article 39 of the Act makes mention of the mission of academic higher education, as being the preparation of persons for creative work in one of the branches of science. The mission of higher professional education is seen as the imparting of highly specialised skills in the domains of social life, national economy, culture or health care.

The higher education institutions enjoy autonomy, and therefore govern themselves in accordance with their by-laws. Article 42 of the Education Law provides that every permanent inhabitant of the Republic of Latvia who has attained the general secondary education level and who meets other national and institutional entrance requirements, has the right to study in a higher education institution.

In 1940 Latvia was incorporated into the Soviet Union and its educational system was then changed to the Soviet model which existed in Latvia until 1990. The sentiments at the heart of the central policy are well reflected in the Government statements according to which the geopolitical situation of Latvia, particularly its limited access to natural resources make the deployment of a highly qualified and educated population the primary factor ensuring the country's global competitiveness.

The Education Law of 1991 introduced important changes. It introduced 5 compulsory and 7 elective subjects and two levels of each subject curricula – core and advanced – in upper secondary education. The Law also granted autonomy to higher education institutions and it opened opportunities to establish private education institutions at all levels. Though the Education Law of 1991 is a frame-law, it did not regulate the relationship between State and higher education in sufficient detail, however, which prompted adoption of the Law on Higher Education Establishments.

On 2 November 1995 Saeima passed the new Law on Higher Education Establishments in Latvia. The higher education institutions enjoy autonomy, and therefore govern themselves in accordance with their by-laws, which they adopt following approval by the Saeima (universities) and Cabinet of Ministers (all other institutions). In the Saeima and within the Government the interests of higher education institutions are represented by the Ministry of Education and Science.

Law on Higher Educational Establishments in Latvia regulates:

·    missions and tasks of the higher education institution (article 5);
·    establishing and re-organization of higher education institutions (article 8);
·    licensing and accreditation of higher education institutions and their programmes (articles 3 and 9);
·    government and establishment regulations of the faculties and other basic structural units (article 12-25);
·    staff structure and selection (articles 26-43);

- student admission regulations, financial and other principles in organisation of studies (articles 46-59);
- regulations of formation and usage of the budget of the higher education
institution; (articles 76-80);
- legal features of the higher education institution (articles 8 and 10).

Autonomy (article 4) and academic freedom (article 6) are guaranteed to
the higher education institutions by the law. The law stipulates the rights
and duties of the already existing Rectors Council (article 64) and Higher
Education Council to be established as an Saeima-approved institution
consisting of academics and professional associations which will work out
strategies of higher education (articles 65-74).

However, the law regulates these issues of the appropriate topics which are
common to all the higher education institutions in Latvia. Each higher
education institution may have its specific regulations stipulated in its Satversme (by-law) such as:

- missions and tasks of the concrete institution;
- structure of the higher education institution;
- governing allocation principles of rights and duties among the governing
higher institutionsof education institution and its structural units;
- institutions checking the operation of higher education institution and
its faculties;
- government and establishment regulations of the faculties and other basic
structural units;
- specific admission regulations;
- legal relations between the structural units, etc.

The declared national priority of education however had no yield to
economic constraints. Economy of Latvia has suffered considerably from
having lost its former access to a wide Soviet market. While recent developments indicate a slow recovery, the higher education system of Latvia still
requires substantial supplementary financial support, particularly, to re-
integrate research and teaching which were split under Soviet rule. The 20
million Lats (40 million US dollars) allocated annually to the higher
education sector represent but a crisis minimum budget, at best considering
the exigencies of over 30,000 students in 15 state-financed institution.

5.14.3   Types and missions of higher education

The Education Act of 1991 does not distinguish between academic and professional higher education institutions but instead between the academic and professional study programmes which can exist in the same institution. The Law on Higher Educational Establishments in Latvia adopted on 2 November 1995, divides higher education institutions into universities, professional higher education institutions and other higher education institutions which may be of university level but operate in a narrower field, e.g. music, art, medicine, etc., (articles 3, 39). However, professional study programmes can still exist in the universities and other higher education institutions. The Law on Higher Educational Establishments contains a new provision regarding "colleges at higher education institutions". These will provide a special kind of short-term professional programmes. Neither such institutions nor the programmes exist at present, more concrete regulations regarding these will be approved by the Cabinet of Ministers in the coming year. The mission of academic higher education is to prepare persons for a creative work in one of the branches of science. The mission of higher professional education is to prepare persons for independent highly qualified work in a given branch of social life, national economy or health care.

5.14.4   The balance of power, accountability and quality assessment.

According to the Law On Higher Educational Establishments, higher educational establishments are autonomous (article 4) and operate on the basis of the Satversme on the Republic of Latvia, the Law on Education, the Law on Higher educational Establishments in Latvia, the law "On Research Activities", its own Satversme and other legal acts (article 10). Article 10 also stipulates that the Satversme of a higher education institution shall contain;

1   the name of the higher educational establishment, its address and legal status;
2   the main directions of its activity and its objectives;
3   the procedure for adopting the Satversme and amendments to it;
4   representation of higher educational establishments and its administrative institutions, in accordance with Article 28 the rights, duties and objective

of this and other administrative institution, the procedure for their formation, election or appointment for these, time periods of their
functioning and the procedure for dismissal of the above;
5   a) the procedure for the foundation, reorganisation and liquidation of
faculties, institutes, departments and other structural units of higher
educational establishments;
   b) regulations which appoint the rights, the obligations and the administrative system thereof,as well as how their governing bodies shall
be appointed and the procedure for their approval;
   c) the procedure for adoption of the documents regulating the internal
order of a highereducational establishment.

A higher educational establishment may include its Satversme other essential
conditions without prejudice to the laws of the Republic of Latvia. The
Satversme of an university shall be adopted by the university and approved
by the Saeima of the Republic Latvia, but the Satversme of any other higher
education institution shall be adopted by the institution and approved by
the Cabinet of Ministers.

The Law on Higher Educational Establishments (article 9) institutes a regular
accreditation of the study programmes and higher education institution as
a whole once every 6 years and the appropriate Regulations of accreditation
have been approved by the Cabinet of Ministers on November 28 1995. The
three Baltic states have decided to carry out higher education quality assessment jointly, therefore a Declaration of intentions was signed by the
Ministers if Education of Baltic countries in October 1994 and a Statute
on cooperation in higher education assessment – in January 1995. Experts
from all the 3 Baltic states must participate in any assessment and participation of experts from outside Baltia is highly welcomed. The quality
assessment will be organized by Latvia Higher Education Quality Evaluation
Centre. Annexes to the Regulations of accreditation: questionnaires for self-
evaluation of higher education institution and peer evaluation, guidelines
and standards are currently being developed.

5.14.5   Competencies, and steering principles and mechanisms of the
         Ministry

The Education Act makes the ministry responsible for monitoring of the
higher education institution's activities, and to represent the interests of
higher education within the Government, as well as licensing and accreditation of higher education institutions and programmes and it (using)
allocates grants, in cooperation with the expert commissions of Latvian
Science Council for both state and market-oriented research.

The new Higher Education Act has expanded the scope of the ministry's
competencies. Using the expertise of Higher Education Council (which will
be represented by the Minister of Education in the Cabinet of Ministers
sessions), it is now responsible for all strategies of higher education starting
from program development up to allocation principles of the budget. The
law also requires new study programmes to undergo evaluation prior to
admission of students. Special grants are designed to help implement new
study programmes that correspond to the present economic situation, practically no funds are allocated to any research projects other than those
supported by the Latvian Science Council and the Ministry of Education
and Science. Thus, the entire research planning is in fact within the authority
of these bodies which decide whether to finance, or to reject research
proposals submitted to them by the institutions.

Public funding is allocated to the institutions within the following categories,
among others:

·   the salary fund is calculated from the actual number of state-supported
    students. This number is divided by 8 and multiplied by the mean value
    of staff salaries, as taken from the pay scale for state employees and
    as approved by the Cabinet of Ministers;
·   re-integration of higher education and research requires distribution of
    integration grants, usually in the form of research grants. Programmes
    involving both research and teaching, therefore, are most favourably
    regarded for funding purposes;
·   additional funding is allocated according to state-approved development
    plans, which are at present equal to zero;
·   allocations for grants and transport compensations.

State investments in higher education, including investments for capital building, are included in the state investment programmes as elaborated by the Ministry of Economics and as approved by the Council of Ministers. The annual budget allocation for these programmes is in turn included in the national budget enacted by the Saeima.

In principle, real and other property utilised by the institutions is state-owned, however, the higher education institutions are beneficiaries under a usufruc-tuary right; unless the property has been purchased by means outside of the state budget, or has been otherwise acquired.

## 5.14.6  Access and selection, tuition fees, loans and grants

Access to higher education is open to all holders of general secondary education certificates. However, the institutions may set out additional requirements, for example, they may condition admission on completion of certain elective subjects at secondary school. According to the Law on Higher Educational Establishments, the regulations for admission shall be made up of two parts:

1  the regulations of the Ministry of Education and Science which apply to all the higher educational establishments in Latvia;
2  the regulations set up by the Senates of higher educational establsh-ments:
   a) what subjects and to what extent shall be mastered in order to begin studies under each of the study programmes;
   b) the volume of entrance examinations and the procedure for examination of the knowledge and skills for successful studies;
   c) the regulations for admission can also stipulate prior specific education, special suitability or preparation or meeting of other prior conditions.
3  In cases when the number of applicants exceeds the number of study places announced by the higher educational establishment, the selection of students shall be through competition.

The main forms of admission procedure in practice may be as follows:

- · 1 to 4 competitive entrance examinations;
- · a competition of diplomas and an interview by the Admission board;
- · just a competition of diplomas on the basis of grades received in subjects relevant to the programme applied to;
- · evaluation of Latvian language proficiency in these cases where the applicant's language of instruction in secondary school had not been Latvian.

The Education Act does provide for yearly tuition fees, though, for some of the students these fees are borne by the State. Grants to state-supported students range from 7.5 to 10 Lats (15-20 US dollars) per month. According to the Law on Higher Educational Establishments, a system of loans has to be established which will start operating in 1996.

### 5.14.7   Conclusion

The higher education legislation in Latvia is currently in a transition. Although the Law on Higher Educational Establishments has recently been adopted and part of the regulations have already been approved by the Cabinet of Ministers, the real implementation of the new Law will take place in the coming year.

The spirit of the Law provides that the higher educations continue to enjoy academic, freedom and autonomy. At the same time, implementation of the law will set up a quality assurance system of higher education thus making the institutions accountable for the state funding they receive. It will also allow to control the quality of private educational institutions. The real outcome of the new legislation depends very much upon the quality of the additional regulations now being creates and upon the real implementation of the Law in the coming year.

# 5.15

## LIECHTENSTEIN

### Franz Messner

### 5.15.1 The current situation

The general structure of the Liechtenstein school and educational system is characterised by the teaching traditions and school systems of the German-speaking countries. Differences exist only in the details of organisation and in the development of the system. The small size of the country prevents the State from offering a complete school and educational system within its own borders. Nevertheless, it provides funds for private schools and organisations in Liechtenstein and other countries and in this way enables Liechtenstein pupils to attend certain educational establishments. A number of treaties with foreign ministries and regional authorities ensures that places are available at schools and institutes of higher education and for vocational training.

The Education Act, which is, to a great extent still applicable, was passed by the Landtag in 1971. The innovations contained in this legislation include the reorganised structure of the school system. The State is primarily responsible for the Liechtenstein education system. According to the Constitution, all educational and instructional institutions, including private establishments, are subject to State supervision. The supreme executive organ for the entire education system is therefore the government. It ensures the application of the laws by the bodies subordinated to it and oversees the management activities of the Educational Council, the Schools Council and the Community School Council.

The Education Council is appointed by the government for a period of four years and consists of a member of the government as the chairman and eight other members. The tasks of the Education Council include counselling the government in all questions of principle concerning the educational system, especially the updating of decrees to take account of developments in the school sector, and in establishing priorities for the development of the educational system as a whole.

The financing of the state educational system is effected largely by the central government and to a lesser extent by the community authorities (50% of primary school staff costs) which are able to exercise independent financial competence within the framework of community autonomy. In some cases, the State also sponsors foreign educational establishments and meets the cost of tuition for Liechtenstein students who attend such schools. Private schools and/or private tuition must always be privately financed. Tuition at the country's state schools is always free.

## 5.15.2   Higher education

The Principality of Liechtenstein has a very limited higher education sector. Consequently it was necessary for the country to ensure that the Matura certificate was officially recognised in the neighbouring states of Switzerland and Austria. Since more than 60% of the persons from Liechtenstein gaining Matura certificate go on to an institute of higher education or university in Switzerland, the country has joined the "Intercantonal Agreement on Contributions for Institutes of Higher Education", to ensure that such students have free access to Swiss institutes of higher education and that students from cantons not possessing such facilities have the same rights as those from cantons with institutes of higher education. At the same time, a treaty was concluded with Austria concerning the mutual recognition of Matura certificates which also recognises the equivalence of Liechtenstein and Austrian students. This means that Liechtenstein students have free access to universities in Austria. An "Agreement on scientific collaboration and admission to studies" has also been signed with Baden-Württemberg for the University of Tübingen which puts candidates from Liechtenstein on an equal footing with those from Baden-Württemberg.

Only recently has Liechtenstein had a non-university higher education sector which is organised in two parts, technical colleges and institutes of higher education. The legal basis is provided by the Law on Technical Colleges, University Colleges and Research Institutes. The technical colleges include the Lichtensteinische Ingenieurschule (LIS: Liechtenstein Technical College) at Vaduz and the Interstaatliche Ingenieurschule Neu-Technikum in Buchs (NTB: Inter-State Technical College) in Switzerland whose sponsors include not only two Swiss cantons and the Austrian Federal State of Vorarlberg but also Liechtenstein. Liechtenstein Technical College offers diploma courses in parallel with employment lasting for eight terms in architecture, civil engineering, mechanical engineering and economic informatics. After four terms, students have to pass a first-part final examination. The courses end with a final examination and a thesis after eight terms. Depending on the particular course taken, graduates are awarded the title of "Dipl.-Ing. (FH)" or "Dipl.-Arch. (FH)". Technical college graduates are also offered post-graduate studies lasting three terms in process automation, ecological engineering and ecology and also a course for qualification as an industrial engineer. On successful completion of the courses, students receive a certificate of the marks awarded and a certificate issued by the "Conference of the Heads of the Swiss Technical Colleges". Students and post-graduate students of the LIS are required to follow a specific professional activity during their studies.

The fees to be paid by students currently amount to Sfr. 700.- per term for diploma students and to Sfr. 2500.- per term for post-graduate students. The qualification for technical college studies or the Vocational Matura certificate, and the qualification for studies at an institute of higher education or the General Matura certificate with specialist professional experience, are required for admission to diploma studies. The Neu-Technikum Inter-State Technical College in Buchs was founded and is sponsored by two of the Cantons of Switzerland and by the Principality of Liechtenstein. The courses offered include:

·   regular studies in electronics, process control and precision engineering in courses of three years each and;
·   post-graduate studies in medical technology, systems technology and technology and automation in courses lasting one year.

The conditions specified for admission to regular studies are a vocational secondary school or vocational school certificate in conjunction with a pass in the examination at the end of the preliminary course, the qualification for studies at an institute of higher education or the Matura certificate with evidence of practical training. Post-graduate studies are open to all mechanical or electrical engineering graduates.

The International Academy for Philosophy in Schaan offers academic studies in philosophy. The general qualification for institutes of higher education is required for admission to studies. The course consists of two parts, comprising a period of basic studies lasting four terms and a further period also lasting four terms. Each part ends with a diploma examination and a thesis must also be submitted. Graduates receive the academic title of "Magister Philosphiae" (Mag.phil). After the diploma course, graduates may study for a doctor's degree for which a doctoral thesis must be submitted. The academic degree of a "Doctor of Philosophy" is awarded on completion of this course. Fees are advanced by the Foundation Council.

# 5.16

## LITHUANIA

### Biruté Mockiené

5.16.1   The Constitution of the Republic of Lithuania provides:

Article 40: Higher education institutions are granted autonomy.
Article 41: Higher education is accessible for everybody in accordance with
a person's abilities. Advanced students of State higher education
institutions are guaranteed education free of charge.

5.16.2   The current legislative situation

The Supreme Council (Parliament, now Seimas) of the Republic of Lithuania
adopted on 12 February 1991 the Law on Research and Higher Education.
The law, on which most of the recent reforms are based upon, provides in
Article 8:

· The Science Council of Lithuania shall be an independent self-governing
institution of research and higher education. It shall be a scientific expert
to the Supreme Council and Government of the Republic of Lithuania
on issues of organising and financing research and higher education.

According to Article 10 of the law, the Council has the following enumerated
functions:
The Science Council of Lithuania:

· shall present development trends of research and assess State research
programmes;

·   shall present proposals to the Government of the Republic of Lithuania
    concerning the formation of the State draft budget;
·   shall assess the distribution of finances for research and higher education
    as well as for the maintenance, development, and establishment of the
    objects of infrastructure of research and higher education;
·   shall organise scientific evaluation of the development programmes of
    the Lithuanian economy, culture, and social sphere;
·   shall present proposals concerning the establishment, reorganisation, and
    liquidation of institutions of research and higher education;
·   shall present to the Government of the Republic of Lithuania its
    conclusions concerning the right of institutions of research and higher
    education to grant research degrees of academic (research) titles.

Article 16 provides:

·   State institutions of higher education and State research institutes shall
    have autonomy, as established by the laws of the Republic of Lithuania,
    and as approved in the statutes of the respective institutions. The State
    may regulate their activities by way of subsidies, orders (agreements)
    financed by the State, and other means provided for in the laws of the
    Republic of Lithuania.
·   The highest decision-making body of higher education institutions and
    research institutes shall be the Council (Senate), which shall be elected
    by the employees of the institution who have research degrees or
    academic (research) titles. The Council (Senate) shall elect and appoint
    the head of the institution (i.e. rector, director) and shall approve deputies
    by means of a simple majority of votes. The same person may not be
    both the head of the Council (Senate) and the head of the institution.
·   The limits of the independence of other institutions, the structure of their
    management, and the procedure for their formation shall be established
    by their statutes and the laws of the Republic of Lithuania.

### 5.16.3   The current situation in higher education and research

The Science Council of Lithuania functions according to the regulations
approved by the Seimas of the Republic of Lithuania. It presents research
trends and assesses state research programmes. It presents proposals to the

Government concerning the state draft budget, and assesses the distribution of funds for research and higher education. It organises scientific evaluation of the development programmes of the Lithuanian economy, culture, and social sphere, and presents proposals concerning the establishment, re-organisation and liquidation of institutions of research and higher education, it also submits to the Government its conclusions concerning the right of research and higher education institutions to grant research degrees or academic (research) titles.

Higher education of one, two or more stages shall be recognised in Lithuania, upon completion of which, a Bachelor's, Master's or other degree or qualification may be awarded. Qualification requirements for these degrees shall be approved by the Government of the Republic of Lithuania on the recommendation of the Science Council of Lithuania. Research degrees of Doctor or Doctor Habilitatus shall be awarded in the Republic of Lithuania. Finally, academic (research) titles of Docent and Professor can be conferred. Qualification requirements for these titles are established by the Government of the Republic. The right of the higher education and research institutions to award academic titles is granted or withdrawn by the Government, on the recommendations of the Science Council.

In recent years, the governmental entities responsible for matters concerning research and higher education have often changed. On May 31, 1994, the Seimas took a decision to establish a new Ministry of Education and Research. Up until then, the Science Council and the Lithuanian Agency for Higher Education, Research and Development were the governmental agencies responsible for the implementation of policy, and the financing and coordinating of foreign relations in research and higher education, as well as responsible for students' and scientists' exchanges, the participation in international research programmes, etc.

The Lithuanian Academy of Sciences is an institution supported by the state, in which the most prominent Lithuanian and foreign scientists collaborate. The Rectors' conference of Lithuanian Higher Education Institutions reunites the rectors of all higher education institutions. Besides the Directors' Conference of State Research Institutes, there also exists the Conference of Senate Chairmen of Research and Higher Education Institutions.

According to the Law on Research and Higher Education, state institutions of higher education are established, reorganised and terminated by the Seimas upon recommendation of the Government. Other state institutions of research and higher education are established, reorganised and terminated only by the Government. Non-state research institutions are fashioned according to the terms set by their founders.

The Regulation for the Establishment and Assessment of Institutions of Higher Education describes the procedure for initiating the establishment, for reorganisation and termination as well as for quality assessment of state and non-State institutions of higher education. These regulations do not control restructuring of institutions in accordance with their statutes.

The allocation of basic financing to state institutions of higher education and state research institutes is approved by the Government. The Funds makes allocations to competitive projects.
State financing sources for higher education, research and development are as follows:

·   basic financing of institutions (subsidies);
·   state research programmes;
·   the Lithuanian Research and Higher Education Fund.


5.16.4   The balance of power

State institutions of higher education and state research institutes have autonomy, as established by the laws of the Republic of Lithuania, and as laid down in their by-laws (statutes). These by-laws of public universities have the same legal status as the framework law that regulates the activities of the institution and must be approved by the Seimas. The by-laws of state research institutes by the Government. The by-laws (statutes) of operating institution are adopted or amended by decision of the institution's employees holding research degrees or academic titles. The statutes of any research and higher education institution must indicate the purpose its activities, its property, including lots of land transferred to its use, as well as the terms for such use, the competence of the Council (Senate) and governing bodies, their structure, and procedure.

The number of enrolments is fixed by the higher education institution which applies a numerus clausus. Persons holding a secondary school diploma or certificate, or an equivalent document, may gain admittance to a higher education institution. Each institution announces its admission procedures and requirements. Additionally, the Ministry of Education and Science publishes a comprehensive booklet "Let's Study in Lithuania". The head of the admission committee is the rector or vice rector, Deans and other faculty representatives are members.

Upon completion of basic studies, a Bachelor's degree, an equivalent qualification and/or professional qualification is awarded, depending on the study programme. Upon completion of basic studies, a Master's course (1.5-2 years) of specialised professional studies may be pursued. Upon completion of specialised professional studies, a professional qualification is awarded. Studies must meet the requirements related to the structure of the content, volume of studies, academic potential and material basis of the higher education institution. The teaching activities of the higher education institution should correspond to the requirements of the Qualitative Regulation for Higher Education.

According to the Regulations for the Establishment and Assessment of Institutions of Higher Education approved by the Government, each institution of higher education should organise continuous self-analysis and self-assessment. Assessment focuses on the study programmes, the methods of instruction, the facilities, and the educational and informational technology. Self-analysis and self-assessment also takes into account the aptitude of academic staff, the material and financial resources of the higher education institution, the research (creative) activities and their conformity with the unity of higher education and research. Last but not least, the institutions shall propose means and ways to maintain an appropriate level of higher education.

The Lithuanian Centre for Quality Assessment in Higher Education was established in January, 1995. The main tasks of the Centre are the following:

· co-ordination and methodological guidance of the regular process of self-analysis;
· organisation of the expert assessment of higher education institutions;

·   informing and counselling on all matters related to the recognition of
    higher education.


### 5.16.5   Conclusion

Establishing a harmonious relationship between higher education institutions
and the State while seeking academic quality under circumstances of serious
budgetary constraints is one of the most pressing issues in Lithuania. The
necessity of defining autonomy of higher education institutions, as well as
establishing exclusive opportunities to finance them, is an equally acute
problem. The statutes of higher education institutions must be endorsed and
their contents should be specified as well. The problems of loans and other
support for students also need to be addressed. Due to the lack of full state
financing, an arrangement for both fully paid and partially paid studies must
be found in the near future.

# 5.17

## MALTA

### *Paul Heywood*

#### 5.17.1  The current legislative situation

After a change of government in 1987, a completely new Education Act
No XXIV of 1988 was passed. The Act was hotly debated in Parliament
which had to hold morning and afternoon sessions for four days in order
to meet the deadline set. It was intended to reform the concept of education
in Malta and introduced a number of innovations in the university set-up.
The new law restored the faculties of Arts and Sciences and made it possible
for government and the Holy Sea to transfer the Faculty of Theology to the
University of Malta. The new law discarded the worker-student scheme and
the system of entry into the university imposed by the 1978 and 1980
amendments to the 1974 Education Act. All students in possession of the
academic qualifications required for entry into the course of their choice
were admitted into the university. Moreover the same law gave greater
academic autonomy to the University of Malta in the formulation and approval of statutes, regulations and bye-Laws. Complete autonomy was
introduced in the administration of its funds, the provision of courses, the
appointment of staff and in the work of its various boards.

#### 5.17.2  The balance of power

In the context of increased measure of autonomy article 29 is of special
interest in so far as the financing and control of the assets of the University
of Malta are concerned.

1   The Government shall allocate annually to the University such a sum
    of money as is voted by the House of Representatives in the General
    Estimates to enable the University to attain the aims for which it was
    founded and refounded and to carry out its activities according to the
    needs of the country as perceived by the Government.

2   The sum voted in accordance with subsection (1) of this section shall
    be paid to the University in equal instalments in advance but the
    Government may at the same time impose a gradual rate of spending
    and may also indicate the limits of future recurrent expenditure in the
    two following years.

3   The Government shall also allocate to the University such capital sums
    as are voted by the House of Representatives for the implementation
    of particular projects. Provided that in the approval of a particular project
    the Government may phase the payment of capital sums by yearly
    amounts but such phasing shall not of itself bind the Government to
    allocate the sum indicated for later years.

4   The University shall provide each year detailed estimates with its
    proposals for expenditure for the following year as well as a detailed
    statement of expenditure for the last completed financial year.

5   Without prejudice to the right of the University to administer, in the
    freest possible manner, money and property received from sources other
    than the government, the Minister of Finance may instruct auditors to
    examine the books and accounts of the University and submit a report
    to him.

Another way in which it is ensured that the university responds to the needs
of the country as perceived by the government is through a majority of
members in the Council (the highest governing body of the University)
nominated by the Prime Minister. In point of fact, these members are mainly
appointed from the academic staff.

A significant innovation in the 1988 Education Act concerns the chancellorship of the university. No longer is it vested in the Presidency of the
Republic of Malta. The chancellor is appointed for seven years by the

President of the Republic acting on the advice of the prime minister after consultation with the leader of the opposition.

Furthermore, the principal posts of the university have now been made tenable for definite terms. The pro-chancellor is appointed by the chancellor for a term not exceeding five years. The rector is elected by the Council for a term of five years; the pro-rector is appointed by the rector for one year; while the secretary of the university (a new administrative post) is appointed by the Council for five years. The deans of faculties are elected by the academic staff of their respective faculties for a term of four years.

The new law also strengthens student representation on all the university governing and academic bodies, including Faculty Boards, Senate and Council.

The 1988 Act confirmed the policy of providing education right up to and through university free of charge, the relevant article being 41 (1): "In State Schools and the University all teaching shall be given to Maltese Citizens without any fee being charged. So as to ensure the full exercise of choice of school by parents the State shall, through agreements of subvention of non-state schools, when such are of a non profit-making character, in accordance with the availability of public funds, provide gradually for the same gratuity of teaching in such schools as is afforded to students in State schools." This provision issues from the rights enunciated in Articles 3 and 4 of the same law:

Article 3:

"It is the right of every citizen of the Republic of Malta to receive education and instruction without any distinction of age, sex, belief or economic means."

Article 4:

"It is the duty of the State:

a) to promote education and instruction;

b) to ensure the existence of a system of schools and institutions accessible to all Maltese citizens catering for the full development of the whole personality including the ability of every person to work and
c) to provide for such schools and institutions where these do not exist."

Until 1987 students received salaries from their employers. The Worker-Students scheme was then wound down and a new system of grants was introduced to ensure that all qualified candidates irrespective of their means were financially assisted by the State. Through this measure the new government implemented the electoral promises of giving higher education the importance it deserved.

As a community-oriented institution with a long history of social and political commitment, the University of Malta patronises and promotes culture for its inmates and the community. In this context, it is important to bear in mind the exceptional growth in the student population since the enactment of the current law. In February 1987, the student intake was less than 300; a few months later the university removed all restrictions to entry and increased the October intake by 550 fully qualified students. This trend continued and with the introduction of new courses and improved conditions yearly entry has now exceeded 2000. In fact whereas the student population in the early months of 1987 stood at 1400, the present figure tops 6000.

The new campus ushered in a period of steady growth in which the University of Malta enhanced its intellectual and social standing. It must be borne in mind that it is the one and only institution of higher learning on the island. This exclusiveness engenders a special relationship with the civil authorities, who cannot but view its operations within the framework of a definite economic and political strategy. The fact that in such a context, the university has enjoyed complete academic and financial autonomy redounds to the credit of both parties. It is in the nature of things that, as long as the university continues to rely heavily on government funds, certain tensions should arise. Different visual angles do not readily blend into a stereoscopic prospect. In seeking the common good both parties have, however, to make the best use of the limited national resources available.

During the last eight years, the University of Malta has been living through a busy period of restructuring after a longish spell of adversity and stress in order to cope with a rapid and exciting spurt of growth.

Students:
· to adapt its structures in order to be able to accommodate up to 20% of the 17 year old age cohort of the Maltese population by increases of about 2% per annum, a process involving measures of administrative decentralisation;
· to increase high-quality foreign student enrolment both for residential and short-term courses and in the distance-learning mode.

Research:
· to develop centres of excellence in determined areas of specialisation, mostly of an interdisciplinary nature, primarily through its Institutes and analogous entities;
· by the same institutional means, to strengthen cooperation with both public and private sector bodies.

Teaching:
· to develop post-graduate study and lifelong education opportunities in all sectors where they do not yet exist;
· to consolidate its assumption of increased provision for diploma and certificate level teaching related to its degree courses, especially in the paramedical, technological and management areas.

General:
· to establish systems to ensure continuous staff development and appraisal of progress;
· to develop its Mediterranean humanist tradition and adapt curricula in the perspective of full participation in the Community of European Universities.

## 5.17.3   Conclusion

The objectives set out in the structure plan harmonise with the government's policy of investing heavily in tertiary education to ensure that the university provides enough flexible professional manpower essential to economic, industrial and commercial growth. Finally, the following comment on the university by the rector sums up current developments: "It has converted itself from an elite to a mass higher educational institution. It is adapting itself to a society in transformation towards the post-industrial condition in which knowledge-workers are fast replacing factory-workers as the leading elements of society. The university has, in fact, rapidly become a multipurpose amalgam of diversely working units with multifarious functions and numerous missions."

# 5.18

## MOLDOVA

## *Petru Gaugaç*

5.18.1   The current legislative situation

The Independence Declaration of the Republic of Moldova (27 August 1991)
gave a powerful incentive to the process of democratisation in the society
and its transition to a market economy. The social, economic and political
changes stipulated a new approach to education, and a reconsideration of
its basic principles. All this necessitated a reform in the system of education,
and the creation of new types of educational institutions, based on the
principles of a harmonious combination of the national, cultural heritage
and the human values common to all mankind, taking into account the social
and economic demands of the country. The idea of new approaches to
education was the focus of the Conception of Education worked out by the
Institute of Pedagogy and Psychology and the Ministry of Education (1990).
It was included into the Law of Education adopted by the Parliament of
Moldova in the first reading (November 1992).

According to the Law the main principles of education are the following:

·   the democratisation and personalisation of education, its accessibility
    in accordance with the students' aptitudes and abilities;
·   diversity of educational institutions, the coexistence of a state system
    of education with different forms of education, including private
    educational institutions;
·   the students' needs and requirements should be the focus of attention.

Unfortunately the Law was not considered by the parliament in the second reading because of the disagreement caused by the discussion of the articles on the language of instruction and education of national minorities.

A new team came to the Ministry of Education. It proceeded with the work on the Conception of Education, which was to be changed in accordance with the current changes in the Republic of Moldova and the experience accumulated during the last few years. The Conception also takes into account the regulations of the new Constitution of the Republic of Moldova adopted in July 1994. The objectives of education have been reconsidered, and the strategic directions of educational development have been elaborated. The integration of the national system of education with the European one has become of primary importance. The new reconsidered Conception was discussed and approved by pedagogues, and was adopted by the Parliament of Moldova in December 1994 and taken as the basis for the new Law of Education adopted in July 1995.

At present the mechanism of putting the regulations of the Law of Education into practice is being elaborated, it will find its reflection in the national programme of education development. Alongside the Law of Education a set of other laws, legislative acts are supposed to be elaborated which must constitute the juridical basis of the education system. Among them there will be the Law of Science and Higher Education, a regulation on pedagogical staff, and the Law of the Vocational Education. In the absence of a new Law of Education, the system of education functioned and developed according to the old Soviet Law of Education, the Presidential Decrees, the decisions of the Parliament, and the government's provisions concerning education. New types of educational institutions, gymnasiums, lyceums, and colleges were opened according to their decisions, which are now stipulated by the new Law of Education. In 1993 there were 1877 preschool institutions, 1496 institutions providing secondary education (including more than 45 lyceums), 78 vocational schools, 48 colleges, 18 higher educational institutions (there were only 9 of them in 1990) while the total number of students equalled 741,200 (the population of Moldova was 4,352,700).

According to the new law of Education there are two types of higher education: long-term or university education provided in universities, academies, institutes and short-term (2-3 years) higher education provided in university colleges. Long-term higher education consists of a basic university education (4-6 years) that leads to the "licentiate" diploma and a specialised university education (1,5-2 years), leading to the "magistru" diploma. Higher education institutions can obtain autonomous university status after accreditation according to the respective rules. Higher pedagogical education functions as a rule in the form of a long-term higher education, destined mainly for pedagogical lyceum graduates.

Short-term higher education is completed by a graduation exam, on the results of which graduates are awarded diplomas certifying higher education. Pre-primary and primary school teachers are trained for 4 years in teacher-training colleges, a short cycle higher education level. Lower-secondary level education (gymnasiums) teachers are trained for 5 years in universities. Upper-secondary level education (lyceum) and higher education teachers are trained in 5 to 6 universities, polytechnics, academies, and institutes.

The admission to higher education institutions is carried out through competitive entrance examinations both on the basis of "Diploma de Baccalaureate" (Baccalaureate/Diploma) and the "Diploma de studii medii" (Matriculation certificate), official documents certifying that the holder has completed upper secondary education (lyceum).

At present the system of higher education includes 4 non-state institutions. About 9,660 students were admitted to the state and approximately 1,200 students to non-state higher educational institutions in 1994. They will be trained in 140 different specialities. Parallel training in two specialities is possible.

A new element in the higher education system has emerged with a market economy: about 20% of the full-time students and about 50% of the extramural students are admitted to state institutions on a contact basis, paying for their education.

The main purpose of higher education is to ensure the training of highly qualified specialists in all spheres of activity. Higher education is integrated with scientific research.

The Ministry of Education is responsible for 8 state higher education institutions, the others come under the responsibility of the Ministry of Agriculture, Ministry of Culture, Ministry of Internal Affairs, and Ministry of Health. All state higher education institutions are financed through the government. Decisions about the allocation of funds are made by the ministry responsible for the corresponding higher education institution.

The institution of higher education comprise faculties and sections. A faculty has a number of departments (catedre).

The languages of instruction are Romanian and Russian. Beginning with the 1991/92 academic year studies at university level may be followed in Ukrainian. Doctorate studies can be followed in Romanian or Russian.

Higher education institutions offer courses lasting 4-6 years according to the subject chosen to study:

·   technical, economic and agronomic sciences – 5 years duration;
·   university studies (exact and natural sciences, law and human sciences) - 5 years duration;
·   medical education: general medicine – 6 years duration, stomatology – 5 years duration; pharmacy 5 years duration;
·   music – 5 years duration; arts – 6 years duration;
·   theatre – 4/5 years duration;
·   physical education and sports – 4 years duration.

All the graduate programmes may be attended by full-time students. Extramural higher education is organised in some subject areas (engineering, building, economics, humanities, agronomy and sports), and evening courses in engineering. Extramural and evening courses,as a rule, last a year longer than the regular courses.

Upon completion of a full course of study, the students sit a final examination (Examen de diploma), including a diploma (project) and thesis (Lucrare-proiect de diploma), proposed by the departments of higher education institutions. The thesis is produced under the supervision of a teacher and is defended in public. The diplomas granted on graduation from higher education institutions are at Bachelor level. Post-graduate training is realised through a doctorate. Access to a doctorate is based on a competitive entrance examination.

A doctorate can be followed either in full time courses (3 years duration) or in extramural courses (4 years duration). The diploma awarded after 3-4 years of study is "Diploma de Doctor". Doctorate activities follow a specific study plan (Plan de activitate individuala) with courses, scientific papers, examinations and a preparation of a doctoral thesis (Teza de doctorat), which is a scientific work containing a new solution or approach to an important scientific problem. The examination consists of a public defense of the doctoral thesis. The name of the degree is "Doctor of ...". It is the first scientific degree at the highest level and is conferred in all branches of science and it is comparable in type and orientation to doctoral degrees in other west European countries. A doctoral degree is mandatory for an assistant professor and a professor. The name of the second scientific degree at the highest level is "Doctor habilitate of ...". This degree is conferred after public support of the doctoral thesis.

As a rule, students from other countries can be accepted to study in Moldova either on their own account or on a basis of bilateral agreements between Moldova and the respective country.

Foreign students begin their studies in Moldova with a preparatory year in order to learn Romanian or Russian. The Republic of Moldova is collaborating in the field of education and science on a contract basis with Romania, Ukraine, Bulgaria, the Russian Federation, Turkey and Azerbaidjan. Under current contracts about 1,200 students and more than 300 post-graduate students from Moldova begin their studies abroad every year. Under similar contracts foreigners study in higher education institutions in Moldova. This kind of activity is supposed to be extended.

# 5.19

## THE NETHERLANDS

### Ernst Hirsch-Ballin

5.19.1    Section 23 of the Constitution provides:

1    Education shall be the constant concern of the Government.

2    All persons shall be free to provide education, without prejudice to the authorities' right of supervision and, with regard to forms of education designated by act of parliament its right to examine the competence and moral integrity of teachers, to be regulated by act of parliament.

3    Education provided by public authorities shall be regulated by act of parliament, paying due respect to everyone's religion or belief.

4    The authorities shall ensure that primary education is provided in a sufficient number of public-authority schools in every municipality. Deviations from this provision may be permitted under rules to be established by act of parliament on condition that there is opportunity to receive the said form of education.

5    The standards required of schools financed either in part or in full from public funds shall be regulated by the parliament, with due regard, in the case of denominational school, to the freedom to provide education according to religious or other belief.

6    The requirements for primary education shall be such that the standards both of denominational schools fully financed from public funds and of public-authority schools are fully guaranteed. The relevant provisions shall respect in particular the freedom of the denominational schools to choose their teaching aids and to appoint teachers as they see fit.

7    Denominational primary schools that satisfy the conditions laid down in an act of parliament shall be financed from public funds according to the same standards as public-authority schools. The conditions under

which denominational secondary education shall receive contributions from public funds shall be laid down by act of parliament.

8   The Government shall submit annual reports on the state of education to the States General.

## 5.19.2   The current legislative situation

A crucial statutory provision referring to (higher) education in the Higher Education and Research Act 1992 is section 1.3: Universities, hogescholen and the Open University:

1   The universities shall be responsible for providing education and performing research. They shall in any event provide initial education programmes, conduct research, provide training for researchers and design engineers and transfer knowledge for the benefit of the community.

2   The hogescholen shall be responsible for providing higher professional education. They may conduct research connected with their teaching. In any event they shall provide initial education programmes and transfer knowledge for the benefit of the community. They shall contribute to the development of those occupations to which teaching in the institution is geared.

3   The Open University shall be responsible for providing university and higher professional education. It shall in any event provide initial education programmes in the form of distance education.

4   The universities, hogescholen and Open University shall pay attention inter alia to personal development of their students and nurture in them a sense of social responsibility. Their teaching activities shall include improving the powers of expression in Dutch of Dutch-speaking students.

Section 1.6: Academic freedom, provides:

Academic freedom shall be respected within the institutions.

Two acts are relevant. On 1 August 1993, the Higher Education and Research Act (Wet op het hoger onderwijs en wetenschappelijk onderzoek, 1992) came into force. This act regulates higher education, teaching hospitals and academic research in the Netherlands and has replaced a large number of acts and regulations concerning higher education and research. The new act does not contain any provision concerning the freedom or principle of autonomy of the institutions. The public universities and some public hogescholen, however, are to be considered as independent corporations according to private law. Furthermore, because of its non-participatory design and the creation of a limited number of government powers, the act renders substantial autonomy to the institutions in the field of higher education.

Since 1 October 1986, the Student Grant and Loan Act (Wet op de Studiefinanciering, 1986) has been in operation. According to this act, every student from the age of 18 has a claim on a state grant and loan during his/her stay at a recognised higher education institution. In its ten year existence, this act has been altered many times because of economy considerations.

*Constitutional rules and principles*

Hogescholen and universities perform functions of education and research in a different way. They have two 'freedoms' of importance: the freedom of education, which is guaranteed in the Constitution and the freedom of science, which is not explicitly guaranteed in the Constitution.

Freedom of education was intended for legal bodies holding private institutions and implies independence from government in internal matters. As a principle; it is not dominant in the higher education field. This fundamental right cannot, for instance, be the basis of teacher freedom within the institutions. It is the basis of the regulation of higher education in an act of parliament and the government's obligation of funding and equal treatment of public and private institutions.

Freedom of science is a composition of guaranteed fundamental rights in the Dutch Constitution, concerning the freedom of information and of speech, academic freedom (statute law) and the right to education. This freedom, which has been shaped in the long tradition of academic life within the universities, is the basis of the prohibition of government interference with education and research in institutions. It is also the basis of functional independence of the public institutions.

*Legal protection*

There is judicial review of government decisions, according to the rules of
the Algemene Wet Bestuursrecht (General Act on Administrative Law). This
law eventually leads to access to an independent administrative court.
Judicial review of an act or decision of one institution by another has been
set up according to the rules of the Burgerlijk Wetboek (the Civil Code),
which eventually leads to access to the civil court.

*Private and public higher education*

There are 63 hogescholen and 13 universities, financed by the State. Three
universities are universities of technology. There is one Agricultural University and one Open University that offers mainly written courses. A distinction
has to made in the field of publicly funded higher education between public
and private education. Public education originates with the government
(national or municipal); private education originates with private organisations. The majority of the hogescholen, 58 out of a total of 63, are
private. Most of the universities, 10 out of total of 13, are public. Of two
private universities one has a Catholic, and one a Protestant basis. Private
education is funded, subject to certain conditions, on the same basis as public
education, in keeping with the Constitution. In practice, this means that the
same rules apply to private and public institutions alike. The difference
between public and private education is apparent in statutory provisions,
concerning regulation of the organisation and administration of institutions,
and the special nature of private organisations, that have to be taken into
account by the Inspectorate of Education when carrying out quality assurance
and quality control activities.

There are 8 approved university level institutions, 3 Protestant and 3 Catholic
theological universities, a university for humanist studies and Nijenrode
University for business administration. There are 30 approved hogescholen
in the fields of health care, interpretation and translation, ballet, theology,
technic, journalism etc. Approved institutions provide study programmes
which lead to the award of diplomas equivalent to those awarded by the
publicly funded institutions. Students of these institutions qualify for student
grants and loans.

*The binary system*

Higher education has two functions, that shall be intrinsically and institutionally separated. Academic education is given at universities; higher professional education at hogescholen. Mergers between universities and hogescholen are prohibited. Furthermore, a university is not allowed to offer higher professional education nor a hogeschool to offer academic education. The reasons for the prohibition of mergers and mixtures are mainly practical:

- Given the short period of study, students should be offered a clear perspective of the study programme as a form of higher education. The annulation of the differences between the missions of universities and hogescholen is not in the interest of such a clear perspective.
- The principal role and mission of universities is not in discussion. In comparison with universities, the hogescholen have their own identity. They came into being in order to meet the practical needs of the labour market and professional world. Among themselves, hogescholen are by nature more diverse than universities, as far as character and quality of the education are concerned.

However, the maintaining of the difference between academic and higher professional education is, although statutorily ordered, not always easy; many study programmes offered by universities lead to a specific profession. The majority of these programmes have been developed in the past decade, in which universities and hogescholen have become competitors in a decreasing student market. At the same time, the existence of the 'mass university' has initiated discussions about the true nature of academic studies and about the present ability of universities to realise 'academic thinking' and 'academic behaviour', whatever they may be.

According to their statutory terms of reference, all institutions are in charge of education and research, but only the research at universities shall be funded by the government. This funding takes place on a basis of independent examinations of research programmes and research results.

The Open University has an unique position in the system. It provides academic as well as higher professional education in the form of written courses.

### 5.19.3   The balance of power

The present act on higher education is, without explicitly providing for it, based on the principle of autonomy of institutions. Autonomy means that the universities and hogescholen are free to decide which study programmes they will offer. The introduction of a new study programme, however, is subject to the condition that the institutions take into account quality requirements, labour market requirements and efficiency requirements at a macro-economic level. All higher education programmes have to be registered in a special public register. Registration is a condition for the allocation of funds and for the right to award a certificate carrying an academic title. It is also one of the conditions which have to be met for the award of student grants and loans. New study programmes can only be registered when they have been submitted to a central advisory committee. On the basis of the committee's examination, the Minister of Education and Science can withhold the legal rights resulting from registration, if the above mentioned quality and efficiency conditions are not fulfilled.

The institutions are free to spend the government's subsidy, within their mission. They are also free to peruse their own policy concerning conditions of employment and personnel. The policy concerning the duration of employment, wages and social security remains a responsibility of the central government.

The internal organisation of the institutions is based on statutory provisions that stem from the early seventies. The appearance of detailed provisions that regulate the relationships within the institutions is contradictory to the philosophy and steering principles of the Higher Education and Research Act. Therefore, the government has held out the prospect of globalisation and change of these statutory provisions in two draft laws: on university and hogeschool governance.

*Accessibility*

Everyone is entitled to enrol in higher education provided he has the necessary educational qualifications. However, access to study programmes may be restricted in three cases: if the institutional teaching capacity is full, the nation-wide teaching capacity is full, or there is an adverse structural situation in a specific labour market. Restriction is made through a ministerial decision and should be seen as an exception to the rule of free access.

On grounds related to their constitutional freedom, private institutions have a right to refuse or cancel enrolment to students if there are well-founded fears that the person concerned will misuse the fact of his enrolment and the rights attached to it by seriously undermining the special nature of the instruction, or if it is discovered that the person concerned has indeed misused the fact of his enrolment and the rights attached to it. These situations hardly ever occur.

At the end of the first year of enrolment, the administration of the university or hogeschool shall advise him on whether to continue with his study programme or choose another. The administration may decide to send a student down if he has not yet completed his first year and, with due regard to his personal circumstances, cannot be regarded as suited to the study programme, because his results do not meet the requirements.

The maximum period of enrolment for full time students is 6 years with the exception of students enrolled in long programmes, such as medicine and theology. For part-time students, it is 9 years. Upon enrolment there is a statutory fixed tuition fee to be payed of nearly 3,000 guilders per year for full-time students and nearly 2,000 guilders for part-time students (situation as of September 1995). In a case when a student does not finish his studies within the period of enrolment, he or she can only be enrolled as an auditor and has to pay a much higher tuition fee.

People of the Dutch nationality and certain foreign inhabitants who want to study at a university or hogeschool can claim a student grant (and loan) from the State for a maximum of 5 years. After this period, which is the maximum in normal cases, they can have a state loan for a maximum of 2 years. Over the past few years the amount of the student grant has decreased gradually.

*Planning, accountability and funding*

The planning of higher education and research is a dynamic process. Facilities are primarily provided in keeping with the intentions of the institutions. These intentions are influenced by the policy of the government as set out in a planning document published every two years: the Higher Education and Research Plan (HOOP). The Minister discusses the draft HOOP with all the institutions of education and research jointly. Before the final version of the plan is adopted, the Minister also consults the Lower House of Parliament.

The institutions submit a report, consisting of an annual report, budget, annual accounts and other financial data, to the Minister every year. The annual report as a whole, together with the institution's budget, should show how well the institute has performed the activities financed by the state and how efficiently the subsidy has been spent. The annual accounts are audited by chartered accountants, and the Minister may ask to inspect their audit reports. The Minister may also instruct the ministry accountant to audit the efficiency with which the institution has been managed.

The size of the state grant is based on a yearly budget and is fixed by the Minister for each institution. The teaching component is calculated on a basis of the number of students and the number of diplomas awarded. In the case of research funds for the universities the government takes into account the profile of the institution and the quality of the research. It is possible that the government may have additional wishes concerning the allocation of funds among the various disciplines in the light of the social relevance of research.

*Curricula*

Every student programme begins with a propaedeutic – preliminary – year (for full-time students) that usually ends with an examination. The objectives of the propaedeutic part are referral, selection and 'insight into the content of the study programme'. After this year, study programme normally lasts another 3 years. The study load for a normal study programme may comprise up to 168 credits; one credit stands for 40 hours study; one year holds 42 credits. Study programmes lasting longer than 4 years are explicitly mentioned in the Higher Education and Research Act. At the moment, there are initiatives to legally guarantee a longer duration than 4 years for the technical study programmes within the universities of technology.

### 5.19.4   Quality assurance and quality control

*Self-regulation*

The institutions are deemed to be self-regulating as far as quality control is concerned. They are free to decide what form quality control should take as long as they adhere to the statutory requirements regarding procedure; there are no uniform requirements concerning content. The system of quality assurance and control incorporates quality exercised by the institutions as well as internal quality assurance. The former is carried out by review committees set up by the institutions and consisting of independent Dutch and foreign experts. The opinion of students on the quality of teaching at the institution they attend is taken into account in the quality control procedure. Since the committees' reports are made public, this puts indirect pressure on institutions to make changes if their standards are too low.

*The role of the Inspectorate of Education*

The Inspectorate's main task is meta-evaluation, that is monitoring the quality of the quality control systems set up individually and jointly by the institutions. It may also carry out complementary evaluation activities of its own in order to assess quality directly, and may appoint a committee of independent experts for this purpose, similar to a review committee set by the institutions. The Inspectorate may also appoint committees as part of its normal work as a supervisory body, or the Minister may instruct the Inspectorate to do so, should he require further information about quality or quality control activities for policy-related purposes.

*Procedure*

The timetable for quality control activities is as follows: internal evaluation should take place every year, whereas an integral survey by a review committee is conducted once every five to six years. If it proves necessary to do otherwise, the reasons can be stated in the institution's annual report. If an internal or external assessment indicates that quality is poor in the areas on which an institution is active, it is assumed that steps will be taken by the institution to improve. Whether quality improves as a result will be revealed by the revised quality assessment by the institution, supplemented if necessary by a further inspection by the Inspectorate. If an institution does not take sufficient measures of its own accord, the Inspectorate, or the Minister acting through the Inspectorate, is free at all times to intensify supervision. There are several remedial measures, ranging from consultation and the issuing of a warning to, as a last resort, withdrawing funding and the effectus civilis from study programmes.

The Minister has no say in the content of quality criteria. Each institution sets out its method of operation in its annual report, effectively justifying its actions. The work of the review committees will have to be organised in such a way as to permit comparison between study programmes in both the short- and the long-term. Although the methods used may differ from one institution to another, the procedural requirements are expected to facilitate comparison.

5.19.5   Developments and recent discussions

The mass nature of higher education has brought the Netherlands large universities and hogescholen that enrol many students, employ many staff and possess a wealth of material goods. In 1960 there were 106,200 higher education students. This number has grown to 418,100 in 1994: 257,300 students at hogescholen and 160,800 at universities. According to the law, all institutions are 100% funded by the government. In practice, the universities earn some 20% of their income by contract activities, an amount of 1 milliard guilders. Furthermore, many of the hogescholen are entering the market. At the moment it is clear that the Netherlands cannot afford a higher education system at the size it had in the 1970s or even the 1980s for much longer. In the struggle to keep up the basics of a western welfare state, higher education is not the most important item on the political agenda nowadays. During the last few decades, the relationship between the size of funding and the numbers of students has become a problem. Over the same period, the financial contributions of students to higher education have risen substantially. The decreasing dependency on government funding makes it possible but also necessary for institutions to have substantial freedom in operating in society and fulfilling the essential tasks. No one argues about the principle of freedom but about the extent to which the institutions are considered capable of doing their job, or the extent to which the government has to withdraw from the field. In the Higher Education and Research Act of 1992 some essential choices have been made in this respect.

In its coalition agreement of 1994, the present cabinet has announced measures to fundamentally reform the Dutch higher education system. The argument put forward for these plans is the necessity for serious budget cuts in the subsidies of the institutions and the student grant system. Soon after publication of the coalition agreement, a heated discussion about the future role of Dutch higher education started between the government, the institutions and students. The following problems are considered serious:

·   The duration of study programmes at hogescholen and universities can be differentiated: some should have the legal length of a maximum of 5 years (e.g. the technical studies at the universities of technology), some 4 years and some 3 years (e.g. some study programmes at hogescholen).
·   The system is rigid, considering the demands of a modern technological society and the requirements of the labour market. Higher education should gain a qualitatively higher standing and be divided into more flexible learning routes.
·   The right to education is not sufficiently optimalised; programme "study-ability" (studeerbaarheid) needs to be improved. That means that universities should pay more attention to teaching in relation to research-activities.
·   The internal organisation of universities is not equipped for the purpose of creating powerful and decisive institutions. The democratically composed 'collectivities' should disappear and a more hierarchical structure, where the centralising aspects of the institutions get more power, should be worked out in new legal provisions.

5.19.6   Conclusion

The structure of the Dutch educational system has been set up by public law and is laid down in the Higher Education and Research Act of 1992. This act renders autonomy to the institutions and is the basis of a stable relationship between the institutions and the government. The stability of the system, however, appears not to be in proper balance with requirements of flexibility stemming from economic and social demands. The objective of the act of 1992 to increase flexibility by introducing steering-principles of market orientation in higher education policy, has not yet been achieved. The institutions are still mainly government orientated: they have not succeeded in acting fully as market parties. The consequence is that the Minister of Education, Culture and Science makes the most important choices, choices that should be the responsibility of the autonomous institutions. In the given circumstances one can imagine why the promises of the Higher Education and Research Act of 1992 have not yet come true. Nowadays, it is extremely difficult for the institutions to know where they stand in their relation to government. Successive and severe budget-cuts, forced mergers between hogescholen and the introduction of a one-sided blueprint in the coalition agreement of 1994 for a fundamentally reorganised higher education system, prevent hazardous behaviour in a market-setting. The incertitude concerning the government's plans and acts drives the institutions from each other and into the arms of that same government.

Functional autonomy of the institutions is an important condition in the public interest for a sound development of education and research, which meet the needs of a pluriform and European society. It implies a basis of mutual trust between the institutions and government. It also implies the government's sense of principle and practical aloofness in the relationship with the institutions.

# 5.20

## NORWAY

### Rolf Kåre Jenssen

5.20.1   The current legislative situation

The Norwegian system of higher education consists primarily of universities, specialised colleges at university level and a number of state colleges (former regional colleges). There are four universities. They are state institutions which have traditionally enjoyed a considerably degree of autonomy. Their autonomy has been widened with the adoption of the Act on Universities and University Colleges of 16 June 1989, put into effect on 1 January 1990. The universities are the University of Oslo – the only university until the end of World War II and still the largest, and the Universities of Bergen, Trondheim and Tromsø.

Although the institutions cover most of the traditional fields of study, with some exceptions for the University of Tromsø, there is some tendency towards specialisation. The University of Trondheim is the central institution for technology, whereas the University of Tromsø has special educational and scientific commitments to studies related to northern Norway.

In addition to the four universities there are six specialised colleges at university level:

·   the Agricultural College of Norway;
·   the Norwegian College of Veterinary Medicine;
·   the Norwegian College of Economics and Business Administration;
·   the Norwegian College of Physical Education & Sport;

·   the State Academy of Music;
·   the Oslo School of Architecture.

The universities and specialised university colleges are represented in the National Council of Universities which has been established to coordinate the activities of the institutions and to contribute to a national policy on higher education. The State Colleges are organised in The National Council of State Colleges.

The universities offer degree programmes at two levels in arts, social sciences and mathematics and natural sciences. The lower level university degree, cand. mag., which is normally obtained after 3,5 to 4 years of study, and the higher level university degree, cand. philol. (humanities), cand. scient. (maths and natural sciences), cand. polit. (social sciences), which generally requires two additional years of study. Currently, the majority of students acquiring the lower level degree continue their studies up to completion of the graduate degree.

The growth and development of the colleges at regional level are closely related to the government policy which has regarded higher education as an important contributor to the economic, social and political life of the regions. The colleges at regional level play an important role in the decentralisation of higher education in Norway, and they have a strong commitment to serve their respective regions. Until now, the most important categories have been the regional colleges of higher education (distriktshøgskoler), colleges of education, colleges of engineering, colleges of nursing, colleges of social work, conservatories of music etc. As a result of Network Norway and the reorganisation of the regional colleges, the number of institutions, in 1994, had been reduced from around 100 to 26.

Research is mainly concentrated in the universities and other institutions at university level. Gradually most of the institutions in the regional system have also developed research activities, often connected to specific problems of the region concerned. Regional research foundations have grown up with links to regional colleges and their boards.

In Norway all teacher training for primary and secondary schools is regulated by the Training of Teachers Act of 8 June 1973, effective from January

1975. According to the Act, teacher training shall comprise both initial and further (post-graduate) training. There are three levels of educational qualification for all categories of teachers (lærer, adjunkt, and lektor), the titles being awarded on the basis of respectively 3-4, 4 and 6-7 years of training. The two latter titles may be compared with B.A. and M.A. degrees.

To assist the Ministry of Education in matters related to teacher training there is a National Council for Teacher Education which has mainly an advisory function.

The majority of the candidates at B.A. and M.A. level receive their academic education at one of the 4 universities, and their practical teacher training in subsequent courses lasting one year. The practical courses are organised by specialised institutions, which are part of each university, and by some colleges of education. One of the colleges has a department which is solely devoted to teacher education and practical training for vocational teachers and also provides courses at B.A. and M.A. level in vocational pedagogy. The models for teacher education in Norway are:

·   4 years' consecutive study of general subjects (class teachers at primary and secondary level;
·   3 years' consecutive study of general subjects (pre-school teachers);
·   3 years' consecutive study for specialist subject teachers, e.g. teachers of arts & crafts, teachers of commercial subjects, teachers of home economics (nutrition, health and environmental subjects);
·   decentralised study for teachers of general subjects or specialist subjects;
·   professional competence as an artist with an additional 1 year practical and didactic training;
·   lower or higher university or college degree (B.A. or M.A.) and 1 year of practical and didactic training;
·   certificate of professional competence, theoretical vocational training and practical experience and 1/2 year practical & didactic training.

Education is given high priority within public activities in Norway. Out of the total population of 4.2 million nearly 900,000 are predominantly occupied with education. In addition, around 700,000 annually participate in adult education courses. The number of pupils or students in the various sectors in 1993-94 were as follows:

| | |
|---|---|
| Compulsory education | 470.000 |
| Upper secondary education | 210.000 |
| Higher education | 160.000 |
| Adult education | 700.000 |
| Private schools (age 7-19) | 16.300 |

The number of students in higher education has increased by more than 60% over the last couple of years, i.e. from about 100.000 in 1988 to 160.000 in 1993. The high priority given to education has resulted in a general rise in the educational level of the population.

The level of education of the population:

| | 1970 | 1980 | 1990 |
|---|---|---|---|
| Compulsory education | 69,4% | 56,8% | 46,1% |
| Secondary education | 23,9% | 32,1% | 39,8% |
| Higher education | 6,7% | 11,1% | 14,1% |

The table shows that only around 30% of the population above compulsory school age (16 years) had secondary or higher education in 1970, whereas more than 50% of the same age group continued their education at upper secondary or higher levels in 1990.

The structure of higher education has been highly decentralised. Up until 1994 there were more than 200 institutions of which only 17 (including the 4 universities) had more than 1000 students each.
In 1991, the government presented a White Paper on Higher Education based on the main issues discussed in the reports of the three above-mentioned commissions. The most important proposals of the White Paper on Higher Education are the following:

·    establishment of "Network Norway", a network of higher education and research based on the principles of specialisation, cooperation and communication;
·    reduction of the regional colleges from 110 to about 30 by merging existing colleges;
·    increasing the transfer frequency from upper secondary to higher education to about 40% of each year group;

- strengthening of core school subjects in teacher training, without extending the study period;
- extending from 1/2 to 1 year the period of study for practical and didactic training which future teachers graduating from universities are required to take;
- increased power of decision and responsibility to the operative units within the system of higher education, and development of better evaluation procedures;
- establishment of a National Academic Information Centre (NAIC);
- increased internationalisation of higher education, for instance by increasing the number of short-term student exchanges between Norwegian and foreign universities and colleges;
- creating similar systems of qualifications and titles for teachers of universities, university colleges and other colleges of higher education.

The Storting, the Norwegian Parliament, supported most of the proposals. The majority decided to extend the period of study for initial general teacher training from three to four years in accordance with the proposal of the Commission on Teacher Training. The Storting also asked the government to present a proposal for a common law for all higher education, including both universities and regional colleges, and to submit a White Paper on student welfare and financial support to students. A White Paper on Student Welfare and Financial Support to Students was presented by the government in November 1993.

The government set up a commission in February 1992 to propose new legislation for universities, university colleges and regional colleges. The commission presented its report in June 1993. Based on the proposals put forward by the commission the government presented a bill to the Storting in June 1994 concerning an Act on Higher Education. The new Act will define a common framework for the management of higher education in Norway and constitute the legal basis for "Network Norway".

As a follow-up to the White Paper on Higher Education and the proposed common Act on Higher Education, the system of higher education is going through a period of reforms. At the same time, the interest for higher education is stronger than ever before. Since the end of the 1980s the student population in Norway has increased by around 60%, from around 100.000

to more than 160.000, due to increased unemployment as well as a change of attitude towards higher education. Thus, the system of higher education is facing challenges, both quantitatively and qualitatively. As a result of merging the regional colleges of higher education, the number of colleges has been reduced from around 100 to 26 in 1994.

The Act on Universities and State Colleges of 12 May 1995 took effect on 1 January 1996. At the same date the Act on Universities and University Colleges of 16 June 1989 is repealed.

# 5.21

## POLAND

### Jerzy Gasiorowski

5.21.1   The current legislative situation

Among the first laws passed by the Polish Parliament at the beginning of the transition period were the 1990 Higher Education, Academic Title and Degrees Act and the 1991 State Committee for Scientific Research Act. The new bills apply to all universities with the exception of military, police and fire-brigade academies, which are subject to special legislation. The Acts confer wide autonomy with respect both to the statutes governing their structure and organisation, and to their every-day activities. The Minister of National Education decides on the allocation of the state budget for higher education and the use of it. He creates the detailed legal framework of higher education and monitors the legality of universities' activities. The minister's actions are to some extent subject to supervision by the Central Council of Higher Education, a democratically elected 50-member body representing the academic community consisting of 35 professors, 10 members of other teaching staff, and 5 students. The Council issues opinions on resource allocation, and on all bills concerned with higher education, academic titles and the organisation and financing of scientific research.

An Act introducing higher professional schools has been prepared for final legislative procedure. The Central Council of Higher Education has given its consent. It will bring in new organisational features as well as some new bodies (i.e. Convent and State Accreditation Commission) and posts (e.g. Chancellor).

5.21.2   The balance of power

*Public and private universities*

Public universities are founded, transformed and dissolved by an Act of Parliament. They are financed from the state budget allocated to them by the Minister of National Education for their maintenance and teaching activities. The universities, their departments and individual academics may apply to the State Committee for Scientific Research for additional research funding. Universities may also recover overhead costs from funds granted by the Committee directly to academics. Public service and economic activities may be also undertaken by the universities. The degree of autonomy enjoyed by public universities depends upon their teaching and research capacity. The Act specifies the minimum number of professors to be employed, the minimum number of departments or institutes entitled to award the degree of doctor habilitus etc., provided a university fits the first of the two categories described below.

The larger universities are completely independent with regard to their statutes, study regulations, and admission requirements. They may establish and dissolve faculties or institutes as required and introduce new fields of study if the proposed arrangements satisfy the staff and curriculum requirements set by the Central Council of Higher Education.

*Self-government*

In smaller universities decisions about matters specified in the above require approval by the competent minister: i.e. the Minister of National Education in the case of comprehensive universities, technical universities, agricultural academies, economic academies, teacher training higher schools and theological academies; The Minister of Health and Social Welfare in the case of medical academies; the Minister of Culture and Art for academies of music, fine arts, theatre, and cinematography; the Minister of Transport and Marine Economy in the case of merchant marine academies; and the Chairman of the State Agency of Sport and Tourism in the case of physical education academies. The Act prescribes that private universities may be established by any person or legal entity, Polish or foreign, authorised by the Minister of National Education. Private universities must comply with the Central Council of Higher Education regulations concerning the curricula for each field of study taught and the level of education (licenciat or master). The promoters of a private university may intervene in its activities only in ways specified in the university's bye-laws or charter. Private universities administer their own funds and may charge tuition fees. The Minister of National Education may also grant funds from the state budget to them.

Every public university is governed by a rector and a university senate, each faculty by a dean and a departmental council. Rectors and deans are elected for a period of three years by the university senate or the faculty council respectively, or by colleges of electors. The composition of senates is usually as follows: professors 50-60%, other teaching staff 15-20%, other employees of university 10% and students 15-20% of the membership. Faculty councils have a similar composition. The university senate frames the university statute and study regulations. All decisions concerning the development of the university such as international cooperation or introduction of new fields of study must be submitted to the senate for approval. Department councils prescribe study requirements and curricula within faculties.

Student self-government plays an important role in every university. The members of its committees are elected by the student body in order to carry out a variety of cultural and social activities. Student self-government participates in the awarding of scholarships and advises on curricula and study regulations. The election of pro-rectors and sub-deans responsible for student affairs are subject to its approval.

*Staff*

There are four categories of teaching post established by the Act. Appointments to the posts of assistant and adjunct are made by the university rector on the recommendation of the dean of the faculty. A master or equivalent degree is required for the post of assistant, and the maximum duration of employment in this position without obtaining a doctoral degree is limited to 8 years. A doctoral degree is required for the post of adjunct, and the maximum employment without achieving doctor habilitus is limited to 9 years. The joint recommendation of the dean and the faculty is required for appointment to the post of extraordinary professor. It is necessary to hold a degree of doctor habilitus to be accepted in this position, and the duration of employment is at least 5 years. Appointments to the post of ordinary professor are made by the Minister of National Education or the competent minister acting on the joint recommendation of the university senate and the department council of the appropriate faculty. It is required to bear the title of professor to be employed in this position, and it is permanent employment. Submission of a recommendation that a person be employed in any position must be preceded by open competition. Persons holding aforementioned positions are obligated to teach and to carry out scientific research. Public universities may employ persons only under the obligation to teach. The appropriate qualifications for such posts are set forth in the university's by-laws. Foreigners may be employed in academic positions at public universities on the same basis as Polish citizens. When employing foreigners a university may however waive the requirement that the holders of a senior position obtained the degree of doctor habilitus or the title of professor.

*Studies*

A condition of admission to study at a public university is the certificate of matriculation. Universities may also hold competitive entrance examinations. Minimum requirements of the curriculum, and the names to be given to particular fields of study are prescribed by the Central Council of Higher Education. Students may follow any number of subjects of study provided that the curriculum of the basic field of study chosen is satisfied. In addition any individual plan and curriculum may be followed which satisfies the rules laid down by the faculty. Study at public universities is free of charge for Polish citizens. However, the Act establishes a basis for charging fees to students who prolong their studies beyond the usual period allowed. The basis according to which fees may be charged to foreign students at public universities is defined by the Minister of National Education. All Polish students have a right to apply for financial support from the State which is granted in accordance with the regulations laid down by the Council of Ministers. All public universities have full autonomy with respect to international cooperation between universities. They may conclude their own agreements with foreign universities, stipulate to admission requirements for foreign students, and grant academic credit for periods of study outside Poland. The Minister of National Education coordinates intergovernmental cooperation in this field, only. However, the universities are obliged to inform ministers of the fact and contents of any agreement concluded with a foreign university or other academic institution. International agreements concerning the equivalence of diplomas are concluded by the Minister of National Education who also establishes the rules and procedures for recognition of diplomas not subjected to international agreements. In practice, however, the Minister allows individual universities to decide such questions themselves.

*Academic titles and degrees*

A new Act (also of 12 September 1990) regulating the award of academic titles and degrees established the following academic ranks (in ascending order):

· the academic degree of doctor of a particular academic subject area within a particular academic discipline;
· the academic degree of doctor habilitus of a particular academic subject area within a particular academic discipline;
· the title of professor of a particular academic subject area.

The degree of doctor is granted to persons who have obtained the diploma of master (or equivalent), have passed the appropriate doctoral examination, and have submitted and successfully conducted a public defense of a PhD thesis which must also be examined by at least two specialists. The thesis written under the supervision of a tutor, should present the author's original solution to an academic problem, and display the author's general theoretical knowledge within the relevant academic discipline and the ability to undertake independent academic research. The degree of doctor habilitus is awarded to persons who have obtained a doctorate, whose scientific attainments are extensive, and who have submitted an habilitation dissertation, successfully participated in an habilitation colloquium, and have delivered a habilitation lecture. The habilitation dissertation must be reviewed by at least three specialists and should be considered a significant contribution to the development of a particular academic discipline. The title of professor is granted to persons who, after obtaining the degree of doctor habilitus, have proceeded to both outstanding academic attainments and important educational achievements. Successful management of a research team could be understood as such an educational achievement. The assessment of these achievements must be supported by the opinions of, at least, three specialists. The degrees of doctor and doctor habilitus can be granted by the faculty councils of university departments (or the academic councils of institutes, including non-teaching institutions such as those of the Polish Academy of Sciences). The right to confer the higher degrees is accorded by the Central Commission for Matters Related to Academic Title and Degrees (Attestation Committee), the members of which are chosen by an electoral college consisting of all Polish professors. In certain cases resolutions granting the degree of doctor or doctor habilitus have the status of law after confirmation by the Central Commission. The title of professor is granted by the President of the Republic of Poland on the basis of a resolution of the Central Commission issued in response to a petition by an academic council of sufficient standing to be entitled to grant the degree of doctor habilitus. Rules governing the equivalence of Polish and foreign academic degrees are established by international agreement. The Council of Ministers prescribes rules and procedures for recognition in Poland of academic degrees not yet subjected to such agreements. In practice the right to nostrification of such degrees is exercised by the faculty or university departments or the academic councils of institutes having the right to grant the degree of doctor habilitus.

# 5.22

## ROMANIA

### *Alexandru Mihailescu & Ioan Neacsu*

5.22.1 The Romanian Constitution provides in Art. 32 "The Right to Education":

- The right to education is implemented through compulsory general education, high-school and vocational education, and through higher education.
- Education at all levels is carried out in Romanian. The educational process may also be organised in a language other than Romanian.
- The right of individuals belonging to a national minority to learn their mother tongue and the right to be taught in this language are guaranteed.
- Education in state establishments is offered free of charge.
- Educational institutions are established and can perform their activities as provided by law.
- Institutional autonomy and academic freedom are guaranteed in Romania.
- The state assures freedom of religious education, according to the demands specific to each culture.
- In state establishments, religious education is organised and guaranteed by law.

5.22.2 The current legislative situation

The Bill of Education was approved by the Chamber of Deputies, and is at present under debate in the Senate. It includes a range of provisions concerning the structure, organisation, management and the financing of higher education. Higher education has an open character and is organised as short term, or as long term university education. Post-university education is offered at accredited institutes of higher education and academies. It involves advanced studies, doctorate studies, post-university academic studies, specialised studies and refresher courses.

Fundamental scientific research, and other programmes of particular concern are financed through research contracts and from annual funds from the Ministry of Education. These allocations are not themselves part of the financing of the education process. The National Council of the University Scientific Research also provides financing of research contracts on a competition basis.

There are 78 higher education institutions in Romania: 36 universities and 42 equivalent institutes, 8 academies, 2 institutes, 1 national school of higher political and administrative studies, 16 military institutes and 15 theological institutes of different denominations. There are also 423 state post-high school institutions which are not included in the higher education, but represent an important component of tertiary education.

During the last four years, the number of private universities has increased spectacularly, but also uncontrolably. According to current statistics, there were 66 private higher education institutions active, with 316 faculties and a total of 118.880 students during the 1993/1994 academic year. At present this sector is undergoing a process of complying with Law 88/93, which is concerned with the evaluation and accreditation of the higher education institutes, as well as the recognition of diplomas.

The legislative basis and, in general, monitoring and regulating higher education development and its administration are still precarious. The new Bill of Education presently under debate in the legislature, will be attentive to the particular needs that arise in a period of transition to a market economy, as well as to trends in the area of human resources training in Europe. It is expected that the 1995/1996 academic year will benefit from the provisions of the new law. Formerly, trials of bureaucratic control had led to a stifling mood at the universities, and at the same time had proved inefficient. Former conditions are highlighted by the fact that more than 2000 legal texts came into effect between 1990 and 1994 alone.

### 5.22.3 The balance of power

The constitutional freedom implies the right of the university community to self administration, to exercise its academic rights without regard to ideology, whether of political or religious provenance.

Today's universities are experiencing increasing tension between their strong inclination towards academic freedom and institutional autonomy, on the one hand, and the Ministry of Education's financing practices, on the other Analyses carried out in the past three years predict some significant changes in the relationships between the Ministry of Education and the university governments, which will be largely favourable to the universities. The studies also indicate, that these developments will be principled by institutional autonomy and academic freedom which are regarded as a means to operate under flexible juridical frameworks. It has furthermore been indicated, that these frameworks will establish functional mechanisms and procedures for academic evaluation and accreditation of institutes and curricula. Until the advent of specific legislation, however, the financing of higher education will be progressively coordinated through mechanisms relatively independent of the Ministry of Education.

The draft Bill of Education guarantees institutional autonomy and academic freedom. These liberties, however, imply essential structural changes in the relations of the government and the institutions, as well as a new out-look on managerial functions. This means, on the one hand, that the Ministry of Education will perform certain strategic functions, such as the coordination and elaboration of educational policies at the national level, by consulting the academic councils, and on the other hand, that the universities will become institutions responsible for the quality of instruction and research, and for services offered to the community. This type of management may eventually permit the instalment of a competitive system of resource allocation to universities, and of intermediary bodies mediating between the ministry and the higher education institutions.

The most important intermediate organisations at present are the National Council of Academic Evaluation and Accreditation, the National Council of University Scientific Research and the National Council for Financing

Higher Education. These bodies will eventually implement performance criteria for higher education.


### 5.22.4   Conclusion

In Romania the general reform of higher education is a national priority. Harmonisation of Romanian with European legislation is expected to lead to an well organised, flexible, continuously adapting system which will be responsive to the needs of society. It is felt, that a democratic society, based on a market economy, does not necessarily imply a super-centralised, state-controlled higher education sector, but a modern, dynamic, open, innovative system. The above-mentioned objectives will remain an illusion without the proper legislative framework adapted to these demands.

# 5.23

## SLOVAKIA

## *Maria Hrabinská, Peter Plavčan & Juraj Švec*

5.23.1   Article 42 of the Constitution of the Republic of Slovakia refers
to higher education and provides:

1   Everyone has a right to education. School attendance is compulsory. Its
length up to the age limit is stipulated by law.
2   Citizens have the right to free education in primary and secondary
schools and, according to the abilities of the citizens and capacities of
the society, also in higher education institutions.
3   The establishment of other than public schools and teaching in them is
possible only under the conditions stipulated by law; in this type of
school education is provided for payment.
4   The law stipulates the conditions under which the citizens, when
studying, have the right to state grants and aid.

5.23.2   The current legislative situation

Furthermore, universities are self-governing bodies, and that their organisation and activities are determined by the law. Members of the academic
community at universities are guaranteed the freedom of scientific research
and of publishing the results. The freedoms of artistic pursuits, to teach and
study, to elect academic self-governing boards, to hold diverse philosophical
views and to profess religious beliefs and to propagate them, to use the
academic insignia and symbols and to perform academic ceremonials are
guaranteed. The exercise and implementation of these rights and freedoms
must be in conformity with principles of democracy, humanism and the rule

of law. The immunity of university academic premises is also guaranteed. Upon a showing of probable cause of a criminal offense, permission of entry is given to agents of the law by the rector, or by proxy. No political party or movement may set up its organisation on the university premises.

Article 15 of the Higher Education Act provides:

1   The Ministry of Education, Youth and Sports of the Slovak Republic:
    a. creates conditions for the promotion of universities and higher education;
    b. co-ordinates the activities of universities;
    c. allocates financial means to individual universities and controls their utilisation;
    d. registers the statutes of universities;
    e. to meet the tasks of universities, sets up on recommendation of the university council, institutes and work places which are legal bodies;
    f. decides, on the proposal or recommendation of the accreditation commission, on withdrawing the right of a university or faculty to hold state and rigorous examinations in relevant subjects of study, habilitation procedures or procedures for nominating professors, or on restitution of this right for universities and faculties; simultaneously it decides at which other university or faculty these procedures or examinations will take place, if the relevant university or faculty agrees to it.

2   On the proposals of universities, the minister submits recommendations to the president of the Czech and Slovak Federal Republic for nominating professors and rectors.

In its initial form the present Higher Education Act No. 172/1990 was adopted during great political changes in the former Czech and Slovak Federal Republic and under requisite pressure to confirm the academic rights and freedoms of higher education institutions. The 1990 Law on higher education was later added to the legal frame of the Slovak Republic. This unusually progressive Act created the pre-conditions for the democratisation and humanisation of higher education institutions. Among the most significant changes set forth in the Act was the definition given of the higher education institutions' status as being the top educational, scientific and artistic institutions

At the same time, the initial Act set down the basic academic rights and freedoms of higher education institutions, in particular, the freedom of scientific research and publishing, the freedom of artistic pursuits, the right to teach and learn. the right to elect self-governing bodies, the right to entertain diverse philosophical views and religious beliefs. In contrast to previous enactments the new law authorises the higher education institutions to determine their internal structure, the content and the organisation of their teaching activities, the filling of managerial posts, their intake and their criteria of selection, and the use of funds allocated to them.

The Act created the Higher Education Council which is composed of representatives of the self-governing bodies of higher education institutions and of the faculties, as well as the governmental Accreditation Commission which assesses the quality of higher education activities in science and in the arts, and annually ranks the programmes in three categories. The Act does not limit the "authority" of the Ministry, but simply divides the competencies between state authorities and ministries. The authority of the ministry has been restricted by the Act. The ministry is now responsible for the creation of conditions of higher education development, higher education co-ordination, distribution and supervision of the use of funds from the state budget, and registration of the higher education institutions by-laws. Under the Higher Education Act it soon became clear that the bye-law registration requirement and the ministry's competencies in regard to financing, in particular, considerably influence the activities of higher education institutions. The Act defined the status of legal entity of higher education institutions and faculties. Nowadays, however, it may be stated that the rectors and deans of higher education institutions and faculties have agreed in principle with the distribution of competencies set forth in the Act.

Nonetheless during the first months of operation of the Higher Education Act of 1990, some new insufficiencies became obvious. The new Act did not delineate with due accuracy the mutual relations of higher education institutions to the State and to the economy, nor did it specify the competencies and the relations between the self-governing bodies of the universities and faculties on the one hand, and the ministry on the other. This is regarded by the academic community as an intervention in the autonomy of higher education institutions as the budget reallocation inside university is the unequivocal right of the university itself. Between 1992 and 1995 various expert groups, ministerial and representative of self-governing higher education institutions and other specialists, drafted amendments and new bills to tackle these problems. The Higher Education Council together with the Slovak Rectors Conference (as defined in the act and its amendments) and the Ministry of Education prepared a draft amendment of the 172/1990 on Higher Education. The draft amendment, considered and adopted by academic senates, other universities and the Legislative Council of the Slovak Government, has been presented to the government for final approval. The government returned the draft amendment to the Ministry of Education with the request to implement given corrections strengthening the central decision making power of the Ministry of Education and authorising the Slovak Academy of Science to independently issue PhD degrees. The revised amendment, elaborated by the Ministry of Education according to government proposals, evoked protests from the academic community. As a result a new version of the draft amendment has been prepared and was presented to the government. Negotiations are under way between the government and the Slovak Academy of Science, and the Ministry of Education, to settle this dispute.

Currently, a new bill is being debated in the parliament, which is expected to remedy some problems. The proposed amendments concern the establishment and dissolution of higher education institutions; the regulation of teaching clinics; the faculty pilot schools and educational establishments; the relations of the higher education institutions with other institutions of science, technology, education, health, service, the fine arts and the economy; the promotion of integration between academic bodies of higher education institutions, academic senates and scientific councils, and the board of university students. Specifically, the amendment delegates to the Slovak Academy of Science the right to organise and perform post-graduate PhD studies independently of universities and then issue PhD diplomas.

The issue of types of higher education institutions, and in particular of higher education diversification, appeared in the legislative drafts at several instances. Also, a greater participation of the 18-23 age group, by increasing the demand of educational institutions and shorter programmes oriented rather at practices, needs to be attained. The draft amendment law of 1993 accordingly called for dividing higher education institutions into four categories: universities, specialised higher education institutions, artistic institutions and professional higher education institutions. This division was opposed, however, by some higher education institutions for fear of discriminatory budgeting, as a consequence, in accord with the amendment proposal, all 14 higher education establishments (with exception of the additional police and military academies) adopted the title "university". It should be mentioned that the revised versions of the amendment in question were elaborated by the Ministry and sent to the government, and all four versions are now circulating in the academic community. All the proposed amendments presupposed and defined the possibility of establishing non-state higher education institutions and set forth the responsibilities of the founder of such institutions especially with regard to financing, study programmes, and teacher qualification. Several proposals dealt with the possibility of misuse of the name "university" and "higher educating institution" and provided sanctions.

Regarding the mission of higher education institutions no substantial changes are required and there are practically no objections to the definition of mission and tasks of higher education institutions. The 1995 draft amendment law emphasises the higher educating institutions' overall responsibility not only to society, but also to science and technology. However, state coordination of research and education at universities has been separated by authorising the newly established governmental Office for Strategic Development, Research and Technology to recognise the financing of research at academic and non-academic research establishments.

Despite the continuously growing number of enrolments, the higher education institutions are still unable to admit all those who fulfil the admission requirements. For that reason, the majority of higher education institutions, or their faculties, hold admission exams, the terms of which are within the competency of the faculty deans.

The question of introducing tuition fees is being considered, with due regard to the need of providing financial assistance to students, likely in the form of low-interest loans. The 1993 draft amendment law set tuition at 50% of actual study costs, which the academic community rejected univocally. The

1995 draft amendment law contains no provision of this kind. However, in conjunction with certain provisions of the Pension and Medical Insurance Acts, it threatens to create a rather disadvantaged situation for PhD students in particular. The "scientific preparation" of graduates at the Slovak Academy of Sciences, leading to Csc (candidate of Science) scientific degree, is based on fellowships that extend PhD fellowships at Slovak universities by 30-50%.

In the domain of institutional self governance, the most critical topic of discussion are the academic senates and their competencies. The 1995 draft amendment law proposes their structure thus, that professors, associate professors and scientific workers form the majority of the senate members. It is furthermore proposed to strengthen their competencies with regard to establishment, merger, division or dissolution of faculties. According to the proposal, the academic senates shall submit recommendations in these matters to the rectors, following a prior statement by the Accreditation Commission. However, the 1995 draft amendment in its last version delegates the right to establish, merge, divide or even dissolve faculties to the rectors or the Accreditation Committee. The founder of the faculty should be the rector who will not be able, however, to act without the academic senate's recommendation. Establishment and dissolution of higher education institutions is one of the most problematic aspects of the otherwise progressive Higher Education Act of 1992.

It is proposed to establish a Council for university students as a new body of special-interest self-governance by students. This proposal was initiated by students seeking a representation at the national level.

Financing higher education is one of the most urgent challenges not yet solved. The latest proposals mention the entrepreneurial activities of higher education institutions, which are not only viewed in terms of income generation, but are expected to stimulate higher education institutions. Allocation of public funds to the institutions is effectuated according to their evaluation by the Accreditation Commission, the opinions of the Higher Education Council being, in this respect, irrelevant, as the final amendment proposal shifted the right of the Higher Education Council to propose criteria for budget reallocation to the ministry. Furthermore, the amendment states that the ministry has the right to reallocate the budget to higher education institutions "in line with the state development strategies and on the basis of own decision". The opinion of the Higher Education Council must be invited. It is expected that the admission of private establishments will unburden the public budget.

# 5.24

## SLOVANIA

*Albin Igličar*

### 5.24.1

The departure point for legal regulation of higher education in Slovenia is Article 58 of the Constitution, which provides, that state universities and other state higher education institutions shall be autonomous and that funding of them shall be regulated by statute. Article 59 of the Constitution furthermore expressly guarantees the freedom of scientific and artistic pursuits.

### 5.24.2   The current legislative situation

On the basis of the provisions of the Constitution, the National Assembly of the Republic of Slovenia adopted the Higher Education Act of 7 December 1993, which governs matters concerning the status of higher education institutions, their activities and their funding. In December 1994, the National Assembly issued two decrees which transformed the legal status of the universities of Ljubljana and of Maribor. Within the six months following the adoption of the acts, both Slovenian universities and professional higher education institutions must adopt their bye-laws. As of 1 January 1995, Slovenian higher education comprised the following institutions:

- the University of Ljubljana, consisting of sixteen faculties, three academies of art and four university colleges;
- the University of Maribor, consisting of eight faculties and two university colleges;

- two independent professional higher education institutions (College of Police and Security – Ljubljana, College of Hotel and Travel Administration – Portorož).

Article 6 of the Higher Education Act grants autonomy to the universities.

Article 9 states that:

"A higher education institution and another institution, member of a university, or student residence halls, respectively, may be established by Slovenian or foreign national or legal persons. In order to provide public service in higher education, the Republic of Slovenia shall establish public higher education institutions and other public institutions, members of universities, and students residence halls, respectively."

General provisions in the Act outline the differences between university and professional higher education institutions, for example Article 3, which provides:

"The University shall be devoted to the development of the sciences and arts and shall transfer knowledge in the various fields and disciplines of science and art, in the educational process performed by faculties, academies of art and vocational higher education institutions;"

Article 5 of the Act provides:

"A vocational higher education institution shall perform teaching in one or more similar and interrelated professional field and shall be committed to the development thereof."

5.24.3   The balance of power

The Constitution and the Higher Education Act provide for the existence of state higher education, it also guarantees the right to establish private higher education institutions. As far as proprietorship of university employed premises and property is concerned, the new law vests these rights with the State, which it stipulates to have founded the universities. However, on the day of enactment of the new law, the management of such property was transferred to the universities. The property status of the universities, therefore, closely resembles an original conception the institutions had championed, according to which universities were to operate and to own their resources as public corporations.

Apart from being thus empowered to manage their resources, the institutions exercise their autonomy furthermore by way of adopting study programmes and regimes, as well as by defining forms and terms of testing and other assessments of academic aptitude. The university's autonomy includes administrating its internal organisation, and also extends to the election of officials, the nomination of professors and to the awarding of academic titles. This autonomy is understood to emanate from the freedoms of research, artistic pursuit, and transfer of knowledge, as a general attribute of modern civilization.

The Higher Education Act introduced a dual system of post-secondary education to Slovenia. The professional higher education institutions will primarily enrol students with final examinations, while the universities require a matura (a special secondary school final examination) for entry. Professional higher education institutions perform educational activities in one or more professional fields, while universities perform scientific-research, and educational activities in the field of one or more scientific disciplines. Accordingly, teachers at professional higher education institutions are required to hold a master's degree, and university teachers must have obtained a PhD Graduates from secondary schools may be admitted to one or other of the higher education institutions. Thus the possibilities of post-secondary education have increased, and the higher education system itself can, to a greater degree, satisfy the diverse educational needs of the Slovenian society. Currently, Slovenia plans the creation of new professional higher education institutions, especially in the fields of administration, tourism, the hotel industry, traffic, and management.

The new Law vests expanded competencies in the universities, which alone have been granted the status of legal entities, while its subdivisions (faculties, academics, and the professional higher education institutions) have not. Also, title criteria, such as the election of professors and research advisers, and the approval of study programmes of university members are now within the competency of the university's senate.

Other agencies of the universities are the rector, the administrative board and the student council. A student council is established at every university and at every faculty or university subdivision. It has a statutory right to prior hearing on all policy issues involving the rights and obligations of students. The student council may issue a suspensive veto on policy decisions taken in violation of this right.

The Higher Education Act also contains provisions governing the status of university students. It created, for example, a one year graduate student status following graduation. It even contains detailed language delineating student work-load and the repetition of courses and exams, although such regulation should, in accordance with the autonomy of the universities, be reserved to the university bye-laws. Under the Act, the government may not prescribe tuition fees to Slovenian citizens for enrolment in public undergraduate study programmes. The act guarantees the conditions of graduation valid at the time of a student's enrolment. The university bye-laws contain more specific regulation on matters ranging from interdisciplinary studies and parallel education, to the recognition of examination results, as well as other rules related to academic advancement and standing. Positions in a public higher education institution are systematically defined by the rector, or by the dean at autonomous higher education institutions, pending approval by the Ministry of Education.

Higher education institutions in Slovenia derive their funds from the budget of the Republic, from tuition fees, payments for services rendered to third parties outside the public programmes, and also from endowments, donations, and legacies. Funding of the national programme of higher education, adopted by the National Assembly – including salaries of teaching and other staff, material expenses as well as depreciation and purchase of real property and equipment – is guaranteed by the State.

An intermediate body in the Slovenian higher education system is the Council for Higher Education. The President and the eleven members of this body are nominated by the government for a term of four years. Six of the members are chosen from nominees proposed by the higher education institutions, other members are the rectors of the universities, the president of the Slovenian Academy of Sciences and Arts, and experts in the area of science, economy and social activities. The Council stimulates and coordinates cooperation between the higher education institutions, and advises the government on legislation, and participates in the strategic planning of higher education policy. The Council for Higher Education also prepares, in cooperation with the higher education institutions, guidelines for the national programme of higher education, and defines standards for evaluating study programmes. It furthermore issues opinions regarding norms on financing the national programme and on criteria for awarding titles to teaching and research faculty. These competencies are intended to enable the Council for Higher Education to balance powers between the State and higher education institutions.

## 5.24.4   Conclusion

The policy behind the new Higher Education Act is to align higher education in Slovenia more closely with modern European concepts. The new Act and the Constitution place strong emphasis, therefore, on the autonomy of the universities, which now also enjoy great normative independence.

The Ministry of Education monitors the legality of higher education activities. A special commission for quality in higher education, formed by higher education institutions themselves, surveys and evaluates educational and scientific research work. The commission reports annually to the senates of the institutions, to the Council for Higher Education and to the Council for Science and Technology. Its reports are published and accessible to the general public.

# 5.25

## SPAIN

### *José Ignacio Cebreiro*

### 5.25.1   Introduction

There are three avenues of higher education in Spain: university education, non-university education and higher vocational education, which are each subject to specific legislation. University education is regulated by the University Reform Act of 25 August 1983, and by its complementary laws. Non-university higher education is provided by establishments dependent on the different organs of the public administration and does not respond to a uniform model. Higher vocational education is regulated by the General Regulation of the Education System Act (LOGSE) of 3 October 1990, and by its complementary laws.

### 5.25.2   The structure of the higher education system

The University Reform Act of 1983 was passed at a time when important political changes had taken place in Spain. These changes led to the adoption of the Constitution of 27 December 1978, which, in its article 27, guarantees the autonomy of universities, and created new regional entities (the Autonomous Communities) with competence in the education sector. The Law accordingly distributes competence as regards university education among the State, the Autonomous Communities and the universities themselves, granting ample autonomy to the latter. The 1983 university reform was not exclusively made in response to political factors, but was also premised by sociological and economic factors which made reforms indispensable. First of all, the dramatic increase in the university population during the last decades from a rate of 100 in 1960 to 513 in 1985 lead to significant imbalances as students concentrated in urban areas, and on a few specific study programmes. This gave rise to an over-burdening of universities and made the adoption of measures, aimed at guaranteeing the quality of education, unavoidable. Among these measures were changes to the student selection procedure, which empowered the establishments to condition access to study programmes upon students showing sufficient academic aptitude. These conditions are determined by the University Council, a body composed of the rectors of all public universities and 15 members of acknowledged prestige in the field of university education and research.

It is also necessary to take into account the rapidly changing international economy and labour market. Many traditional subjects have become obsolete, making it necessary to modify the structure of university studies in order to achieve increased flexibility.

It should be underlined that the growing financial needs of universities had made it urgent to create new funding models through joint participation of both the representatives of universities and of the communities in university-governing bodies. This new approach fashioned a type of university that is more open to, and serving, the society from which it receives the necessary support. The 1983 University Reform Act guarantees adequate representation of the different sectors of the university community in all the governing bodies of the university. The Act also created Social Councils, in which representatives of the various sectors outside the university form a majority, so that they can serve as a link between the university and the communities.

To give an adequate response to these needs, the University Reform Act of 1983 contains provisions devising a Model University founded upon the following principles:

- the principle of academic freedom, which manifests itself in freedom of teaching, research and study, as mentioned in its article 2, that applies in the University sector the right to freedom of teaching recognised, in general, in article 27 of the Constitution;
- the principle of institutional autonomy, that manifests itself in four basic aspects:

a.  each university develops its own bye-laws;
b.  the universities prepare and approve the study plans of the courses they provide;
c.  the universities approve their own budgets and manage and administrate their resources;
d.  each university is free to select and promote its teaching staff, with due respect for the principles of merit, publicity and non-discrimination.

For teaching and research the Law shapes a new structure in which departments appear as the basic organs. Courses conveying official degrees are structured in three cycles. The first cycle lasts two or three years; the second cycle lasts three years and the third cycle includes those programmes of study leading to the doctoral degree. The system is also characterized by a diversification of universities in order to promote competition and improve the level of quality, although a minimum of homogeny and quality is guaranteed. The Law distinguishes between two types of universities: public and private, and lays down the procedure to be followed by the latter for their official recognition. Since no one shall be prevented from going to university for financial reasons, the Law provides in general terms for grants, as well as for financial aid. The basic norms of the University Reform Act have been complemented by the other ordinary laws that have been modified to adapt them to the new realities appeared in the last few years. There are provisions to make reforms of the basic norms related to teaching staff.

### 5.25.3   Non-university education

Supplementary Provision Nr5 of the University Reform Act of 25 August 1983 refers to higher education teaching establishments and states that those institutions not considered universities by the law – given the nature of the curricula or the degrees they issue – shall be governed by specific legislation. There does not exist, therefore, general regulation for this type of establishment. One can however distinguish two groups:

·   establishments that offer study programmes assimilated to university programmes (tourism, military, music, singing);

·   establishments that offer study programmes not assimilated to university programmes (civil aviation, occupational therapy, restoration of works of art).

### 5.25.4   Higher vocational education

Higher vocational education was established by the Law on the General Regulation of the Education System (LOGSE) of 3 October 1990. This type of education has a theoretical and practical basis, and part of the latter involves practice in private business. The duration of higher vocational studies varies with the type of programme. The senior high school or A-level certificate is required for admission. Upon completion of a course of study not exceeding two years, students are issued a diploma of "técnico superior" in their chosen profession; the degree is comparable to that of "master technician". Higher vocational education is intended to facilitate the incorporation of young people into active life, and satisfies the ever growing demand for more practical qualifications, especially from industry. However, rapidly changing cultural and technological systems have also prompted the public administration authorities to extend educational programmes to these sectors where they had not been previously present.

### 5.25.5   The balance of power

Ever since the University Reform Act of 1983 became effective, the competence for university education has been shared between the central government, the government of the Autonomous Communities and the universities. The University Council and the Social Council of each university have also been assigned roles in the governance of universities. Central government powers include the approval of norms regulating the rights of citizens to education and the conditions of admission at universities. The central government also determines the requirements of issuing "official qualifications". It furthermore approves the basic provisions governing teachers. Powers of the Autonomous Communities include subsidising the universities in their region, as well as enacting norms complementary to those of the central government. The universities make their own bye-laws, approve their curricula, and manage their funds. They select and appoint their teachers and professors. In the event of the government issuing a Royal Decree or Ministerial Order affecting the powers of a university, it may challenge the decision before a court of law. The University Council serves as an advisory committee to the central government, the Autonomous Communities and the universities. It participates in coordination and planning of new official qualifications, as well as in the adoption of basic norms on the creation or suppression of departments.

Establishments providing non-university education depend upon the central government (e.g. military education) or the Autonomous Communities (e.g. tourism, music, singing). They lack the autonomy retained by the universities.

Higher vocational education is carried out by establishments which depend upon the Autonomous Communities. They can be public or private. In each establishment there exists a "Consejo Escolar" (School Council) in which teachers, students and parents are members. It is one of the functions of the School Council to elect a director of the establishment. Teachers in the public establishments are selected by the Autonomous Community which also pays their salaries.

## 5.25.6 Conclusion

In the field of higher education legislation, university education is elaborately, and has been timely regulated. The autonomy given to the universities in 1983 is wide in scope and has enabled them to efficiently meet the needs of research and education. The newly created University Council has especially proven useful in coordinating the Autonomous Communities' work in the field of university education. The newly created University Social Councils also deserve mention, these bodies have succeeded in connecting the universities more closely with the communities, thereby securing support, including financial support, of both public and private organisations in their regions. The number of students has been growing with increased number of new careers and during the course of 1994-95 there were 1.435.732 students registered in the Spanish universities, that is 48,09% more than during the course 1987-1988.

The university reform, which has been under way since 1983, has successfully adapted Spanish universities to the rapid, far-reaching changes within the socio-economic, technological, cultural and political environment, improving both the quality of education and equal opportunity in education. Non-university education, however, has not yet seen any significant changes during these last few years. Higher vocational education is only now being introduced, an analysis of its successes and impact appears, at this time, premature.

# 5.26

## SWITZERLAND

### *Christen Lenzen*

5.26.1  The current legislative situation

Article 27, para 1 of the Federal Constitution states:

1  The Confederation is entitled to create, in addition to the existing federal institute of Technology, a federal university and other higher education establishments or to subsidise establishments of this type.

The Federal law on aid to universities, Article 1, paras 1 and 2 provides:

1  In conjunction with the cantons, the Confederation shall foster the implementation of a co-ordinated policy on universities, which shall also take account of international co-operation.
2  The Confederation shall encourage, through financial support, the operation and development of officially recognised canton universities and university institutions.

The Law on federal polytechnic colleges, Article 1 states:

1  The present law applies to the domain of the federal institutes of technology, which include:
   a.  the Federal Institute of Technology of Zurich;
   b.  the Federal Institute of Technology of Lausanne;
   c.  research establishments attached to Federal Institutes of Technology;
2  These establishments are under the control of the Confederation.

The eight canton universities of Zurich, Basel, Bern, Fribourg, St Gallen, Lausanne, Neuchâtel and Geneva are each governed by a specific canton law. In Zurich, it is a section of the general law on education.

The federal polytechnic colleges (FPCs) are exclusively funded and governed by the Confederation. A new law on FPCs, which entered into force on 1 February 1993, entailed a major devolution of powers, considerably increasing the autonomy of FPCs, which now are legal entities. The FPCs are now under the control of the Board of the Swiss Federal Institutes of Technology, which itself comes under the Federal Department of the Interior. The Board of the Swiss Federal Institutes of Technology is composed of 9 members who are external to the FPCs and appointed by the Federal Council. The Board of the Swiss Federal Institutes of Technology has a part-time chairman, who is assisted by a full-time deputy. The main tasks of the FPC Council are to:

·   establish general policy directives for FPCs and set basic objectives for
     each institute;
·   approve plans for developing FPCs and monitor their implementation;
·   establish directives concerning studies;
·   decide on the setting up and closure of teaching and research units;
·   directly supervise the domain of FPCs;
·   play a co-ordinating role.

Each FPC has its own management and in particular a chairman appointed by the Federal Council. The chairman has overall responsibility for running the FPC and accounts for its management to the FPC Council. The management of the FPC organises teaching, research and scientific services; in this connection, it plans, co-ordinates and controls the resources of the FPC. It lays down policy, issues instructions and takes decisions of principle in the following areas:

a.   education, continuing education, research;
b.   staff, finance and buildings;
c.   information and relations with outside partners and the public.

A draft federal law on specialised high schools (SHS) is being debated in parliament at the moment. It concerns the organisation and funding of high schools in the fields of industry, services, agriculture and forestry, which are run at canton level. The SHS provide practical training for jobs requiring scientific knowledge and methods. They offer vocational refresher courses, undertake practical research and development work and provide services. They also work with other training and research establishments in Switzerland and abroad.

The Confederation contributes to the funding of canton universities through subsidies granted for four-year periods on the basis of a programme drawn up by the Conference of Swiss Universities. There are three categories of subsidy:

a.  Operating (or base) subsidies. Funding of operating costs and investments below 300,000 Swiss francs (CHF). These are calculated in proportion to the number of students, lecturers' salaries, expenditure on equipment and investments below 300,000 CHF. At present, base subsidies cover some 15% of universities' costs (the subsidy rate varies between 35 and 60% of the qualifying amount, depending on the financial resources of the cantons). The financial difficulties of the Confederation have resulted in several reductions in recent years (-15% in 3 years).

b.  Subsidies for building investments. Every four years the Confederation establishes a framework loan which makes it possible to subsidise the building investments made by cantons for education, research, student welfare or university administration. Subsidies are granted to sound projects satisfying the criteria of the division of tasks and co-operation between universities. Up to the beginning of the 1990s, the loans were always available to cover all requests for subsidies. For the subsidy period 1992-95, however, an order of priority had to be established. The same will apply for 1996-99. From 1996 onwards, a fixed proportion (15%) will be reserved for subsidising university medical clinics; this new measure is intended to limit the funds used to build medical clinics and simplify procedures.

c.  Extraordinary subsidies. The Confederation may grant extraordinary subsidies if ordinary grants are insufficient. These subsidies are governed by a time limit and are intended for projects in the national interest which respond to an urgent need. To date, the Confederation has used this facility in four areas: student and lecturer mobility (until the end of 1995), continuing higher education, information technology and promotion of junior academic staff.

The aims of federal policy in the field of science for the period 1996-99 are as follows:

1   to strengthen the position of Switzerland in research and university education;
2   to meet the needs of society;
3   to draw greater benefit from the resources invested.

Swiss universities are education and research establishments in the tradition of Humboldt. They are divided into faculties (sections in St Gallen). The executive authority of the university is the rectorate. The rector is a lecturer appointed for a fixed term.

Most university legislation is undergoing reform to varying degrees. The main reforms are:

1   the creation of a "University Council", an interface between the government and the rectorate, which has strategic management powers; it generally includes persons from outside the university sector;
2   greater power for the rectorate (administrative authority) within the university, with the rector appointed by the government or the University Council; longer terms of office (often 4 years, renewable);
3   greater autonomy for universities to which certain state powers are being transferred. It includes legal personality; budgetary package;
4   establishment of a legal basis for limiting access to studies;
5   systematic evaluation of teaching and research programmes.

All the above-mentioned elements illustrate the links between different levels of the system (State, intermediate body, university or high school). The trend is towards greater autonomy, as has been the case for the FPCs since 1993.

The universities and the FPCs have no legal means of contesting the decisions taken by the higher authorities. Their new powers, legal status and academic freedom, however, amount to an ample space for manoeuvre.

# 5.27

## TURKEY

### *Mustafa Akbulut*

5.27.1   The current legislative situation

Article 130 and 131 of The Turkish Constitution provide in pertinent part:

For the purpose of training manpower to meet the needs of the Nation, universities shall be established by the State in the form of autonomous public corporations. They shall engage in teaching, research, and act as consultants to the state and the community at large.

Institutions of higher education maybe established by non profit foundations in accordance with the procedures and principles set forth in the law provided that they do not pursue lucrative aims. They shall perform their activities under the control and supervision of the state.

The law shall provide for a balanced geographical distribution of universities throughout the country.

Universities, members of the teaching staff and their assistants may freely engage in all kinds of scientific research and publication, however, this shall not include the liberty to engage in activities directed against the existence and independence of the State and against the integrity and indivisibility of the Nation and the Country.

University rectors shall be appointed by the President of the Republic, and faculty deans by the Higher Education Council, in accordance with the procedures and provisions of the law.

The administrative and supervisory organs of the universities and the teaching staff may not be removed from their office by authorities other than those of the competent organs of the university or by the Higher Education Council.

The budgets drawn up by universities after being examined and approved by the Higher Education Council shall be presented to the Ministry of National Education and shall be put into effect with the principles applied to general and subsidiary budgets according to the principles applicable.

It shall be regulated by law :

- the procedures applicable of the establishment of higher education institutions including and their organs;
- their authorities and responsibilities;
- the procedures applicable to state supervision and inspection;
- the duties of the teaching staff;
- the training of the teaching staff;
- matters related to titles, appointments, promotions and retirement;
- the relation between the universities and the teaching staff with other organisations and public institutions;
- the level and the duration of education;
- the admission of students;
- attendance, requirements and fees;
- disciplinary and penal matters;
- financial matters;
- personnel rights;
- the assignment of the teaching staff as regards interuniversity requirements.

As regards the institutions of higher education established by private foundations they shall be subject to the provisions set forth in the constitution for State institutions of higher education. The same constitution shall apply to the recruitment of the teaching staff and security, not however to financial and administrative matters.

## 5.27.2 The structure of the higher education system

The Higher Education Council shall be established for the purpose of planning, organising and supervising the education provided by the institutions of higher education. It shall also ensure the conformity of these activities with the objectives and principles set forth by law as well as ensure the effective use of the resources allotted to the universities, and to plan the training of the teaching staff. The Higher Education Council shall be composed of members appointed by the President of the Republic from among candidates nominated by the Council of Ministers.

In the decades preceding the 1981 University reform, the Turkish higher education system consisted of three types of institutions:

· the universities;
· the "academies", which specialised in engineering and economic studies;
· vocational schools and teaching institutes.

The academies, vocational schools and teacher training institutes were affiliated with the Ministry of National Education.

Owing to the absence of an efficient and coordinated central plan for all the levels of higher education, and also because of the rapid growth, especially during the 1960s and the 1970s, of the number and variety of higher education institutions and correspondingly of the student population, this tripartite system of higher education began to show signs of failure and degeneration. During the last two decades, political, social and economic problems contributed further to this process of deterioration. Thus, as reforms became inevitable, the 1981 Higher Education Act was put into effect.

With the 1981 Higher Education Act, higher education underwent major academic, institutional and administrative changes. The most significant of their kind since the great university reform in 1993. The provisions of this Law and of Articles 130 and 131 of the Constitution of the Republic vest the supreme authority for higher education in the Higher Education Council, which is now a fully autonomous body administered by a national board of trustees without political or governmental affiliations.

The reform introduced a unified system of higher education and a coherent and interrelated pattern of institutional diversity. All the academies, teacher training institutes and vocational schools were re-organised, while some of them, wherever viable and convenient, were amalgamated to form new universities, others were transformed into new faculties and affiliated with universities in their regions. Thus, with the establishment of eight more state universities in 1982, and one foundation university in 1984, the total number of universities rose from 19 to 28. In 1992 24 new state universities were established in different regions of the country. At present there are 57 universities all together in Turkey, four of which have foundation status.

According to Article 130 of the Constitution, and Article 3/de of the Higher Education Act universities are autonomous and degree-granting corporate institutions of higher education, with recognised rights and functions.

Higher Education Institutions in Turkey are under the protection of the Constitution and the Higher Education Law of 2547 enacted in 1981. This law was amended several times during the ensuing years.


5.27.3   The Higher Education Council

The Higher Education Council consists of 24 members, 14 of whom come from and represent the universities, while the other ten members represent the government; four of the latter are full professors. Once nomination and selection is completed, final appointment to the Council is made by the President of the Republic for a renewable term of four years. The president of the Council is also elected, and appointed by the President of the Republic for a term of four years.

The Council has two governing bodies, the General Assembly and the Executive Committee, both are chaired by the president. The General Assembly, whose proceedings are final and need not be ratified by another authority, is the main decision and policy-making body. It consists of all the Council members and meets, at least three times every half-year, at the president's invitation or upon a written proposal of one third of the members. It may also convene extraordinary meetings. The quorum needed for the transaction is 14.

The Executive Committee is a permanent body primarily concerned with the implementation of policies and the General Assembly's resolutions. It is composed of eight members including the president and two vice-presidents. One of the vice-presidents is appointed by the president and the other is elected by the General Assembly. The quorum is six.

Through its president, the Council reports only to the President of the Republic. Any communication with the government is maintained through the Minister of National Education, who may, if he/she so wishes, attend and preside over meetings of the General Assembly but does not have the right to vote. For instance, it is through the Minister of National Education for submission to the Council of Ministers or to the Parliament, that the Higher Education Council makes its proposals as regards the annual higher education budget, the establishment of new universities or amalgamation, where necessary, of the institutions of higher education.

According to the Constitution of the Republic, universities are established only by an Act of the Parliament.

In all of its proceedings and deliberations the Higher Education Council always works in close cooperation with the universities, the Interuniversity Board and the Rector's Committee. Such cooperation being of vital importance to develop and coordinate higher education policy, some of the essential responsibilities of the Higher Education Council are listed below:

· it is the duty of the Higher Education Council to prepare short-term and long-term projections relative to the establishment and improvement of institutions of higher education;
· it must likewise prepare guidelines for the rate of growth of universities, compatible with their capacity at maximum efficiency;
· the Council is charged with providing facilities and drawing up programmes for the training of junior academic staff;

- the Council monitors and assures the efficient allocation of resources in higher education;
- the Council drafts proposals and plans for the establishment of new universities, which are submitted to the Minister of National Education who in turn makes his proposals to the Council of Ministers, or the Parliament;
- it determines the enrolment capacity of the universities and defines the general principles of admission;
- the Council makes recommendations to the Minister of Higher education, the Council of Ministers and the Parliament concerning the annual higher education budget as proposed by the universities;
- it nominates candidates for vacant rector-positions at universities. The selection of three candidates is made from a list of six, elected by faculty members of the university. Final appointment is made by the President of the Republic;
- the Council appoints deans of faculties from among three candidates recommended by a rector;
- the Council defines principles governing minimum requirements for curricula taking into account recommendations of the Interuniversity Board;
- it drafts regulation governing the transfer of students from one university to another;
- it makes recommendations to the government as to the amount of tuition fees to be charged for different education programmes in each academic year.

The universities, with their own governing bodies, have full autonomy to make their own by-laws, academic and curricula. They are also fully free to determine their own academic standards and policies.

*The Higher Education Supervisory Board*
On behalf of the Higher Education Council, the Higher Education Supervisory Board evaluates the performances of the universities, the units attached to them, and the teaching staff and makes recommendations. The Board consists of 5 professors nominated by the Higher Education Council; 3 members elected and appointed by the Council from among 9 candidates proposed in equal numbers by the Court of Cassation, the Council of State

and the Court of Accounts; and 2 members, one selected by the General Staff and the other by the Ministry of National Education.

### The Student Selection and Placement Centre

The Student Selection and Placement Centre (OSYM), which was established in 1974 and affiliated to the Higher Education Council in 1981, is primarily concerned with the selection and placement of students in higher education programmes. In addition to this main function, it provides services administrating examinations which are either interuniversity in nature cr are being held on a large scale. Its other activities include the collection and processing of statistical information concerning the teaching staff and students, and the administration of examinations for recruitment and promotion of personnel in public organisations. The President of OSYM is appointed by the President of the Higher Education Council.

### The Inter-university Board

Members of the Interuniversity Board are the rectors of all the universities and the elected representatives (one full professor from each university); in the order of the year of its establishment, the rector of one university serves as the Board's chairman for one calendar year. The Board coordinates interuniversity academic activities and sets down educational standards. The Board makes general regulations and principles related to research activities, publications, higher degrees, equivalence of titles and degrees earned abroad, academic procedures for the promotion of senior faculty members. The Board also elects seven of the Higher Education Council's 24 members.

### The Rector's Committee

The Rector's Committee of Turkish Universities is an advisory administrative body for the Higher Education Council and the Interuniversity Board. It has no executive functions. Members of the Committee are the incumbent and five former rectors, and the President of the Higher Education Council serves ex officio as chairman of the Committee.

### 5.27.4   The current situation

Universities comprise of faculties, institutes, vocational schools for higher learning and research centres. Faculties consist of departments and subdepartments. The head of a faculty is the dean. Each department has a chairman appointed by the rector upon the proposal of the dean of the faculty. The institutes are concerned only with research and graduate studies. All the institutes – whether primarily concerned with the coordination and organisation of graduate courses or research work only – are directly affiliated with the office of the rector, who also appoints their directors. There are three categories of institutes for graduate studies: social sciences, health sciences and basic sciences, each is responsible for one group of courses.

## Higher Schools and Vocational Higher Schools

Higher schools and vocational higher schools offer educational opportunities in various professions through either a 4-year course of study, or 2-year course of study which is directed at the training of ancillary manpower. The annual enrolment of students into these institutions is planned, and ultimately determined, by the Council; which takes into consideration the country's manpower needs, the physical and staff capacity of the institutions, budgetary resources and other similar criteria.

## Teaching Staff

According to the provisions of the Higher Education Law, full professors, associate professors, assistant professors, instructors, lecturers, and the ancillary staff (research assistants, translators, educational planners) are all designated as teaching staff. The senior teaching staff (full, associate, and assistant professors) are mainly concerned with teaching, with applied work at undergraduate and gradate levels, with project preparation and seminars, in addition to undertaking scientific research and publication. They also advise and guide students, and undertake administrative duties within their own higher education units.

## Staff Training and Development

The training of teaching staff is of vital importance. According to the Higher Education Law, (art. 35) higher education institutions are responsible for the training of their academic staff, both at home and abroad, in order to meet their own needs and those of other institutions, either newly established or yet to be established. In recent years, the Higher Education Council and universities have focused their attention on graduate study programmes, since these are the first step in the training of staff. Thus the need for more qualified academic staff members has paved the way for the re-organisation of graduate programmes.

*University Budget*

Although the Higher Education Council was established at the end of 1981, and became fully operative thereafter, it was only in 1983 – when the higher education budget was separated from the general budget of the ministry of National Education Council – that the autonomous authority in higher education began to coordinate university budgets. For the universities and the affiliated institutions, the main source of income is the State subsidy allocated each fiscal year by Parliament, as based on the budget proposals mentioned above. The budget allocated to each university consists in essence of two parts: infrastructure investments and recurrent expenditures. Infrastructure investments are coordinated by the State Planning Organisation, and require this Organisation's approval.

Aside from the annual State subsidy, which makes up the total of major infrastructure investments and recurrent expenditures, the universities are free to create extra-budgetary sources of income, by procuring contracts, by conducting research projects, by functioning as consultants and by way of providing health services, or engaging in semi-industrial operations such as, for example, dairy farms, fisheries, agricultural produce, printing and computer services.

All income from these sources is channelled into revolving funds which are set up by the universities or their affiliated institutions individually. The management and utilisation of these funds is regulated and controlled by the universities themselves within the framework of special revolving fund bye-laws created by the universities or their affiliated institutions and ratified by the Higher Education Council. Since each revolving fund is independent of other revolving funds, balance sheets are kept at the Office of the Revolving Fund for inspection by the state Court of Accounting. These funds are controlled by the universities; they are used to finance various university services, research projects, study trips and expeditions, purchase of laboratory and teaching equipment, and improvement and maintenance of university facilities.

*Institutional Autonomy*
The universities have full academic autonomy in terms of teaching and research activities. Thus, within the framework of the Higher Education Law and also of the general statutes of each university, a certain degree of administrative autonomy is enjoyed by all the sections of the universities. Of course, above all of this is the full and unrestricted enjoyment of academic autonomy. Yet, to safeguard autonomy against its abuse as a means of apathy and irresponsibility, the system is based on the principle of hierarchical accountability; every administrator is answerable to his immediate superior and each year every faculty member submits to his/her faculty board a detailed report of his/her academic work.

*Tuition and Fees, Scholarships, Awards and Loans*
Turkish university students are required to pay a tuition fee which varies according to the discipline studied. Tuition fees, as proposed by the Higher Education Council, are determined by the Council of Ministers. Foreign students pay in convertible currency generally five times the amount Turkish students are charged. To help university students meet the costs of their education, the government, and private organisations provide financial aid in the form of loans, scholarships, grants and awards. Many students benefit from student loans given by the Ministry of National Education, on a monthly basis. The amount is increased every year according to the inflation rate. Those students who received loans are required to repay them once they start working after graduation.

*Research*
According to the statistics by the Institute for Scientific Information in Philadelphia, Turkey was rated 44 in scientific research between 1981-1986 in the world. This figure rose to 34 in 1995. The role of Turkish universities was significant in this achievement. Indeed, among the countries which increased their scientific and technical publications by more that 62% annually, Turkey occupied third place. The number of publications increased three times in 1993 compared with that of 1986. There were 520 publications in 1986, this figure rose to 1789 in 1994.

### 5.27.5    Conclusion

The current state of Turkish higher education was brought about by the 1981 Higher Education Law, which transformed it from a diluted and degenerated version of the old traditional Continental model to a system which has many affinities with the Anglo-American model. The establishment of the Higher Education Council (YOK) as a national intermediary body was the first significant evidence of this transformation. The Council is fully autonomous and, in its structure and powers, greatly resembles a state board of trustees for a multi-campus system such as is found in the United States. Furthermore, the 1981 reform law, introducing a unified system of higher education, paved the way for the creation of a coherent and interrelated pattern of institutional diversity in Turkey.

# 5.28

## THE UNITED KINGDOM

### John Aslen

#### 5.28.1 The current legislative situation

The United Kingdom has no written constitution. In the absence of a single piece of overriding legislation referring to higher education, the following are statements describing the basic characteristics of the UK higher education system.

The UK government does not plan or direct the higher education system in detail. It has no locus to intervene in the internal affairs of higher education institutions as such; these are independent, self-governing bodies and responsible for managing their own financial, administrative and academic affairs. The government is effectively prohibited from intervening in matters of higher education admissions, curriculum or examination.

From the mid 1960s to the late 1980s there were two separately-funded higher education sectors: traditional self-governing universities and local education authority controlled polytechnics and colleges. The period saw significant changes in teacher training with many teacher training institutions merging with universities, polytechnics and colleges. Around 1 in 8 young people entered full-time higher education.

Since then, the main policy and legislative developments have been the creation of a single higher education sector and the significant increase in participation in higher education. Approaching 1 in 3 young people now enter full-time higher education and the number of mature entrants has risen by some 140% since 1979.

The 1988 Education Reform Act took the former polytechnics and the higher education colleges out of local education authority control and established them as self-governing institutions.

The 1990 Student Loans Act broadened the higher education funding base by introducing repayable publicly-subsidised loans to supplement the maintenance grants made to full-time students.

The 1992 Further and Higher Education Act provided a mechanism for the polytechnics to gain university status and the power to award their own degrees and established a single higher education sector funded through the Higher Education Funding Councils for England and Wales. There are similar arrangements in Scotland. The 1992 Act also required the Funding Councils to provide for the assessment of the quality of teaching provision in higher education institutions. Previously only the polytechnic and college sector was subject to independent inspection.

With the establishment in 1992 of the Office of Science and Technology, the government reaffirmed its longstanding commitment to supporting the science and engineering base and to maintaining the dual funding system for university research.

The 1994 Education Act created the Teacher Training Agency to support courses for the initial training of school teachers. Part 1 of the Act requires the Agency to carry out its functions in pursuit of various objectives – namely, raising the standards of teaching, promoting teaching as a career, improving the quality and efficiency of all routes into the teaching profession and securing the involvement of schools in all ITT courses. The Act gives schools the power to provide courses of initial teacher training for graduates.

Finally, there are two principal sets of Regulations which govern student local education authority grants and tuition fees:

·   The Education (Mandatory Awards) Regulations 1995, made under powers conferred by sections 1 and 4(2) of the Education Act 1962, provide for mandatory awards to be made to eligible students on the following kinds of courses: full-time or sandwich courses leading to a first degree or comparable qualifications; Diplomas of Higher Education or Higher National Diplomas and certain other designated courses.

· The Education (Fees and Awards) Regulations 1994 (as amended), made under sections 1 and 2 of the Education (Fees and Awards) Act 1983, provide the framework within which institutions decide the appropriate fee status of students. The Regulations allow for a higher rate of fees to be charged to overseas students than to home or EU students, whose fees are subsidised by the United Kingdom government.

## 5.28.2   The higher education system

Higher education is decentralised in the UK. Each higher education institution is self-governing and, as such, is responsible for managing its own financial, administrative and academic affairs. The UK government is effectively prohibited from intervening in matters of higher education admissions, curriculum or examination.

The internal governance of the new universities and non-university higher education institutions is referred to in two Acts of Parliament:

· Part II of the Education Reform Act 1988 and,
· Part II of the Further and Higher Education Act 1992.

Separate Royal Charters govern the internal administration of the older universities.

Higher education in the United Kingdom is characterised by great diversity of size and mission amongst its institutions. Some institutions – mainly from the former polytechnic and college sector – have put a strong emphasis on providing vocational education, enhancing access and serving the needs of their locality. The older universities, by contrast, have few sub-degree students and tend to focus on courses with an academic perspective and also on research. A few institutions admit post-graduate students only. Institutions also vary widely in the proportion of mature and part-time entrants that they accept.

Higher education institutions comprise universities, teacher training colleges and other colleges of technology, art and professions allied to medicine. Universities are multi-faculty institutions awarding their own degrees whilst colleges of higher education include both general and specialist institutions. Most of the latter award degrees validated by universities.

The United Kingdom has 89 universities and 70 other HE institutions. The creation of a unified higher education sector in 1992 required the establishment of new quality assurance arrangements that would operate across the whole sector. These have been established in accordance with the following principles:

·   that prime responsibility for academic quality and standards rests with the higher education institutions, acting individually and collectively; and
·   that there also needs to be proper accountability for the substantial public funds invested in higher education.

5.28.3   The balance of power: quality assurance and financing

The quality assurance arrangements now in place, following the 1992 Act are as follows:

·   each higher education institution maintains its own quality assurance arrangements. One aspect, found in few other countries, is the external examiner system, through which the standards of examinations for degrees are checked by experts from other higher education institutions. This helps to ensure that standards really are comparable across the system.
·   With the encouragement of the government, the higher education institutions have collectively established the Higher Education Quality Council. This undertakes "academic audits" of the quality assurance arrangements of individual institutions. Its reports are published. For institutions which validate degree courses at other institutions, these audits include a scrutiny of the quality assurance arrangements through which validation operates. The Council also undertakes activities designed to promote and enhance quality in higher education.

· The Quality Council advises the government on applications from colleges seeking the powers to award their own degrees and use the title of university.

· The Higher Education Funding Councils undertake "quality assessments" of the quality of teaching and learning in the different subjects within the institutions they fund. These reports are also published. They seek to ensure that public funding for British universities and colleges is well spent.

These arrangements were supplemented by the government's publication in 1993 of the Charter for Higher Education. This sets out the standards of service which universities and colleges are expected to provide. The government is encouraging all HE institutions to produce their own individual charters.

Higher education in the UK is funded from a variety of sources, including employers, students and parents as well as the taxpayer. The government accepts that public funds will remain the main source of income for higher education. But this is an increasingly expensive commitment. And overdependence on a single funding source is not compatible with institutional independence. There is therefore an established trend towards further diversification. Recent expansion of HE has been funded by broadening the funding base as well as increasing public spending and making efficiency gains. Apart from Government funding, universities and colleges attract general funding through sole privately paid fees; endowments, donations and subventions; charges for residence and catering; and other sources. They also attract specific funding – for research grants and contracts from charities and industry, as well as Government and EC sources; and for other services rendered, again from various sources.

Public funding for institutions flows through two main channels: about three quarters are now paid to the Higher Education Funding Councils for England, Scotland or Wales for distribution in grant to institutions – in Northern Ireland grant is paid to institutions by the Department for Education for Northern Ireland – and the remaining quarter is paid through publicly-funded tuition fees which follow the students. In order to promote responsiveness by institutions to the needs of students and employers and to provide an incentive to use spare capacity, institutional funding for teaching has been linked more closely to recruitment. This involved a shift in the balance of funding from Funding Council grant to tuition fees and the adoption of competitive funding methodologies by the Funding Councils.

The government's intention is that funding should enable institutions to consolidate the growth already achieved. To remove the incentive for further expansion, it has introduced a shift in the balance away from tuition fees back towards Funding Council grant.

Funding Council funds for research are mainly for basic and strategic research: either universities' own research or projects supported by the Research Councils or others.

Research Council funds are provided through the dual support system: Research Councils meet all costs other than academic salaries and premises; the Funding Councils meet the rest. Funding Council research grant is allocated selectively based on the volume and quality of research. Quality ratings derive from a research assessment exercise conducted by peer review every 3 or 4 years. Neither recurrent grant nor research grant from the Funding Councils are earmarked. It is for institutions to decide how to use their funds.

In addition to grant, institutions receive tuition fees for each student. The great majority of full-time undergraduates are automatically eligible to have their tuition fee paid for them by local authorities. Each year the government specifies maximum fees payable by local authorities through awards for individual students. Institutions may set their own level of fees, but in practice they have charged the maximum specified for reimbursement by the government.

Fee rates are banded to reflect the relative cost of courses based in classrooms, laboratories or workshops, and medical, dental or veterinary clinics. The government recently increased the differential between the fee classroom and laboratory/workshop courses in order to provide an incen- for institutions to recruit students to science courses.

ernment does not control precisely the numbers enrolled: that is a individual institutions. But it can influence recruitment by shifting the balance of public funding between grant and fees. By reducing the maximum tuition fees reimbursable through student awards, for instance, it can reduce the incentive for universities and colleges to recruit extra students above the government's plans. Corresponding adjustments to the Funding Council grant at the same time ensures that the planned funding available to institutions is maintained. The Funding Council can also act through its funding for universities and colleges to encourage stability in student numbers – or growth when the need arises.

Government-funded support for HE students mainly takes the form of student awards and loans. Local authorities are obliged to make awards for maintenance costs and tuition fees to all undergraduates who meet stated criteria Central government reimburses their costs in full. In 1990 the government introduced student loans to supplement awards. Loans are available for all eligible students who apply. The Research Councils provide stipends for a certain number of post-graduate students in each scientific or engineering field according to demand and in consultation with universities, employers and the government. The British Academy offers post-graduate studentships in the humanities.

Grants are means-tested. Parents, spouses and students themselves may be expected to contribute towards their maintenance. Loans are not means-tested. Students are expected to start re-paying them only after they finish or leave their course. Payments may then be deferred if the borrower's income is not more than 85% of national average earnings. The amount to be repaid is indexed to inflation so that it will be broadly the same in value as the amount borrowed. In 1993/94, loans were made to 430,000 students, 47% of those eligible in the UK.

The Government is accelerating the shift from grants to loans so that the loan and grant should be broadly equal by 1996/97. The cost of student maintenance will thus be shared more equitably between tax-payers, parents and graduates themselves. Since 1990, the government has also made available access funds to institutions so that they can provide selective help to students who have serious financial difficulties or who might not otherwise have been able to afford to enter higher education. Universities and colleges decide which students should receive payments and how much payments should be.

Institutions are constituted as chartered bodies, higher education corporations or as companies limited by guarantee. In this respect institutions are no different from other corporate bodies and would be exercising the same statutory rights of appeal as any other corporate body.

In matters concerning public administration it also is possible for an institution to challenge a disputed administrative decision through a process called "judicial review". Judicial review is available against a body exercising, broadly speaking, public functions and thus applies generally to central and local government when exercising statutory or other powers. It is the method by which the Courts supervise the way in which ministers, government departments agencies or other public bodies exercise their powers or carry out their duties. It is therefore a means by which institutions (or, indeed individuals) can apply for a remedy against the improper exercise of administrative power. Grounds for an application for judicial review could include:

·   the exercise of powers which have been in excess of those provided for in legislation;
·   decisions which have been reached unreasonably or "irrationally", defined as a decision which is "so outrageous in its defiance of logic or of accepted moral standards that no sensible person who had applied his mind to the question to be decided could have arrived at it";
·   a procedural unfairness in the decision making process, for example where an institution had not been given an opportunity to state its case.

It is, however, important to note that judicial review is not concerned with the merits of decisions or with government policy and it is not for the Courts to enquire into these matters.

### 5.28.4   Conclusion

 summary, higher education in the United Kingdom is characterised by
ntralisation. The government does not plan or direct the HE system in
Institutional autonomy in both academic and administrative affairs
recognised and supported by the government. Where institutions
ly to respond to intergovernmental initiatives on academic or

administrative matters or when the government needs to consult the higher education sector on matters which are the responsibility of the individual institutions, it does so through the institutions' representative bodies.

# 5.29

## UKRAINE

### *Mikhail Stepko*

5.29.1    The current legislative situation

Article 43 of the Constitution of the Ukraine grants equal rights to all citizens to obtain an education. On 25 June 1991, the Law on Education became effective. This Law is currently under revision by parliament. The major issues of discussion national higher education are:

- autonomy;
- the revival and development of the national cultural heritage;
- accessibility of education and its international prestige;
- the future of continuous and graduate education;
- equality of different world outlooks in education.

The principles of conceptual innovation in the field of higher education take into account political, ethical and administrative social exigencies. Among the most pressing concerns in the political arena are preserving the sovereignty of the Ukraine in the sphere of education, vesting the powers to determine the State's educational policy with the Supreme Council of the Ukraine, and assuring non-interference by political parties and religious organisations. In the sphere of ethics and of human rights, the main purpose of education is seen in the development of the individual's personality, his/her talents, mental and physical abilities, and moral standards. The formation of citizens able to make conscious social choices in a humanistic, democratic environment which is organically linked with national culture and heritage, is indeed proclaimed as the quintessence of education.

With regard to the administration and management of higher education institutions a policy of decentralisation is being pursued. The new draft envisions a division of competencies between the central and local government, the intermediary bodies and the institutions themselves. The basis for drafting curricula and study programmes as well as of quality assessment have been changed as well, though, the State continues to determine the necessary requirements of the level and quantity of education, and controls their implementation. A binary licensing and accreditation system has been introduced for vocational and higher education.

The need to secure the social net has led to the establishment of average salaries for teachers in higher education establishments at a rate of about twice the average pay of industrial workers. Bonuses and fringe benefits are also available to all personnel engaged in the educational process. Public funding of education may now amount to no less than one tenth of GNP.

The direction of the reforms in higher education are set forth in the Decree of the President of the Ukraine, of 12 September 1995. According to this decree, the network of state higher education institutions includes 14 classical and 45 technical universities, 30 academies, 72 institutes and 740 special higher schools on different levels of accreditation. There are now more than 90 higher education institutions other than those created by the decree. Some of them were established by public entities, cooperatives and other associations, as well as by private citizens.

Vocational and higher education institutions now accommodate over 1,5 millions students in nine disciplines. The new system provides training at six levels. The first level, junior specialist, consists of a three-year course at a technical school or college after secondary education. A bachelor's degree is awarded following successful completion of a 3,5-4 year course after secondary education. A specialist degree is conferred after completion of a five-six year course at a university, an academy, or an institute, or through completion of an additional 1-1,5 year course of study following college. The specialist degree qualifies the holder to practice as a teacher, engineer, economist, lawyer, doctor, manager, etc. The fourth level of academic achievement, the magister degree follows a six year course of study at a university, academy, or institute, all of which are establishments of the third and fourth levels of accreditation. The magister degree may also be obtained after two supplementary years of study following a bachelor's degree or one year of study upon completion of the specialist degree. There is a fifth level for candidates of science degrees which includes post-graduate study for scientific and pedagogical specialists. Post-graduate studies last 3-4 years and entail the successful defense of a thesis, after which the nominee becomes a holder of the scientific degree of Candidate of Sciences. The sixth and last level of academic merit is the doctorate which is gained after 3 years study following completion of the candidate degree.

### 5.29.2   The balance of power

Ukrainian higher education administration is public. The Ministry of Education manages the higher educational system, which also determines and implements the State's educational policy. The self-governing bodies in the education system are the General Meeting of the Scientific Council of the Regional Conferences of the Educational Personnel, and the Ukrainian Congress of Educational Personnel.

Higher education establishment administration is provided on the basis of autonomy, which is understood to imply the right to determine:

· planning of higher education establishment work, scientific, research and economic activities;
· the number of students admitted on the basis of contracts;
· the concept of higher education, its forms and methods in order to meet the regional and economic requirements;
· the contents of student's training;
· the composition of faculties.

Autonomy furthermore confers the right:

· to enter into contracts with foreign students and scientists;
· to independently dispose of all allocations;
· to register a lecturer or professor for scientific degrees.

The higher education establishments can delegate these rights to the Ministry of Education. Intermediate organisations do not exist in the Ukraine. All

institutions for higher education are protected against decisions of the
Ministry of Education by the Cabinet of Ministers. However, in practice
there are no State decisions against education institutions.


### 5.29.3   Conclusion

The Ukraine inherited a highly developed and broad system of education
from the former Soviet Union. Currently there is a need to reduce the surplus
of engineers, and to increase the number of lawyers, economists, sociologists,
and managers. The Ukrainian higher education system is undergoing radical
changes, and its current legislative situation is not yet stabilised, but is still
adjusting to the requirements of a modern society.

# BIBLIOGRAPHY

Bernt, Jan Fridthjof
*Universities, colleges and others: Diversity of structures for higher educa-tion,* Report of the 3rd LRP workshop, Strasbourg, 1994, Council of Europe.

Bîrzea, César
*Educational policies of the countries in transition,* Strasbourg, 1994, pp. 68-77, Council of Europe Press.

Clark, Burton R.
· *Plans of Engineering,* Berkeley/Los Angeles, University of California Press.
· *The Higher Education System,* London, 1983, p. 28.

Dahrendorf, Ralf
*Betrachtungen über die Revolution in Europa,* Bergisch Gladbach, 1992, p. 187, Bastei Lübbe.

De Groof, Jan
· *The Legal Status of Teachers in Europe,* Leuven, 1995.
· *Droit à l'instruction et liberté d'enseignement,* Bruxelles, 1984.
· *Subsidiarity and Education,* Leuven 1994, p. 105.

Goldschmidt, Dietrich
'Systems of Higher Education in Academic Power', in Van de Graaf, Clark et al. (eds), London, 1978, p. 154.

Gellert, Claudius
'Germany', in: Burton R. Clark, ed., *Advanced Graduate training systems: Germany, Britain, France, Japan, United States,* Berkeley/Los Angeles, University of California Press, 1993.

Goedegebuure, Kaiser, Maassen, Meek
  Goedebuure, L. (ED) Van Vught, F. (ED), 'Comparative policy studies in higher education' E.04:115, *Management and policy in higher education,* no 19, 1994, M NL: Utrecht, Lemma.
Karcyewski, Witold A.
  *Western Paradigms and Eastern Agenda,* Vienna, 1995, p. 38.
Kazemzadch & Steube
  *Verbesserung des Validtät und der internationalen Vergleichbarkeit von Bildungsausgabenindikatoren,* Hannover, 1995.
Johnstone, D.B.
  'Financial Issues facing Hungarian Universities in the 1990's: Containing costs and enhancing revenues', *Higher Education in Europe,* vol XVII, no. 3, 1992, p. 30.
Kogan, Maurice
  'Models of Governance and Development in the United Kingdom', *Higher Education in Europe,* vol XVII, no. 3, 1992, p. 49.
Litt, Th.
  *Führen oder Wachsenlasse,* Leipzig/Berlin 1927.
Noll, Peter
  *Gesetzgebungslehre,* Reinbek bei Hamburg, 1973, chapter II.2, Rowohlt GmbH.
Maassen & Van Vught
  1994, p. 37 quote Clark (1983).
Nossom, Karen
  Bie (1981), *The Norwegian Regional Colleges,* 1981, Paris European Institute of Education and Social Policy.
Nowak, Manfred
  'The Right to Education, its significance and limitation', *Academic Freedom,* 2, London 1993.
Rasmussen, T. Kornbech
  *Equality, Proceedings of the joint conference on Access to Higher Education in Europe,* Parma, 1992, p. 89.
Russel, Conrad
  *Academic Freedom,* London, E.14/22 1993 M.GB/ London: Routledge.

Šebková, Helena

'Institutions of Higher Education and the Czech Academy of Sciences in the Transitional Period', *European Journal of Education,* vol 29, no 1, 1994, p. 97.

Swanson, G.

'Frameworks for Comparative Research: Structural anthropology and the Theory of Action', in: I. Vallier, ed., *Comparative Methods in Sociology,* Berkeley, 1971, p. 145.

Toffler, Alvin

· *Future shock,* New York, 1970, Bantam Books Inc.

· *The third wave.* New York, 1981, Bantam Books Inc.

Vallier, I.

*Comparative Methods in Sociology: Essays on Trends and Applications,* Berkeley, 1971.

# INDEX

**A**

'academic audits' 288

academic behaviour 225

academic freedom(s) 2, 57, 71, 77,
97, 113, 121, 130, 138, 141, 142,
151, 160, 181, 188, 189, 193, 198,
222, 231, 245, 247, 257, 259, 264

academic thinking 225

accountability 9, 67, 80, 84, 194,
198, 228, 288

accountable management 59

accreditation 63-65, 131, 141, 143,
154, 192, 196, 296

Accreditation Collegium (Czech
Republic) 138, 139, 141

Accreditation Committee (Hungary)
61/62, 186-188

accreditation committees 5, 65, 250,
251

Accreditation Regulations (Latvia)
195

affirmative action programmes 69

age groups (of any −) 25

Agency for Higher Education,
Research and Development
(Lithuania) 205

agrégation 169

American type (of university) 48,
77, 85

'ancien regime' 64

Assessment Committee (France) 164

Association of Co-operating Dutch
Universities 61

AStA (Allgemeiner Studentenausschuss [Germany]) 178

Attestation Committee 244

Autonomous Communities (Spain)
263, 266, 267

autonomy 2, 8, 59, 75, 78, 80, 83,
84, 97, 112, 130, 139, 141, 146-
149, 151, 153, 160, 161, 176, 177,
179, 186-189, 191-193, 198, 200,
204, 206, 208, 209, 223, 226, 232,
233, 239, 240, 245, 247, 252, 257-
259, 261, 263, 264, 267, 272, 273,
295

Azerbaidjan 219

**B**

baccalauréat 164

bachelor study programme 138, 139

Baltic Higher Education Coordination
Committee (BHECC) 62

Belarus 28, 62

Belgium 56, 61, 62

state reform of 1988  108
BLK (Bund-Länder-Commission for
    Educational Planning and Research
    Promotion [Germany])  175
Board of the Swiss Federal Institutes
    of Technology  270
BTS (higher technical studies
    certificate [France])  168
budget cuts  7
budgeting  67
'buffer organisations'  34
Bulgaria  54, 58, 219
bureaucratisation  80, 83, 85, 86
business administration  128
business community  64, 128, 131
business companies  134

*C*
CAPES (diploma of secondary
    education [France])  169
catedre  218
Cellule de prospective pédagogique
    122
Central Council of Higher Education
    (Poland)  239-242
Centre for Quality Assessment in
    Higher Education (Lithuania)  207
CESS (certificat d'enseignement
    secondaire supérieur)  116
Chair of Arts College Directors
    (Hungary)  186, 188
chancellorship  210, 211
checks and balances  64
CIUF (Francophone Inter-University
    Council [Belgium])  122
civil disobedience  74
codification  10
codification-modification distinction
    71
collective leadership  64

College Directors' Conference
    (Hungary)  186, 188
Colleges at higher education
    institutions (Latvia)  194
Committee on Engineering
    Qualifications (France)  166
comparability  51
competition  179
Conception of Education (Moldova)
    215, 216
Conference of the Heads of the
    Swiss Technical Colleges  201
Conference of Senate Chairmen of
    Research and Higher Education
    Institutions  205
Conference of Swiss Universities
    271
Congress of Educational Personnel
    (Ukraine)  297
Conseil Général des Hautes Ecoles
    (Belgium)  122
Conseils supérieurs sectoriels
    (Belgium)  122
'Consejo Escolar'  267
Council of Educational Institutions
    (Belarus)  61
Council of Europe  1, 70, 97, 132
    Legislative Reform Programme
    135
counselling  200, 208
credit system  187
Croatia  60, 63
cultural quality  71
cultural rights  56
curricula development  7
Czech Republic  54, 58, 64

*D*
DAEU (higher education entrance
    certificate [France])  164

DEA (certificate of advanced studies [France]) 167
decentralisation 73, 80, 81, 83, 84, 146, 149, 234, 236, 296
deconcentration 80
definitional disparities 52
degree 23, 25
degree structure(s) 23, 24
degrees (external –) 60
degrees (recognition of –) 63, 188
degrees (standardisation of –) 22
degrees (structure of –) 22
democracy (representative parliamentary –) 21
democratic control 83
democratic security 2
democratisation 130, 138, 186, 215
Denmark 64
'density' 80
deregulation 189
DESS (certificate of specialised higher studies [France]) 167
DEUG (general certificate of university education [France]) 165
DEUST (university diploma in science and technology [France]) 167
Directors' Conference od State Research Institutes (Lithuania) 205
disciplines 70
discretionary powers 59
districthøgskoler 234
diversification 7, 65, 138, 140, 142, 189, 265
  (vertical –) 66
diversity 54, 90
  (systematic –) 66
  (programmatic –) 66
  (structural –) 66
divisions of responsibilities 59

DRT (certificate in technological research [France]) 167/168
'duplex ordo' 86
DUT (university diploma in technology [France]) 168
'dynamic conservatism' 85

**E**
economic, social en cultural rights 159
economies of scale 68
education (– for Europe as a whole) 34
Education and Training Council of the French Community (Belgium) 122
egyetem 185
'enterprise' 59
'entrepreneurial' 75
'envelopes' 111
equal opportunity 68, 127, 160, 268
Estonia 54
European Bank for Co-operation and Development 132
European Court for Human Rights 68
European Network of National Information Centres (ENIC) 70
European Union 132, 143, 289
external degrees 60

**F**
Fachhochschulen (Germany) 55, 58, 126, 176
fair competition 74
fees (student –) 28
fees (users –) 68
financial autonomy: see autonomy
Flanders 61, 62
foiskola 185

FPCs (Federal Polytechnic Colleges
  [Switzerland])  270, 272
freedom of education  56
freedom of expression  56, 173
freedom of religion  56
freedom of speech  56
fundamental rights  57, 113, 159,
  160
funding councils  5
Fund for Structural Reform & Technological Development (Bulgaria)
  129, 132

**G**
General Estimates (Malta)  210
General Meeting of the Scientific
  Council of the Regional Conferences of the Education Personnel
  (Ukraine)  297
General State Requirements for Admission of Students (Bulgaria)  130
geographical distribution of universities  273
Germany  55, 56, 58, 64, 65
(self) governance  10, 110, 112, 127,
  134, 141, 155, 186, 254, 266, 285
governments  5
grades légaux  118
grades scientifiques  118
Graduiertenkolleg (Germany)  54

**H**
Higher Education Evaluation Council
  (Estonia)  62, 154, 157
Higher Education and Scientific
  Council (Hungary)  186-188
Higher Education Funding Council(s)
  (United Kingdom)  62, 288
Higher Education Quality Evaluation
  Centre (Latvia)  195

Hochschulrektorenkonferenz
  (Germany)  61
HOKT (higher education of the short
  type [Belgium])  108
HOLT (higher education of the long
  type [Belgium])  108
HOOP (Higher Education and
  Research Plan [The Netherlands])
  228
HRK (Conference of the Rectors and
  Presidents of Higher Education
  Institutions [Germany])  178
Humboldtian tradition  47, 73, 85,
  178, 272
Hungary  54, 63
hybridity  75, 76, 85, 89, 90

**I**
immunity (of university premises)
  250
implementation  2
incentive structures  79
Inspectorate of Education (The
  Netherlands)  229, 230
institutional autonomy:  see
  autonomy
institutional freedom:  see academic
  freedom
'integral manager(s)'  80, 84, 86, 89
inter-active learning  43
Intercantonal Agreement on
  Contributions for Institutes of
  Higher Education  200
intermediate bodies  5, 64, 101, 105,
  148, 157, 188
internal governance  74
internalisation  72
International Academy of Philosophy
  (Liechtenstein)  202
international co-operation  70
'international standards'  70

internationalisation 4. 110, 131, 237
Inter-University Council (Flanders)
61
IUFM (university teacher training
institutes [France]) 167
IUT (university institute of
technology [France]) 166, 168

*J*
joint tasks 173, 175, 176
judicial review 292

*K*
KMK (Standing Conference of the
Ministers of Education and
Cultural Affairs of the Länder
[Germany]) 175

*L*
labour market(s) 22, 30, 57, 77, 96,
110, 227, 264
legal protection 7
legal status (of universities) 153
legiferation 73, 75
legislative melting-pot 4
Lehr- und Lernfreiheit 47
licence 165
licencié 117
Licensing Standards (Estonia) 154
Lithuania 28
Lucrare-proiect de diploma 218
lump sum funding 68

*M*
'machine bureaucracies' 86
maître 117
maîtrise 165, 166
Malta 55, 58
management 3
management culture 5
marginal costs 68

marker demands 96, 128
market mechanisms 66
market regulation 161
market requirements 131
marketing 128
Marxism 18
mass higher education 26, 90
mass university 225
master study programme 139
Matura certificate 200-202, 259
Mediterrean University Community
98
meta-legislation 83
Model University 264
models 8
modification 10
modularisation 58
monotype university 76, 77

*N*
NAIC (National Academic
Information Centre [Norway]) 237
Napoleonic tradition 46, 73, 85
nation state 20, 24
National Academic Foundation
(Bulgaria) 132
National Academic Recognition
Information Centres (NARICs) 70
National Assessment and
Accreditation Agency (Bulgaria)
62, 132
national consciousness 100
National Council of Academic
Assessment and Accreditation
(Romania) 62, 247
National Council for Financing
Education (Romania) 62, 247/248
National Council for Teacher
Education (Norway) 235
National Council of State Colleges
(Norway) 234

National Council of University
  Scientific Research (Romania) 62,
  246, 247
National Council of Universities
  (Norway) 234
National Equivalence Information
  Centres (NEIC) 70
National Science Fund (Bulgaria)
  129
Netherlands 55, 62, 64, 79
Network of Information Bodies on
  Recognition and Mobility
  (UNESCO) 70
Network Norway 234, 236
'new public management' 77/78
Newmanian concept 48, 77
*numerus clausus/fixus* 9, 116, 207

**O**
OECD 30, 79, 132
Office for Strategic Development,
  Research and Technology
  (Slovakia) 253
'official qualifications' 266
Onderzoeksscholen 54
Open Society Fund (Bulgaria) 132
Open University 222, 225
OSYM (Student Selection and
  Placement Centre [Turkey]) 279
out-of-hours programmes 117
output-orientation 59

**P**
panels 117
parity 61
peer review 81, 111
performance-budgeting 59
personnel administration 111
plan de activitate individuala 219

Planning Committee for Higher
  Education Construction (Germany)
  176
'plea for internal democracy' 74
policy development 2
'policy prison(s)' 84
'political business cycles' 84
post-secondary sector 185, 186
PPGS (programmes of post-graduate
  studies [Greece]) 183
primary process 87-89
'prisoner's dilemma' 80
private sector 57, 75, 111, 154
'Ptychio' (Greece) 181

**Q**
Qualitative Regulation for Higher
  Education 207
quality assessment 2, 7, 62, 111,
  131, 230
quality assurance 3, 61, 63-65, 116,
  131, 135, 198, 229, 288
quality care 81, 83
quality care systems 81
quality consciousness 63
quality control 63, 77, 78, 111, 146,
  229
quality evaluation 62
quality guarantee 265

**R**
Rechtsstaat 34
recognition (of qualifications) 165
Rectors' Conference(s) 5, 279
  of Bulgaria 61, 132
  of the Czech Republic 141, 142
  of Germany 178
  of Hungary 61, 186, 188
  of Lithuania 205
  of Romania 62
  of Slovakia 252

reflexivity 77
reform(s) 3, 96, 97, 131, 146, 248, 263, 268, 275, 276
reform of university research 140
registration fee 116
research (teaching and –) 53
Research and Development Council (Czech Republic) 141
Research and Higer Education Fund 206
respect for democracy 100
reunification (German –) 174
Romania 219
Russian Federation 219

**S**
Sacima 192
Saeima 191, 192, 195, 197
safeguarding of fundamental rights 57
safeguards 60
Satversme 191, 193-195
scaling-up operation 112
Science Council (Lithuania) 203-205
'scientific preparation' 254
scientific research 94, 96, 128, 249
'second generation legislation' 9
Seimas 203, 204, 206
self-administration 177, 247
self-analysis 63, 207
self-assessment 62, 111, 207
self-control 86, 89
self-steering 90
semi-higher institutions 126, 135
'sense making processes' 89
site visit 111
Slovak Republic 58, 63, 64
Slovenia 55
Social Councils 264, 266
social-advancement programmes 117
'social engineering' 9

social welfare 68
society (an enabling, prosperous, democratic and open –) 2
solidification 75
Spain 55, 62, 64
'spectral' system 54
stabilisation 153
standardisation 22, 80
State Higher Certifying Commission (Bulgaria) 129
state investment programes 197
state license 105
steering/steering instruments 5, 36, 71, 78, 161, 186, 196, 232
steering at a distance 75, 77, 80
steering by incentives 78
steering by regulation 78
Storting 237
STS (section for higher technical studies [France]) 166
student self-government 241
'study-ability' 231
'study-market' 55
'study programme' (Czech Republic) 138
subsidiarity 56, 59, 64, 70
Switzerland 64

**T**
Teacher Training Agency (UK) 286
teaching (– and research) 53, 140
technical universities 65
'técnico superior' (diploma of –) 266
teza de doctorat 219
throughputs 75, 80, 83
top-down administration 85
treasure chamber(s) 87-89
trends 6
tripartite system 275

tuition fees   104, 127, 128, 140, 186,
   197, 198, 227, 253, 260, 282, 290
tuition loans   140
Turkey   55, 58, 219

**U**
Ukraine   219
UNESCO   132
unit costs   68
United Kingdom   55, 58, 79
United States   63, 68, 80
university administration   160
University of California   69
University Research Institutes
   (Greece)   183
'user's market'   68

**V**
verasste Studentenschaft   178
vertical diversification   66

**W**
welfare state   26
Wissenschaftsrat   175
World Bank   30, 132

**Y**
YOK (Higher Education Council
   [Turkey])   273-283

# ACKNOWLEDGEMENTS

Each book in this series is a joint effort of experts involved in higher education, in a process that deliberately includes the creativity of many people in the inception of the texts and the process of the series as a whole.

- The European network of national correspondents. Each participating country designated, in principle, two experts: the government correspondent and the scientific correspondent (a representative of the academic sector) who co-ordinated, at a national level, the co-operation between all the authors involved. They are jointly responsible for the content and accuracy of the written contributions of their country.
- The Editing Board. Formed by six eminent scientists with a variety of experience in higher education and research, the Editing Board is a collegiate body responsible for the publication project as a whole. It fulfils an overarching role for the development of the series, the structure of the volumes and their co-ordination.
- The volume editors and the general editing consultant. Each member of the Editing Board has taken up the primary responsibility for one volume. Together with a second editor, he or she is responsible for the assessment of country reports, and the drafting of the introduction, the comparative analysis and the conclusion. In conjunction with the Editing Board and the LRP Secretariat, the volume editors are responsible for all substantial elements of the preparation and publication of the volume. The general editing consultant, one of the members of the Editing Board, acts as the permanent advisor to the editors, overseeing terminology and avoiding overlaps and gaps between the volumes.
- The authors of country reports and respondents to questionnaires. It was left up to the countries to organise their written contributions.

The LRP Secretariat developed the structure of the series, gave advice to its editors, and arranged the logistics; Peter Kwikkers and Andreas Kleiser of the Secretariat also contributed to the volume's theoretical foundations.

*Volume editors:*

Roeland IN 'T VELD
Hans Peter FÜSSEL

*General Editing Consultant:*

Guy NEAVE

| *LRP Editing Board:* | *First editor of:* |
|---|---|
| Roeland In 't Veld | Volume 1 |
| Jan de Groof | Volume 2 |
| André Staropoli | Volume 3 |
| Guy Neave | Volume 4 |
| Alenka Šelih | Volume 5 |
| Ulrich Teichler | Volume 6 |

*LRP Steering Group:*

Peter Fischer-Appelt
Ko Scheele
Juraj Švec
Jan de Groof
Alexandre Draguiev
Peter Soltesz
Ergün Togrol

AUTHORS OF THE COUNTRY REPORTS

| | |
|---|---|
| Albania | *Ilia Prifti*<br>Director of the Higher Education Department Ministry of Education, Tirana |
| Belarus | *Boris Kopissky*<br>Head of the Analytical Department, Ministry of Education and Science, Minsk<br>*Nikolai Listopad*<br>Director of the Computer Centre, Ministry of Education and Science, Minsk |
| Belgium (Fl) | *Jan Fiers*<br>Researcher, University of Ghent<br>*Joan Lesseliers*<br>Researcher, University of Ghent |
| Belgium (W) | *Chantal Kaufmann*<br>Head of the Higher Education Section |
| Bulgaria | *Tsvetomir Georgiev*<br>Expert, Ministry of Education, Science and Technology, Sofia |
| Czech Republic | *Emanuel Ondráček*<br>Vice Minister, Ministry of Education, Youth and Sport, Prague<br>*Helena Šebková*<br>Director of the Centre for Higher Education Studies, Prague<br>**Stanislav Hanzl**<br>Rector of the Czech Technical University, Prague |
| Denmark | *Jane Planck*<br>Head of Section, Ministry of Education, Department of Higher Education, Copenhagen |
| Estonia | *Voldemar Tomusk*<br>Head of the Division for Higher Education, Ministry of Culture and Education, Tallinn |
| Finland | *Eila Rekilä*<br>Senior Adviser, Ministry of Education, Helsinki |

| | |
|---|---|
| France | *Claudine Bachy* |
| | Ministry of Higher Education and Research, Paris |
| Germany | *Wolfgang Mönikes* |
| | Referatsleiter, Federal Ministry of Education, |
| | Science, Research and Technology, Bonn |
| | *Cornelia Haugg* |
| | Referatsleiter, Federale Ministry of Education, |
| | Science, Research and Technology, Bonn |
| Greece | *Roy Hourdakis* |
| | Head of the Interuniversity Relations Section, Ministry of Education, Athens |
| Hungary | *Anna Imre* |
| | Research Fellow, Hungarian Institute for Educational Research |
| | *Janos Setenyi* |
| | Senior Researcher, Hungarian Institute for Educational Research |
| Latvia | *Andrejs Rauhvargers* |
| | Head of the Academic Information Centre (Latvian ENIC), Riga |
| | *Janis Čakste* |
| | Director, Department of Higher Education and Research, Ministry of Education and Science, Riga |
| Liechtenstein | *Franz Messner* |
| | Department of Education, Principality of Liechtenstein |
| Lithuania | *Biruté Mockiené* |
| | Deputy Director and Head of the Lithuanian ENIC, Vilnius |
| Malta | *Paul Heywood* |
| | Pro-Chancellor, Malta Equivalence Information Centre |
| Moldova | *Petru Gaugus* |
| | Minister of Education |
| Netherlands | *Ernst Hirsch-Ballin* |
| | Professor of Law, Tilburg University |

| Norway | Rolf Kåre Jenssen |
|---|---|
| | Senior Executive Officer, Department of Higher Education, Royal Norwegian Ministry of Education and Church Affairs |
| Poland | Jerzy Gąsiorowski |
| | Director of the Department of Science and Higher Education, Ministry of National Education |
| Romania | Alexandru Mihailescu |
| | Expert, The Department of Strategy, Development and European Integration, Ministry of Education |
| | Ioan Neacsu |
| | General Director, Ministry of Education |
| Slovakia | Mária Hrabinská |
| | Head of the Centre for Equivalence of Diplomas, UIP, Bratislava |
| | Peter Plavčan |
| | Expert, Ministry of Education, Bratislava |
| | Juraj Švec |
| | Rector of the Comenius University, Bratislava |
| Slovenia | Albin Igličar |
| | Professor of Law, University of Ljubljana |
| Spain | José Ignacio Cebreiro |
| | Legal Adviser, Ministry of Science and Education, Madrid |
| Switzerland | Christen Lenzen |
| | Adjointe Scientifique, Conférence Universitaire Suisse, Berne |
| Turkey | Mustafa Akbulut |
| | Foreign Relations Department, Higher Education Council, Ankara |
| United Kingdom | John Aslen |
| | Department for Education, London |
| Ukraine | Mikhail Stepko |
| | Head of Department of Higher Education, Ministry of Education, Kiev |

LIST OF PERSONS WHO COMPLETED THE QUESTIONNAIRE

| | |
|---|---|
| Albania | *Gjergji File* |
| | Director of the Education Department, Ministry of Education, Tirana |
| Belarus | *Boris Kopissky* |
| | Head of the analytical Department, Ministry of Education and Science, Belarus |
| | *Nikolai Listopad* |
| | Director of the Computer Centre, Ministry of Education and Science, Belarus |
| Belgium (Fl) | *Noël Vercruysse* |
| | Director, Ministry of Flemish Community, Higher Education Department, Brussels |
| | *Tony Keuleers* |
| | Assistant Director |
| | *Jan Fiers* |
| | Researcher, University of Ghent |
| | *Joan Lesseliers* |
| | Researcher, University of Ghent |
| Belgium (W) | *Chantal Kaufmann* |
| | Head of the Higher Education Section |
| Bulgaria | *Ivanka Yordanaova* |
| | Coordinator for the Cooperation with the Council of Europe, Ministry of Education, Science and Technology, Sofia |
| Cyprus | *Christodoulos Cleopas* |
| | Director, Higher and Tertiary Education, Ministry of Education and Culture, Nicosia |
| Czech Republic | *Emanuel Ondráček* |
| | Vice Minister, Ministry of Education, Youth and Sport, Prague |
| | *Helena Šebková* |
| | Director of Centre for Higher Education Studies, Prague |
| | *Stanislav Hanzel* |
| | Rector of the Technical University, Prague |

| | |
|---|---|
| Denmark | *Jane Planck* |
| | Head of Section, Ministry of Education, Department of Higher Education, Copenhagen |
| Finland | *Elia Rekilä* |
| | Senior Adviser, Ministry of Education, Helsinki |
| Germany | *Frank Reifers* |
| | Referent, Federal Ministry of Education, Science, Research and Technology, Bonn |
| Hungary | *Anna Imre* |
| | Research Fellow, Hungarian Institute for Educational Research, |
| | *Janos Setenyi* |
| | Senior Researcher, Hungarian Institute for Educational Research, |
| Latvia | *Andrejs Rauhvargers* |
| | Head, Academic Information Centre (Latvian ENIC), Riga |
| | *Janis Čakste* |
| | Director, Department of Higher Education and Research, Ministry of Education and Science, Riga |
| Malta | *Paul Heywood* |
| | Pro-Chancellor, Malta Equivalence Information Centre |
| Moldova | *Petru Gaugaş* |
| | Minister of Education |
| Netherlands | **Ko Scheele** |
| | Inspector of Higher Education, Inspectorate of Education |
| Norway | *Rolf Kåre Jenssen* |
| | Senior Executive Officer, Department of Higher Education, Royal Norwegian Ministry of Education and Church Affairs |
| Romania | *Iulian Beju* |
| | Deputy Director, Ministry of Education, Slovakia |
| | *Mária Hrabinská* |
| | Head of the Centre for Equivalence of Diplomas, UIP, Bratislava |

| | |
|---|---|
| Slovenia | *Albin Igličar* |
| | Professor of Law, University of Ljubljana |
| Spain | *José Ignacio Cebreiro* |
| | Legal Adviser,Ministry of Science and Education, Madrid |
| Switzerland | *Christin Lenzen* |
| | Adjointe Scientifique, Conférence Universitaire Suisse, Berne |
| Turkey | *Mustafa Akbulut* |
| | Foreign Relations Department, Higher Education Council, Ankara |
| United Kingdom | *Sue Garner* |
| | Head of International Students Team, Department of Education, London |
| Ukraine | *Mikhail Stepko* |
| | Head of Department of Higher Education, Ministry of Education, Kiev |

*The LRP Secretariat:*

| | |
|---|---|
| Peter Kwikkers | Programme Manager |
| Andreas Kleiser | Programme Officer |
| **Markus Adelsbach** | Programme Officer |
| Theresa Lad | Assistant |
| Debbie Orme | Assistant |
| Caroline Ward | Assistant |
| Genevieve Woods | Copy editing |

# STRUCTURE OF THE SERIES

| THE STRUCTURE OF THE FIRST THREE VOLUMES OF THE SERIES | | | |
|---|---|---|---|
| | VOLUME 1 | VOLUME 2 | VOLUME 3 |
| TITLE | RELATIONS BETWEEN STATE AND HIGHER EDUCATION | INSTITUTIONAL GOV-ERNANCE | INSTRUMENTS OF CHANGE |
| Subtitle | Mission, autonomy, accountability | Central legislation and institutional regula-tions | The process and di-rection of legislative reform |
| Planned | 28 March 1996 | 4 November 1996 | 1997 (March) |
| Scope | Higher education in politi-cal, legal, educational, economical, cultural, socio-logical context. | Democratic govern-ance of higher educa-tion institutions. | The process of legis-lative change in Europe |
| First Editor | Roeland IN 'T VELD | Jan DE GROOF | Guy NEAVE |
| Second Editor | Hans Peter FÜSSEL | Juraj ŠVEC | Tibor NAGY |
| Editing consultant | Guy NEAVE | Guy NEAVE | Editing Board |
| Elements | · The legal framework: international conventions, constitution, legislation.<br>· Types of institutions: scientific-professional; public-private; general-specialised.<br>· The domain of higher education: mission/task/role of institutions<br>· Relationships: principles and instruments of minister-ial planning, State-students-other organisations.<br>· Dimensions: responsibil-ities and competencies, financial relations, human resources policy.<br>· Subjects: access and labour market, accountability/quality con-trol, teaching and research<br>· Legal protection of insti-tutions, case-law | · The legal frame-work: definitions, international conven-tions, legislation, case-law<br>· Regulations: demo-cratic governance, responsibilities<br>· Principles and struc-tures: standard prac-tice. 'model' Statutes management of staff, students, teaching, research, infrastruc-ture.<br>· Democracy: staff/students, elections, nomination.<br>· External influence: social, economic, political, intermedi-aries<br>· Hidden State govern-ance<br>· Legal protection | · The genesis of legis-lative reform within the general policy within the individual country<br>· The trust and prior-ities of national pol-icies<br>· The process of legis-lative reform<br>· The institutional impact of legislative enactment upon agencies and estab-lishments in individ-ual systems of higher education<br>· Trends in legislative reforms |

| THE STRUCTURE OF VOLUMES FOUR, FIVE AND SIX OF THE SERIES | | |
|---|---|---|
| | VOLUME 4 | VOLUME 5 | VOLUME 6 |
| TITLE | ACCOUNTABILITY | STAFF | STUDENTS |
| Subtitle | Administration; quality management and allocation of money. | The position of staff | Admission, education and graduation |
| Planned | 1997 (January) | 1997 (November) | 1998 (March) |
| Scope | Administration: accountability, self-assessment and finance. | Academic staff | Full-time students |
| First Editor | André STAROPOLI | Alenka ŠELIH | Ulrich TEICHLER |
| Second Editor | Ioan MIHAILESCU | | |
| Editing consultant | Guy NEAVE | Guy NEAVE | Guy NEAVE |
| Elements | · The legal framework for accountability and administrative structures.<br>· Financial management, authorisation: property (funds and real estate) decentralised allocation.<br>· Self-assessment and quality control/quality assessment: relation between quality and allocation<br>· Certification.<br>· Legal protection, case-law.<br>· International Conventions | · The legal framework: types of staff, legal status.<br>· Labour conditions and Unions.<br>· Contracts: types, main elements, requirements, nomination, dismissal.<br>· The academic profession: tasks of staff academic freedom teaching, research sabbatical leave other rights and duties.<br>· Legal protection, case-law<br>· International Conventions | · The legal framework: status, taxes, loans, grants, repayments, social benefits, housing, student aid, other services,"in loco parentis" function.<br>· Access and admission: legislation and institutional regulation, restrictions.<br>· Democratic rights: participation in governance, student unions.<br>· Study systems, credits<br>· Study programming.<br>· Study-ability.<br>· Graduate profiles<br>· Graduation and beyond: the labour market international academic, professional recognition<br>· Legal protection, case-law<br>· International Conventions |